Urban Development Planning

Urban Development Planning

Lessons for the Economic Reconstruction of South Africa's Cities

Richard Tomlinson

Contributing authors

David Dewar
(University of Cape Town)

Roland Hunter
(for Planact)

Jennifer Robinson and Carlos Boldogh
(for Built Environment Support Group)

Witwatersrand University Press
JOHANNESBURG

Zed Books Ltd
LONDON AND NEW JERSEY

First published in 1994 in the Republic of South Africa by

Witwatersrand University Press
1 Jan Smuts Avenue
Johannesburg, 2001
South Africa

ISBN 1 86814 258 2

In the rest of the world by

Zed Books Ltd
7 Cynthia Street
London, N1 9JF
United Kingdom

and

Zed Books Ltd
165 First Avenue, Atlantic Highlands
New Jersey, 07716
United States of America

ISBN 1 85649 307 5 (Cloth) ✓
ISBN 1 85649 308 3 (Paper)

A catalogue record for this book is available from the British Library
US CIP is available from the Library of Congress

Cover drawing by Derrick Nxumalo,
        reproduced with permission of the Tatham Art Gallery, Pietermaritzburg
Cover design by Andrew Lord

Typeset by Photoprint, Cape Town
Printed and bound by The Penrose Press, Pretoria

Contents

Foreword

This book, compiled between mid-1991 and early 1993, is based on an understanding of international trends in policies intended to promote development in urban areas. It covers the agencies responsible for formulating and implementing development policies and what those policies consist of. The essence of these strategies informs local economic development planning.

Development planning strategies are undertaken by development partnerships and focus on increasing investment in the local economy, thereby contributing to the number of jobs and expanding the tax base. The development tools have shifted away from the use of location concessions and 'beggar thy neighbour' competition towards the strategic restructuring of the metropolitan economy, marketing, the support of indigenous medium and small enterprise, and working with community organisations to reach into low-income neighbourhoods.

This foreword interprets these policy trends in the light of the African National Congress's *Reconstruction and Development Programme* (RDP) that dominates the development debate in mid-1994.

The RDP constitutes a socio-economic policy framework that has won considerable acceptance. It is a product of wide consultation and many influences with the result that it can be interpreted in a number of ways. This diversity of potential interpretations contributes to its acceptance. The specific implications of the RDP for development programmes, projects and budgets are still being debated. While central government is actively involved with RDP strategies, the provincial governments' attempts to formulate RDPs are moving much more slowly. This is due in part to the lack of clarity regarding the still evolving roles of the central, regional and local governments in promoting economic development. We therefore have to refer to the intentions and values underlying the RDP rather than to subsequent documents that might suggest how cities and provinces will function to promote development.

Of particular importance is Chapter 4 of the RDP where it is stated:

> The fundamental principles of our economic policy are democracy, participation and development. We are convinced that neither a commandist central planning system nor an unfettered free market system can provide adequate solutions to the problems confronting us. Reconstruction and development will be achieved through the leading and enabling role of state, a thriving private sector, and active involvement by all sectors of civil society which in combination will lead to sustainable growth. (4.2.1)
>
> The RDP will foster a new and constructive relationship between the people, their organisations in civil society, key constituencies such as the trade unions and organised business, the democratic government, and the workings of the market. (4.2.6)
>
> In order to foster the growth of local economies, broadly representative institutions must be established to address local economic development needs. Their purpose would be to formulate strategies to address job creation and community development. (4.3.5)

These statements, in addition to the central role accorded provincial and local government in implementing the RDP, read like a manifesto for local economic development planning as portrayed in this book. Whether this plan will be fully implemented depends on the actual division of labour between cities and provinces. As a result this book also constitutes an argument for a particular allocation of responsibilities, one wherein cities play a prominent role.

Richard Tomlinson
July 1994

Acknowledgements

During 1985 and 1986 I spent a sabbatical at the Massachusetts Institute of Technology while researching material for an earlier book on urbanisation in a post-apartheid South Africa. I took the opportunity to attend some courses at MIT and Harvard University, and it was during a lecture by Professor Avis Vidal at Harvard's Kennedy School that the idea for this book was born. It seemed to me that regional planning in South Africa was hopelessly outdated and that local economic development planning offered a more effective vehicle for promoting development.

Later, having moved from the University of the Witwatersrand to the Development Bank of Southern Africa, I was put in charge of the Planning Unit whose job it was to facilitate development planning. It became apparent to me that the development planning initiatives in South Africa's cities were conducted with more enthusiasm than substance. The time had come to act on the idea born during Professor Vidal's course. Happily, the Development Bank of Southern Africa indicated a preparedness to grant me (unpaid) leave.

As difficult as writing a book is the raising of funds for such an enterprise. I was fortunate to win a Robert S. McNamara Fellowship from the World Bank which enabled me to spend a period as a Guest Scholar at the Brookings Institution in Washington DC while conducting comparative research. Brookings proved a challenging institution and I spent a long time keeping my intellectual peas on the plate while being impressed by the acumen of those around me. I am extremely grateful to the Bank and Brookings.

I am also grateful for support from the Anglo American and De Beers Chairman's Fund, and for a consulting project commissioned by the

Pretoria office of USAID. Their support enabled me to spend an additional period as a Research Associate at the Programme for Research in Planning at the University of the Witwatersrand, while working in association with Planact. This period allowed me to contextualise the comparative material.

I owe a debt of gratitude to many individuals. Avis Vidal again provided encouragement. Robert Mier opened many doors in Chicago. I stayed with Robert Beauregard in Pittsburgh, held fruitful debate with him, and gained a number of important introductions. Norman and Susan Fainstein provided a base in New York City, moral support, and guidance. Roland Hunter read and commented on the text. Kathy Eales translated my academic prose into more reader-friendly material. Ivan Vladislavić did the same job at the behest of the Witwatersrand University Press. We should all thank them! I should also credit the Urban Institute in Washington DC for the use of its library. Finally, I thank my wife Mary and my daughters Catherine and Lisa for putting up with my poor pretence at being a husband and father.

It goes without saying that, except in respect of the chapters contributed by David Dewar, Roland Hunter, and Jennifer Robinson and Carlos Boldogh, the views expressed in this book are mine and do not reflect on the individuals or institutions with which I have been associated.

Abbreviations

ANC	African National Congress
BESG	Built Environment Support Group
BQE	Brooklyn Queens Exports
CBD	Central business district
CBM	Consultative Business Movement
CBP	Community Banking Project
CDC	Community development corporation
CDT	Community development trust
COSATU	Congress of South African Trade Unions
DBSA	Development Bank of Southern Africa
DCC	Durban City Council
DFR	Durban Functional Region
EDC	Economic Development Committee
EPZ	Export processing zone
ESOP	Employee share ownership
EWIDCO	East Williamsburg Valley Industrial Development Corporation
FMN	Flexible manufacturing network
GLC	Greater London Council
GNP	Gross National Product
Habitat	United Nations Commission for Human Settlement
JCI	Johannesburg Consolidated Investment
JETRO	Japanese Export Trade Organization
LIMAC	Local Initiatives Managed Assets Corporation
LISC	Local Initiatives Support Corporation
MANCO	Management committee
MITI	Ministry of International Trade and Industry
NCUED	National Council for Urban Economic Development

NEF	National Economic Forum
NGO	Non-governmental organization
NP	National Party
NPA	Natal Provincial Administration
NUM	National Union of Mineworkers
OECD	Organization of Economic Cooperation and Development
OJ	Operation Jumpstart
PEBCO	Port Elizabeth Black Civic Organization
PIDC	Philadelphia Industrial Development Corporation
PSC	Project steering committee
PSDO	Private sector development organization
PWV	Pretoria-Vaal-Witwatersrand
RLF	Municipal Revolving Loan Fund
RSC	Regional Services Council
SACTWU	South African Clothing and Textile Workers' Union
SAIRR	South African Institute of Race Relations
SANCO	South African National Civic Organization
SAPOA	South African Property Owners' Association
SBI	Small Business Initiative
SCA	Soweto Civic Association
TPA	Transvaal Provincial Administration
UDC	Urban Development Corporation
UNIDO	United Nations Industrial Development Organization
USAID	United States Agency for International Development
WDB	Women's Development Bank

Chapter 1
Introduction

Prior to 2 February 1990 and the unbanning of the African National Congress (ANC), the strife in South Africa's cities centred on 'bread and butter' issues – housing, transportation and services; and on broader political issues – the black local authority system, divided cities with unequal tax bases, and apartheid itself. The conflict was led by civic and residents' associations[1] and took the form of bus and consumer boycotts, refusals to pay for rents and services, and often violent opposition to the black local authorities. The result was that even before De Klerk's reforms, there were numerous instances of local negotiations intended to address these matters. The civics led these negotiations; and since the civics formed part of the United Democratic Front – a proxy for the ANC – they provided an organisational base and undertook mass action to further the ANC's national political agenda.

Conditions have changed since 1990. Civics are now cast as apolitical, in the sense that they focus on 'civic' issues and seek support from a town's inhabitants regardless of their political persuasion. The nature of the struggle has changed: where before the style was combative, now it has shifted to address 'the politics of development'. Indeed, some civics are trying to assume the role of development agencies, supplying services and amenities in their area.

As the focus of local initiatives has shifted from conflict resolution to development, the range of participants has broadened. Negotiations prior to February 1990 were essentially between a civic and a branch of government, commonly a provincial authority. Now, there is a tremendous diversity of participants in the local development process. In Johannesburg, for example, the protracted negotiations which led to the Soweto Accord and the formation of the Metropolitan Chamber[2] began in 1988. The main negotiations involved the Soweto Civic Association (SCA) and its ally, the nominated Soweto People's Delegation, the Transvaal Provincial Administration (TPA) and Soweto's black local authorities. Current participants include adjacent white local authorities, the Congress of South African Trade Unions (COSATU), major utility companies, and chambers of commerce and industry. In Durban, development planning was initiated by a large private corporation and evolved into a process incorporating the major political parties, the private sector and affected local authorities. By contrast, in Port Elizabeth local representatives of the ANC and the Democratic Party took the lead in convening a forum. There the negotiating partners include the Port Elizabeth City Council, the ANC, the Democratic Party, the Institute for a Democratic Alternative for South Africa, the National Party, the Midland Chamber of Industries, and the Port Elizabeth Chamber of Commerce.

There is a willingness now to confront development issues. Of course, the motives diverge. For white local authorities, the inevitability of the post-apartheid era acts as a spur to begin negotiating; the sooner they engage, the better their prospects of pre-empting an imposed national settlement which determines municipal borders and fiscal responsibilities against their interests. For civics, their credibility is contingent on their ability to pressure local authorities to deliver services and housing. Business people, for their part, have a vested interest in resuscitating a crumbling local economy. Clearly, the motives vary and depend on context, but what is important for this book is the willingness of the parties concerned to undertake collaborative efforts, at the local level, to promote development.

A problem which arises at this point is that there is neither a tradition of local responsibility for development nor an awareness of how to promote such development. Decision-making in South Africa has been controlled from the centre, whether by central government in Pretoria or by the major corporations in Johannesburg. The fact that local economic development planning is only now being introduced into the curricula of a few South African universities highlights this lack of familiarity and experience.[3]

The question addressed in this book, therefore, is whether local initiatives – by local authorities, community organisations, unions and business people – can help to promote economic development and ease urban poverty in South Africa. One way of addressing this question is to examine local development needs in the light of foreign experiences in development planning. What can South Africa learn from experiences elsewhere, and how can these lessons be applied?

ISSUES TO BE ADDRESSED

It is hard to anticipate what impact development planning might have in the South African context. My hope is that this book will demonstrate the relevance of development planning in:

- reducing poverty;
- facilitating redistribution and empowerment;
- remedying the consequences of the apartheid city;
- outlining an alternative approach to development, in relation to the prescriptions of the World Bank and the United Nations;
- enhancing the role of civics as development agents; and
- contributing to debate on the distribution of powers between central, provincial and local government.

Beyond this, I hope the book will serve as a useful text on development planning, both for participants and students.

Poverty

Poverty is a difficult concept to define; I struggle with its causes and characteristics in the next chapter. None the less, it is appropriate at this point to identify a problem which bedevils this text: is it sufficient to promote economic development and employment creation in general, or must the benefits be targeted at specific low-income groups? For example, when addressing small enterprise, should the focus be on micro or informal enterprises or on relatively larger enterprises which, it is often claimed, are more efficiently served by assistance strategies?[4] My inclination is to focus on informal enterprises, and throughout this text I struggle against the alluring pull of strategies which would serve larger enterprises.

Yet even if one strives for targeted development, development planning cannot be regarded as a panacea. For the 'ultra-poor', the problem is less one of economic development than sheer access to the food and medical services which are a precondition to participation in the economy. I believe it is fanciful to proffer economic development strategies when the health and nutritional status of the ultra-poor make a mockery of, say, images of a wealth-creating informal sector. There is a point at which redistribution and subsidy must take first place.

Redistribution and empowerment

Another measure of poverty is relative inequality. As a country becomes more developed, so distributive measures become more pertinent. The reason for this is that when a country has a low per capita income, inevitably the basic needs of a significant proportion of its population are not met. However, as a country's per capita income rises, the incidence of poverty more clearly reflects the unequal distribution of resources, both public and private. In South Africa, of course, this measure is especially sensitive because apartheid has predetermined who benefits from the economy.

In South Africa, the white share of national income is declining – from 71 per cent in 1970 to 54 per cent in 1990 – and is expected to drop below 50 per cent by 1995. Yet whites constituted only 14 per cent of the total population in 1990.

Figures such as these reinforce one's sense that an essential component of an urban development programme must be redistribution, not least for political reasons. It is in this context that one should note the parallels between the policies contemplated within development planning and the emerging conception of 'black empowerment' in South Africa. As Duncan Innes (1991) has explained, the need for empowerment is rooted in the history of expropriation to which Africans have been subjected. The Freedom Charter states that 'our people have been robbed of their birthright', and calls for the restoration of the country's wealth to the people. Historically, it has been assumed that redress requires nationalisation, yet recent international developments, especially in Russia and Eastern Europe, have raised doubts about nationalisation and the wisdom of a socialist path of development. But these doubts have not lessened the desire for redress. Consequently economic empowerment is being considered carefully as an alternative means of redistribution.

From the point of view of Planact, a pivotal planning and development agency based in Johannesburg, 'empowerment should be the overriding objective of all activities and interventions at the local level, and necessitates intervention in four distinct spheres: planning, control, capacity and finance' (Planact 1992a: 207). It is in this light that development planning – which involves civics in the preparation and implementation of development strategies, or requires that a given percentage of municipal purchases be directed to African-owned businesses – becomes particularly interesting.

The apartheid city

The apartheid city has four components:

i. A **spatial system** that allocates populations in urban space according to their colour. The result is a deconcentrated urban form that simultaneously:
   (a) facilitates the reproduction of cheap urban labour power; and, in contrast,
   (b) generates enormous inefficiencies with respect to land use, industrial location, commercial development, local taxation, job creation, transport, bulk service provision and housing.
ii. An **urban management system** predicated on the notion that towns and cities can be compartmentalised into separate units presided over by separate local governments, with their own fiscal, legal, administrative and representative systems.
iii. A **system of urban service provision** that provides land, infrastructural services, transport and community facilities in a way that severely disadvantages the urban poor and subsidises the white ratepayer with surpluses generated from black consumption.
iv. A **housing delivery system** that subsidises whites and relegates the black majority to either homelessness or rental status with no security of tenure. (Planact 1989/90: 5)

This formulation usefully depicts the apartheid city as it was in 1991.[5] The establishment of functionally-defined municipalities, sharing a tax base and institutional and technical capacity, is imminent, and so a number of these characteristics will soon be a thing of the past. But, for a long time yet, South Africa will continue to carry the burden of inequalities and inefficiencies created by the dispersed apartheid city. Of course, it is the poor who carry the heaviest part of this burden; it is they who suffer most from exhaustion, it is they who have to commute vast distances, using inefficient and expensive transport, it is their time with their families which is cut, and it is their productivity which suffers.

An alternative approach

Under a majority government, South Africa will gain access to the resources of the World Bank, the United Nations and the United States

Agency for International Development (USAID), amongst others. (The World Bank has already sent a number of preparatory missions to South Africa and USAID has established offices in Pretoria.) How these agencies perceive the contribution that community organisations and local authorities can make to the formulation of urban economic development policy will profoundly influence the relative power these local organisations enjoy. Already there are indications that these agencies do not favour giving community-based groupings a significant role in *policy formulation* The World Bank, the United Nations Commission for Human Settlement (Habitat) and the United Nations Development Program already have an Urban Management Program in place which advances the view that local authorities should promote development indirectly, through efficient administration and an enhanced role for the private sector in providing services and shelter (Clarke 1991). This does not bode well for community organisations and local authorities seeking to influence how resources are allocated and how they are used.

One of the problems which assistance from bodies such as the World Bank introduces is the vast power of their intellectual and financial resources. They have the capacity to influence how a country defines its urban problems, how it allocates resources, who participates in decision-making, and who benefits. One does not have to be a hardened cynic to ask: if the poor are not party to decision-making, might they be secondary to the benefits? My task, therefore, is to delimit 'turf': to describe some practical arenas for action which demonstrate how communities can engage in development planning and economic initiatives.

Civics

While the theory holds that communities should participate in development planning and implementation, one seldom sees development agencies putting the theory into practice. Of course, non-governmental organisations (NGOs) receive much support – and, indeed, assistance to NGOs is highly fashionable; but it is not the role of NGOs to engage in policy formulation. Even if the World Bank wished to involve community organisations in policy formulation, it would find this difficult since host governments are typically averse to redistributing power in this area.

So far as participation by community organisations goes, the South African reality is different to the international norm – at least for the time being. In many areas the civics are powerful actors which cannot be ignored. But since most civics, regardless of calls for non-alignment, support the ANC, and since their leadership often holds office within the ANC, a critical question remains: will the ANC allow civics the autonomy to lobby over local development issues?

In its journal *Mayibuye* the ANC asserts that 'organisations of civil society – trade unions, community organisations, women and youth organisations – need to be empowered' (July 1991: 45). But the extent of the independence envisaged for civics seems to vary considerably. Natal Midlands ANC activists Blade Nzimande and Mpume Sikhosana have called for close ties between civics and local ANC structures:

> The strengthening of the ANC as a national liberation movement depends on the ability of its branches to respond and take up people's demands at local, regional and national levels. Civics ... have very limited ability to relate local to national demands ... Failure of the ANC branches to take up 'civic' issues will not only weaken the ANC locally but nationally as well. ... It is therefore important that where there are civics, ANC branches should work closely with them, but where there are no civics, our efforts should be directed towards strengthening ANC branches and not the formation of civics. (*Mayibuye* June 1991: 39)

And according to a key national civic movement strategist, Zora Ebrahim, independence for civics means they would make 'demands like affordable and accessible housing, land and services regardless of what government is in power' (cited in *Mayibuye* June 1991: 11).

Yet in the Pretoria-Witwatersrand-Vaal region (the PWV), for example, there are civics that are well organised and prepared to adopt positions of which the ANC disapproves. This was evident in the negotiations that led to the Soweto Accord, during which local civics engaged with black local authorities (albeit as members of the delegation of the Transvaal Provincial Administration), contrary to ANC policy.

The Soweto example suggests that whether civics do, in fact, mobilise around local issues will be more a reflection of their organisational strength than ANC policy.

In considering the role of community organisations within development planning, it is more interesting to move beyond formal ANC policy and, instead, examine what civics are presently doing – and question their likely future role. Currently, civics are engaging in negotiations and development efforts in major and intermediate cities like Johannesburg, Port Elizabeth, East London and Kimberley, and in small towns as far afield as Stutterheim in the Eastern Cape. The implicit planning processes in these initiatives, albeit more by default than by design, have many parallels with development planning.

The future role of civics is less clear. It appears they have a number of options; these are explored in Chapter 5. In brief, there seem to be three paths: many – perhaps the majority – will not survive the transition; some will probably continue as advocacy groups without clear mandates from their communities; and it is likely that the better-organised civics with clear mandates will create development agencies which they control. For the last group, in particular, the question that arises is whether a more self-conscious exploration of foreign experience can enhance their contribution to urban development.

The role of local authorities

Local authorities play an obvious and pivotal role in development planning and in the negotiations presently underway. This rather complicates matters, because the future powers and responsibilities of South Africa's municipalities have not yet been decided. At present, white local authorities are assuming primary responsibility for promoting development, while, it seems, the government and the ANC dither. One illustration of this apparent indecision can be found in the report of the government's 1990 Thornhill Commission, which proposes various local government models. The last of the six possibilities outlined is simply 'any other model' which proves acceptable!

According to State President De Klerk, National Party policy supports 'the greatest possible devolution of power to the lowest effective decision-making level. This embraces, *inter alia*, the maximum shift of government functions to the local government level, and the minimum central administrative control' (cited by Croeser 1991: 142). Arguably, the goal is to minimise the power of a future central government likely to be dominated by the ANC.

Until fairly recently, the ANC focused on national constitutional issues and appeared to take the view that local government constitutions would evolve from central negotiations. More recently it has called for interim local authorities, and has even accepted that black local authorities might form part of these. Nevertheless, while it urges devolution 'to empower the masses', there is reason to doubt whether the ANC, which anticipates being the future government, would permit constitutions which enable local authorities to challenge its power at national, central level.

This point has crucial implications, as the capacity of a local authority to intervene in the development planning process is clearly enhanced if it has significant powers.

A manual and text

One final reason for a book on development planning is the hope that it can provide a service to those engaged in development planning and serve as a text for students of the subject.

Awareness of the need for appropriate development planning has been raised in several quarters. In South Africa, events are outstripping existing local capacity to anticipate, manage and direct the process. There has been a tremendous inflow of overseas expertise, from Americans in particular, who are lending their skills to local service organisations,[6] NGOs and civics. At the same time, South Africans who encountered the topic while studying abroad have brought it back to local universities, where it has begun to filter into academic curricula. This book is intended to serve as a text for teaching purposes, and as a manual for those engaged in development planning so that they might develop their own capacity.

PERSONAL COMMITMENT

While writing this book I was torn between my academic self, which presents a distant, jaundiced picture of development planning, and a more activist self taken with enthusiasm for the potential achievements of local initiatives. Consequently the text swung from scepticism to committed optimism and back again. After much reflection, I came to the conclusion that I would be doing readers a disservice if I inflated the potential for development planning without due regard to the broader realities of development.

My impression is that purveyors of development planning in the United States and the United Kingdom search incessantly for communities (clients), funding, and students. They tend to hype up enthusiasm for development planning and create false expectations that generate a dangerous mythology of self-help. In a context of national and international economic restructuring, it might well be that local initiatives can do little to relieve urban poverty. As Rodwin (1989:18) has said

... regions have become increasingly dependent on decisions and forces outside the country as well as outside the region. This, in turn, has led to a considerable loss of influence and control over industrial and other development by national as well as by regional and local authorities.

We have to remember that development planning can make a contribution to alleviating poverty, but on its own it is not *the* answer.

It is important that we are clear on this. All too easily, civics can become victims of the interest in development planning. Civics will want to do something for their constituents, and local initiatives may offer a seemingly promising course of action. But if attempts at development fail, the civics themselves will suffer the harsh consequences of being unable to meet unrealistic expectations. Civics should have an idea of the likelihood of success – premised on more than my own enthusiasm. For this reason I have not entirely abandoned my cynicism; after all, cynicism is closely related to realism.

Approach

'There are two ways of looking at cities, neither incorrect' (Fainstein 1990a: 31). One approach examines the restructuring of the international economy – the decentralisation of production and service functions, global financial and commodity markets, the centralisation of control functions within giant corporations – and then considers the implications of this for the 'movement of capital and labour throughout the entire world system of cities and regions' (Fainstein and Fainstein 1989: 18). Within this approach, the fortunes of individual regions and cities are determined not by their specific locational advantages, but by the strategies of capitalists and the manner in which they are affected by state policies.

The second approach examines specific places: their economic bases, the predominant political interests and social divisions operating there, and the potential for coalitions which promote development. It is obvious that this book is oriented to the second approach.

However, in a given situation, it is difficult to assess whether the urban development strategy is exploiting existing and perceived potentials, or simply tilting at opportunities which an understanding of the movements of capital and labour and the place of the city within the international economy would reveal as ill-considered. There is unavoidable ambiguity in all of this: if the strategy succeeds, the development committee is visionary; if it fails, it has wasted the public's money.

For these reasons, I adopt a comparative approach in this book. I examine strategies that have worked or failed in other countries and try to interpret their potential application in South Africa. With few exceptions, though, development planning has been practised primarily in North America and Western Europe, and so it is inevitable that my material is drawn largely from these areas. In particular, the material is weighted to the USA. There are two reasons for this. The first is that the extent of competition in the USA – cities against suburban counties, cities against one another, states[7] against one another, and all of the above against foreign countries – means that experimentation with development strategies is more advanced there than in other countries where central government plays a dominating role. The second is that American community-based organisations are 'more advanced' due to the pressures exerted by the relative absence of welfare support and the greater need for self-reliance.

I sought the assistance of the Built Environment Support Group (BESG), Planact, and Professor David Dewar in areas in which they are South Africa's experts. BESG commissioned Jennifer Robinson and Carlos Boldogh to assess development initiatives in Durban. Planact commissioned Roland Hunter to describe the history of negotiations and development planning on the Witwatersrand. Professor Dewar shows how the form of future urban growth, the supply of shelter, and small-scale entrepreneurship can be combined to help alleviate the hardships imposed by the apartheid city.

The writing of this book was complicated by the range of goals I set myself. I wanted to refer to theory, to advance practical suggestions, and contribute more generally to the urban policy debate. The readership I had in mind includes local government officials, academics and students, members of the community, community organisations and business people. This required an accessible text, one which avoids 'academic prose' and is not littered with quotations and references. Of course, littering is relative, and as an (ex-)academic I have probably only succeeded in tidying up a little. As a compromise with my roots, I have striven for a clear text, and then resorted to notes to acknowledge debts or when I felt that further elaboration was necessary.

STRUCTURE OF THE BOOK

Chapter 2 undertakes three preliminary tasks: a presentation of demographic and economic trends, clarification of who the poor are, and discussion of how they will be affected by economic change.

Chapter 3 describes the emergence of development planning and presents a 'genealogy' of the various approaches to development. The chapter constitutes a family tree rendered complex by the attempt to traverse time, continents and countries at different levels of development. The chapter also explains why labour unions tend to participate in development planning on the metropolitan scale only and why they are often left out of the practice of development planning.

Chapters 4, 5 and 6 address the strategies and types of projects which might interest local authorities, community organisations and the private sector. These chapters reflect on comparative theory and experience, and then suggest specific local courses of action including ways of organising for participation in the development planning process.

In Chapter 8 Jennifer Robinson and Carlos Boldogh assess Operation Jumpstart, which began in the Durban Functional Region in 1990. They examine Jumpstart in political-economic terms, moving beyond an assessment of its developmental ramifications to consider the underlying struggles between central government, business and local authorities on the one hand, and the ANC and community-based organisations on the other. The terms under which the second group participated reveal that political capital is not to be underestimated and can be translated into both material gains and a redefinition of the development agenda.

In Chapter 9 Roland Hunter explores the issues which arise in the development and implementation of local economic strategies when the 'local' under consideration also happens to be the heart of the South African economy. The perspective adopted is that the overall aim of a local economic strategy is to ensure a sustainable improvement in the living conditions of the poorest urban residents. With this in mind Hunter examines the two major 'local economic' initiatives in the PWV: the PWV Economic and Development Forum and the Economic Development Working Group of the Central Witwatersrand Metropolitan Chamber. He identifies the different forces driving these initiatives and argues the need for one strategy.

In Chapter 10 David Dewar looks at shelter strategies and small-scale enterprise, and proposes how they can be combined to overcome many of the negative characteristics of the apartheid city. In particular, the sprawling settlements outside the cities impose severe time and money costs on the movement of people; and, because shelter densities are low and the land is zoned for one use only, the settlements forego entrepreneurial opportunities. Inefficient and inequitable cities are the result. There is a danger, too, that attempts to address the shelter problem will be located in areas outside the city where land is cheap. The effect will be to reproduce the physical form of the apartheid city, although this time it will be through economic means.

The book concludes with my suggestions on how local authorities, civics and the private sector can work in partnership to promote both urban development and the targeting of the benefits to the poor.

NOTES

1. For the sake of convenience I refer to civics and residents' associations as 'civics'. A description of the role they envisage for themselves is that they are now to represent civil society's fight for resources and power in the post-apartheid order. They must enjoy independence from political movements and the state; must be open to members of all political groups; are to become 'watchdogs' on the new state and are to play a major role in development. They will focus on 'day to day community issues' rather than fight for state power. (Friedman 1991b: 9)
2. See Chapter 8 for a description of both.
3. Development planning has two branches: economic development and community development. Economic development focuses on economic growth, employment creation and an enhanced tax base, often in run-down parts of towns. Community development looks to improving the quality of life through housing renovation, improved engineering and social services, job training and political advocacy. This book is directed at the economic branch of local development planning. Economic development has been the subject of many books and articles, for example, Blakely (1989), Bingham *et al.* (1990), Kane and Sand (1988), Lassar (1990), Luke *et al.* (1988), Sharp (1990), Eisinger (1988), and Peterson *et al.* (1991). The journal *Economic Development Quarterly* is devoted to the topic.
4. A common definition of small enterprises is that they are owned and managed by one person; employ 20 or fewer persons; have an annual turnover of less than R400 000; and employ capital of R160 000 or less (excluding immovable property). The terms 'micro' and 'informal' are often used more or less interchangeably to refer to unregistered and untaxed enterprises that employ simple financial and management systems and technology. Since the imagery surrounding the informal sector more clearly conveys the situation of the urban poor, it is the preferred term.
5. I am not entirely in agreement with this depiction. For example, see Tomlinson and Addleson (1987a) on the question of cheap labour power.
6. Service organisations are non-profit organisations which offer technical, professional, organisational skills and assistance to communities, political parties and unions. After the elections, these services will be extended to government itself.
7. It is convenient to refer to states as the level of government between the central and local levels in federal systems, and to provinces as the equivalent level in unitary systems.

Chapter 2

Economic Decline and Urban Poverty

This chapter constitutes an introduction and a context for the rest of the book. The first section provides a broad sweep of existing demographic and economic trends. The second narrows in on the urban poor: how should they be characterised, and how are they located in terms of urban labour markets? In the conclusion I speculate about the impact of the economic trends on the urban poor and whether they can be served by development planning.

DEMOGRAPHIC AND ECONOMIC TRENDS

In the ensuing data there is a relative focus on Africans. My reason for distinguishing between Africans, Asians and coloureds is that the urban conditions confronting these groups are markedly different. Asians and coloureds have higher urbanisation levels, superior monthly household incomes, and better services. In addition to having the lowest household incomes, Africans also constitute an ever-increasing majority in South Africa's cities. From the point of view of identifying the urban poor, it makes sense to focus on Africans. It is they who should be the primary beneficiaries of development planning.

Urban growth and poverty

Table 2.1 shows South Africa's population size and growth rate, urbanisation levels, the racial proportions of the total population, and the racial share of personal income. The striking feature of the table is the revealed inequality. In 1990 South Africa's white population, who make up 14 per cent of the country's total, earned approximately 54 per cent of the national income.

Table 2.1 also explains why Africans are becoming such a majority in the cities. They have the highest population growth rate and already contribute more than three-quarters of the country's population.

Table 2.2 shows that the geography of African urban growth is biased in favour of the metropolitan areas and the immediately adjacent areas located just within the homeland borders.[1] No area will lose population; the disparities arise due to the different growth rates. A fact which will later prove significant when explaining differences in income between men and women is that men outnumber women by 1,3 to 1 in the cities and 1,1 to 1 in the towns (Budlender 1992).

The associated incidence of poverty is shown in Table 2.3. A common measure of poverty in South Africa is the Minimum Living Level – defined as the income required to provide basic food, clothing, fuel and lighting, washing and cleansing, rent and transport, medical expenses, education and household equipment for an average family of 5,45 people. In 1990 the Bureau of Market Research calculated this level to be R695[2] per month. Table 2.3 shows that poverty predominates among rural Africans (69,9 per cent) and rural coloureds (51 per cent), and is also

Table 2.1 *South Africa: Demographic and income profile*

	African	Asian	coloured	white	total
Population total and proportion (a)					
1990	74,2%	2,7%	8,7%	14,4%	38,05m
2000	78,1%	2,5%	8,0%	11,5%	47,74m
Urbanisation level (b)	53%*	90,6%	80,6%	89,4%	62%
Population growth rate (c)					
1990 – 2000	2,8%	1,5%	1,4%	0,02%	2,29%
Share of personal income (d)					
1985	29%	4%	8%	59%	
1995	37%	4%	10%	49%	

Sources: (a) & (c) Development Bank of Southern Africa, Development Information Group, 1992.
(b) The Urban Foundation, n.d.
(d) The Urban Foundation, 1991. (The 1995 data assume a 2,5% economic growth rate between 1990 and 1995.)
*   1985

Table 2.2 *African population distribution, 1985 and 2010*

	1985		2010	
	%	**Actual**	**%**	**Actual**
Metropolitan areas	21	5,2m	30	14,3m
Homeland metropolitan	14	3,5m	19	9,3m
Other urban	10	2,4m	12	5,7m
Homeland dense settlements (a)	8	1,9m	8	3,9m
% urban/sub-total	53	13,0m	69	33,2m
Rural outside the homelands	14	3,4m	7	3,4m
Homeland rural	33	8,0m	25	11,9m
% rural/sub-total	47	11,4m	32(b)	15,3m

Source: The Urban Foundation, n.d.
(a)   This refers to informal settlements in homeland rural areas where people are minimally engaged in agriculture and have family members who engage in long-distance commuting to urban areas.
(b)   The sum equals 101% due to rounding.

Table 2.3 *Households in poverty*

	Asians	Africans	coloureds	whites
1985	%	%	%	%
Metropolitan	10,2	31,9	11,6	3,9
Urban	10,8	40,9	5,8	4,4
Rural	10,4	69,9	51,3	4,8
Homeland metropolitan	52,7			
Homeland urban	64,7			
Homeland rural	84,0			
1985	%	%	%	%
Metropolitan	7,2	30,9	8,9	4,4
Urban	6,1	33,8	10,4	4,9
Rural	5,4	65,2	31,6	5,4
Homeland metropolitan	46,8			
Homeland urban	58,8			
Homeland rural	80,0			

Source: The Urban Foundation, 1991. (The 1995 data assume a 2,5% economic growth rate between 1990 and 1995. Ten per cent of the income of urban, single African males has been deducted and added to rural households in order to account for migrant remittances.)

found among a significant proportion (33 per cent) of urban Africans.[3] Overall, survival is the primary concern of nearly half (45 per cent) of the country's African households.

One illustration of what this means is that about seven million people currently live in informal settlements, including more than half the population of the Durban Functional Region (DFR). The number of people living in informal settlements is expected to increase to 12 million by 2010. In effect, South Africa is experiencing the urbanisation of a low-income African population which is unable to afford housing and services.

Urbanisation under apartheid

South Africa is notorious for its attempts to constrain African urbanisation. The salient factors of this endeavour are well known.[4] I deal with these factors expeditiously, not with a view to describing the sins of the past, but to conveying how urban apartheid came to place an insupportable strain both on the poor and on the country's urban system.

Perhaps the most notable feature of urban apartheid is the 'apartheid city'. One form of this is residential segregation, caused by racial zoning and low incomes among Africans, but there are others – forced removal of Africans, coloureds and Asians to formal townships outside the city, or the consignment of Africans to informal settlements just inside homeland borders, usually some distance from the city.[5]

Restrictions on the movement of Africans into urban areas did not prevent African urbanisation so much as displace it. Despite influx controls and pass laws, informal settlements developed apace with backyard shacks in formal townships and widespread overcrowding. African urbanisation was already happening at levels comparable with other countries at similar levels of development. The demise of apartheid would not cause an 'urban flood'.

The resulting form of the apartheid city is something akin to a doughnut: the highest population densities are on the fringes of the city. Associated with these areas of high-density settlement are grossly inferior engineering services and dependence on illegitimate black local authorities.[6] Despite the poor quality of these services, institutional duplication and the relatively recent supply of services to historically African parts of towns means that residents of these areas pay more for the services they receive. The capital cost of Johannesburg's electricity supply network, for example, has effectively been paid off; Soweto's on the other hand is a fairly recent installation, and an amount in the order of R400 million is still owing on it. Because Soweto has a separate local authority, the city cannot benefit from cross-subsidisation by Johannesburg. Exacerbating this problem is the fact that the Johannesburg and Soweto local authorities have historically operated in different financial markets, and capital is less easily come by and costs more for Soweto (Swilling and Shubane 1991).

These problems have been aggravated by restrictions on economic activity in the townships. In official terms, African urbanisation was permitted simply to provide urban labour. Quite apart from the negative impact this had on African entrepreneurship,[7] the townships and informal settlements were left without any kind of fiscal base.

The result of these policies and developments has been dysfunctional cities with a host of problems. The location of African housing or dispersed informal settlements relative to commerce, industry and services is wholly impractical. Africans are required to commute on average 37 kilometres each way, and this imposes severe burdens of time, money, exhaustion and harshly diminished family life. Not surprisingly, labour productivity among workers is comparatively low due to exhaustion.[8] Massive state bus and rail transportation subsidies for commuters are required – an amount of R1,9 billion was spent in 1992. But despite this, commuting typically consumes around 10 per cent of an urban family's household income. The costs of providing services are inflated. Black local authorities have been left without fiscal potential and institutional capacity. Informal sector opportunities are diminished due to the isolation of low-income communities.

South Africa's cities are both extraordinarily inefficient and inequitable. Fortunately, negotiations are presently underway to address the delimitation of functional urban areas that share a tax base and institutional and technical capacity. Similarly, racial zoning and restrictions on African enterprise are now a thing of the past. Yet the consequences of this history will not easily be reversed. South Africa will long be burdened by the form of its cities, inequalities in the supply of land, housing and services, and by disadvantages arising from impediments to economic advancement.

Economic malaise

The notion of inequality underlies most thinking about economic policy, but this emphasis is probably misplaced. African incomes are rising considerably faster than those of whites,[9] while the white share of household income, as a proportion of the national total, is declining rapidly. Once one moves away from the cruder racial inequities, rather different problems come to the fore. Almost half the African population lives in poverty. Formal unemployment among Africans is now about 50 per cent. Table 2.4 shows the marked decline in employment opportunities – in 1992 less than 7 per cent of new African entrants to the labour force could find formal employment. A 1 per cent increase in GDP leads to an increase of only 0.3 per cent in employment.

Table 2.4 Decline in employment opportunities[10]

	Average annual increase in labour force	Average annual increase in formal employment	Average annual absorption capacity of formal sector
1966-70	197 000	145 000	73,6%
1971-75	249 000	156 000	62,7%
1976-80	288 000	102 000	35,4%
1981-85	310 000	68 000	21,9%
1986-90	366 000	33 000	9,0%

Source: Ligthelm and Kritzinger-Van Niekerk 1990: 630.

By contrast, the improving income distribution reflects the fact that wage differentials between the races have been dropping since the early 1970s. Fallon's explanation (1992: 23) is that 'African wages have largely responded to influences other than market forces that have led to an increase in real wages despite higher African unemployment; [whereas] white wages have adjusted much more strongly to market forces ...' and in the 1980s fell in the face of slower economic growth. He credits the resilience of African wages to increased strike activity, the abolition of influx controls, the demise of job reservation and other discriminatory practices, pressure on employers to do away with inter-racial wage differentials, and some convergence in skills. Thus Hofmeyr (1990) observes that the labour market is becoming increasingly unified as segmentation between races and sectors, and among men and women, declines. In his view education is now the leading determinant of wages.

This contradictory situation – declining income differentials and increasing unemployment and poverty – has been greatly exacerbated by the country's poor economic management. This is particularly evident in the country's import substitution industrial strategy and in the economy's rising capital intensity.

Growth under an import substitution regime depends on an expansion of the internal market, but the skewed income distribution inhibited the development of a mass market and promoted the growth of a market for consumer durables such as cars. Such consumer markets are dependent on scale economies which the size of the internal market was unable to sustain, and this created a dependency on the import of components and capital goods. The problem with scale economies is more pronounced in the production of components and capital goods and the country's manufacturing sector soon lost hope of being internationally competitive. The possibility of exports was lost.

The economy's capital intensity reflects negative real interest rates for most of the 1970s and 1980s, generous tax write-offs and incentives, 'strategic investments' such as petrochemicals which were intended to enhance the independence of the apartheid state, and successful labour organisation that led to higher wages and uncertainty due to work stoppages. In addition, the exchange rate was frequently overvalued, which contributed to difficulties in promoting exports. The consequence is that employment growth in the private sector has been static since 1982; the increases which have occurred must be attributed largely to the public sector.

In the absence of economic growth, African youths will have to turn *en masse* to alternative income sources. The government's Central Statistical Service (South Africa 1991) estimated that in 1990 the informal sector provided full-time employment for 1,7 million persons and part-time employment for 2,8 million persons. The Service estimated that this was comparable to about 20 per cent of the full-time labour force, and that this number increased by 20 per cent between 1989 and 1990. The informal sector produced the equivalent of six to eight per cent of the country's GDP. However, these figures exclude the 'independent' homelands, informal settlements, domestic servants, and Africans in 'white areas'. A more accurate estimate of overall informal sector employment is in the order of 4,5 million persons.[11]

The foreseeable future is bleak. Table 2.5 shows that growth rates have been declining for three decades and that since 1981 per capita GDP growth has been negative. Especially striking is the fact that gross domestic fixed investment as a percentage of GDP declined by 10 per cent between 1975 and 1990 (to 19,6 per cent). The economic malaise has parallels elsewhere in the world and is not unique to South Africa. Yet it is unfortunate, to say the least, that South Africa's economy is in such a dire state at a time when growth in employment and incomes is critical for a successful transition to democracy.

Table 2.5 *Deterioration of economic performance in South Africa (average annual percentage change)*

	1961-70	1971-80	1981-90	1991-93
Private consumption	5,3	3,8	2,8	-0,7
Government consumption	7,2	5,5	3,4	1,5
Gross domestic product	5,7	3,4	1,5	-0,7
Gross domestic product per capita	2,9	0,7	-0,9	-2,9
Employment	3,5	2,7	1,0	-2,1
Inflation	2,8	10,6	14,7	12,9

Source: South African Reserve Bank Quarterly Bulletin, June 1994.

There is general acceptance that the country is confronting an economic crisis, and there is now considerable debate around future economic policies. A key site of this debate is the National Economic Forum (NEF). The factors underlying the formation of this forum can be traced through material cited in the *Bilateralism Review* (1992, 1, 1: 17). Dr Japie Jacobs, special adviser to the Minister of Finance, states that

the government has embarked on a policy of restructuring the economy, of which the main ingredients comprise the reduction in the public sector's share in the economy, the promotion of effective competition, including foreign competition, improved education and training, restricting the rise in government spending, reducing the overall tax burden, implementing tax reforms which include lowering the nominal corporate tax rate and the high marginal personal income tax rates and shifting a greater share of the tax burden to indirect taxes, the promotion of industrial growth which is more export oriented and maintaining financial discipline with the aim of curbing the high rate of inflation.

For its part, COSATU, the massive trade union federation, has been concerned with

the Government's refusal to negotiate burning economic issues on the one hand, while on the other hand unilaterally imposing

economic restructuring programmes. The proposal that these negotiations must be postponed until national political negotiations
take place, [was] viewed as a transparent delaying tactic ... by the
Government ... in order to impose its own economic programme.

For this reason, during the transition process COSATU has focused on
the creation of a forum to initiate negotiations around restructuring the
economy. Major employer bodies are participating in the National
Economic Forum; more recently, the Minister of Finance, Derek Keys, has
not been reluctant to participate, as the government was in the past. The
NEF now represents a tripartite relationship between government, organised labour and major employer bodies. The NEF has two broad working
groups. The short-term group focuses on job creation and industrial strategy and restructuring, and the long-term group concentrates on industrial strategy.

Against this backdrop, the local development initiatives described in
Chapter 1 are prompted, at least in part, by frustration at the inability of
government to manage an economic recovery. As a counter to further
mismanagement at the centre, business groups, civics, unions and local
authorities are leading strategic planning at the scale of cities and
regions, while urging that the resulting development policies should
correspond with those of the NEF.

POVERTY AND URBAN LABOUR MARKETS

It comes as a bit of a shock to discover that the poor are not clearly
delineated in the South African literature. Belinda Bozzoli[12] explains that
one reason for this is that most research has been intended to demonstrate the failings of apartheid, rather than examine township social
structures. Alternatively, as Charles Simkins[13] puts it, the areas in which
people conduct research are closely related to the interests and constituencies of funding agencies, and the poor are not included in those.[14]

Were it not for apartheid, we would ordinarily claim that the origins of
urban poverty lie in the performance of urban labour markets. That is,
the 'disparities and differentials found in the labour market, the various
institutions and mechanisms governing job access and security, and the
legal and social frameworks, all form part of a broader social process
governing the use and remuneration of labour ... Poverty ... derives in
large part from the structure of the labour market and of the associated
labour processes' (Rodgers 1989: 1). We therefore need to interweave a

concern with apartheid with the qualities of urban labour markets which give rise to poverty, and then describe the characteristics of the poor in a manner which contributes to targeted urban policy.

Urban labour markets

Vulnerability

The notion of 'vulnerability' is useful for conceptualising the likelihood of poverty – although data are seldom available in a form which facilitates an analysis of this sort. Rodgers (1989: 9) identifies five categories of vulnerability:

i. Protected wage work (contracts and legal constraints operate; jobs are protected from market forces by restrictions on entry).
ii. Competitive regular wage work (entry is relatively open and market forces operate, but employment is nevertheless continuous and perhaps subject to contract – i.e. one can identify continuing jobs).
iii. Unprotected wage labour (heterogeneous: includes much casual labour, domestic service, wage workers in petty trade; characterised by insecurity and/or irregularity). Various forms of disguised wage labour (e.g. outwork) might also be included here.
iv. Self-employment and family labour in 'productive' small-scale production.
v. 'Marginal' activities, which range from peripheral low-productivity work such as shoe-shining and hawking to semi-legal and illegal activities.

The poorest persons are generally casual labourers and those engaged in marginal activities, followed by workers in small enterprises, and then the self-employed. (Admittedly it is often difficult to differentiate between self-employment and marginal activities.) When unemployment among such people is high, the effects ripple upwards through the labour hierarchy.

In an economic downturn, informal sector activity declines in proportion to that in the formal sector. This is because formal sector workers provide a market for the products of the informal sector. As their economic situation deteriorates, they consume fewer informal sector products. Informal sector incomes then decline, creating another round of declining consumption. In broad terms, as conditions within protected wage work and competitive regular wage work deteriorate, the decline in Rodgers's other three work categories will be even more marked.

Job access

In a smoothly functioning market economy, access to jobs depends on an individual's leisure preference and productivity and the issue of job access becomes redundant. In the South African reality, access is critical. As McGrath and Van der Berg (1991: 6) note, 'in recent years many "apartheid" obstacles have been removed, and education and access to the internal labour market of major employers, and access to employment in the public sector, are now becoming the major determinants of racial distributions of occupations'.

Access depends on:
*   inter-personal networks;
*   qualifications;
*   skills and experience;
*   personal characteristics, for example, docility, initiative, age, sex;
*   access to capital from one's family, one's own savings, and public and private financial institutions;
*   residential location;
*   access to a market for the products of self-employment; and
*   negative personal effects on motivation, health, appearance, employment record arising from one or more periods of unemployment.

Contrary to the common assumption that the 'informal sector is easy to enter', the informal sector can also be highly protected. For example, it is to be expected that persons with profitable stalls on a street corner with much passing traffic will oppose the encroachment of other stalls. Similarly, prostitutes control 'turf'. Ultimately it is unclear whether there are any sectors with unconstrained access. Certainly as unemployment deepens, control of access to jobs becomes an increasingly contested arena.

Unemployment

It used to be argued that the poor could not afford to be unemployed, and that perforce they engage in some marginal activity. It has become clear that this is not true. Unemployment is higher among the poor, and when it is the head of household who is unemployed the implications for household poverty are particularly severe. Unemployment forces changes in labour supply strategy, intensifies the job search, and increases subsistence activities.

The unemployment situation in South Africa has already been touched on. Additional features worth mentioning are the distribution of unemployment between men and women and between adults and children. After expressing a variety of qualifications about the data, Fallon (1992) observes that unemployment among African women is about double that of African men. He hypothesises that this is especially true of less-educated women and women with young children who do not wish to travel far from the household in order to seek work.

Fallon also found that unemployment is disproportionately concentrated among younger groups. This, of course, is to be expected in the light of the declining employment opportunities for new entrants to the labour force.

Supply of labour

The supply of labour depends on the life-cycle and demographic characteristics of the household. For example, poverty within a family is often greatest when the head of household is between 35 and 44 years old, for this is when the number of new non-working members of the family is greatest and when women may be out of the labour force. Poverty induces changes in labour supply strategies, particularly of 'secondary' workers – women and children – and may lead to children being taken out of school in order that they contribute to household income. Sometimes the poorest may show a low labour force participation, but individuals may be handicapped, ill, underfed or discouraged, and there may be undercounting of subsistence workers. (These are all categories for which there are no reliable data in South Africa.) Lipton (1988) holds that discouraged workers are invariably men rather than women, but fails to explain why this should be so.

The legacy of apartheid

Apartheid has so predetermined the life chances of the majority of South Africans that any discussion of labour markets and poverty has to mention the history of unequal expenditure on education, job reservation, harassment of unions, restrictions on African entrepreneurship, and the form of the apartheid city. The problem, however, is that much of this is not unique to South Africa. For example, there have been attempts to control population mobility in many countries, as well as attempts to control informal enterprise. Repression of unions is all too common. And Janet Abu-Lughod (1980) was not being merely provocative when she titled a book of hers *Rabat: Urban Apartheid in Morocco*. We should not make the mistake of attributing to apartheid features which are often found in totalitarian middle-income countries with a labour surplus.

Yet, two features stand out: institutional racism and an extraordinarily skewed distribution of income. The latter is so extreme as to refute the claim that apartheid has structured inequality along racial lines; in fact it has accentuated that inequality. For example, the shortage of skilled labour, due to unequal education and legislated or informal discriminatory practices, is commonly held to have retarded the country's economic growth. Due to their inferior education, the burden of slow economic growth falls most heavily on Africans, for it is they who most suffer from high unemployment.

The characteristics of the poor[15]

Broadly speaking, there are four criteria for measuring poverty:

- **absolute consumption** – the 'destitute' are those whose incomes are insufficient to purchase a food basket, while the 'poor' are those whose incomes are below the arbitrarily defined value of twice the cost of the food basket;
- **relative consumption** – a measure of income inequality;
- **access** to public and semi-public goods and services; and
- **subjective criteria** based on the perceptions and responses of the poor.

The last criterion explains the behaviour patterns and labour market responses of the poor. Destitution, poverty and relative consumption are the most commonly employed measures and are properly assessed in terms of household income per capita. This text has rather tended to focus on inequalities. Here it is useful to consider poverty in more absolute terms.

The characteristics of the urban poor described below are borrowed from the comparative literature. I have used them as a guide to narrow in on the particulars of poverty in South Africa. The absence of a migrant category should perhaps be explained. In other countries, migrants are not represented disproportionately among the poor, nor are they more prone to unemployment. It appears that the decision to migrate is based on contacts and influence, and may even be preceded by the availability of a job. Similar factors seem to be at play in this country. In the DFR, for example, Cross *et al.* (1992: 41) observe that 'new in-migrants tend to be the *middle poor*, i.e. young nuclear families with comparatively few dependents, headed by a man, who is often employed or at least employable. In short these families are not the very poor or destitute.'

Household structure

A useful insight into household income is gained by referring to household income per capita. This includes the income of the head of household and that of other household members who are working. In these terms, a household with a small income may be better off than a household with a larger income – the crucial question is the number of dependants among whom the income has to be divided.

In practice, though, even household income per capita fails to account for the distribution of income within a household. For example, whereas women commonly devote all their income to necessities, men retain a portion of their earnings for 'extras' and enjoy a higher standard of living.

A household is defined as a unit of social organisation which usually combines shared residence, reproduction (income generation, consumption and domestic activities such as cooking and eating) and, most often, family organisation.[16] The household is a dynamic entity and can take different forms – nuclear households, women-headed households and extended households. An extended household may resemble either of the first two examples and, in addition to children, may include other income-earners who spread the risk of survival, or other persons who share the residence. The additional members are usually family, or at least come from the same clan or village. The advantage of extended families is that through dispersing members between sectors and, perhaps, across space, the household minimises the risk of destitution.

As Mabin (1991) points out, most urban commentators were misled by restrictions on urbanisation into believing that once those restrictions were lifted, there would be rapid migration to the cities of *entire family units*. This has not happened to the extent anticipated. Frequently some members retain a base in rural areas or in non-formal urban areas, some proceed to town and others go on to another rural area. To complicate matters, the duration of all these migrations might vary. Households combine urban and rural incomes, spread the risks of economic hardship and might thus have every intention of continuing with a process of circular migration.[17] For example, gold miners represent a conspicuous example of circulatory migration and it has been estimated that each gold miner supports nine dependants.

Low education level

Low levels of education are characteristic of poverty. In other countries the poor generally lack secondary education. However, Fallon (1992) reports that in South Africa unemployment among Africans peaks at Standard 7, and that unemployment among those with no education is lower than among those with Standard 10. Among those with tertiary qualifications there is no unemployment. It appears that in an environment where there are a limited number of jobs which require an education, education raises thresholds and acts as a rationing device.

Perhaps the most important manner in which education interacts with poverty is inter-generational: the children of people who are poor and have low levels of education often drop out of school and enter the labour market early.

Hofmeyr (1990) found that education is a highly significant variable in explaining South Africa's wage distribution. Inequality in educational expenditure in the country is notorious. Half of all African schoolchildren drop out before Standard 5, the level of schooling generally regarded as necessary for lasting literacy. And, for every 10 000 African children who start school, 113 pass their school-leaving examination in Standard 10, 27 obtain a sufficiently high mark to enter university, and only one does so in Science and Mathematics. Obviously, conditions are now changing, but it remains true that most Africans are condemned to compete in an overcrowded, unskilled labour market. This helps to explain why the wages of unskilled male workers in manufacturing in Johannesburg dropped by 3 per cent per annum between 1975 and 1985.

Large number of dependants

Poor households are generally large and have high proportions of dependent children and older non-workers. Poverty among such households may have little to do with labour market mechanisms. Instead, when the problem is too many children, poor health or old age, the issue is less one of government interventions to ensure access to jobs than it is one of formal or informal social support systems.

More formally, the dependency ratio describes the total number of persons supported by every employed person, excluding the employed person. It is unclear what we should make of the dependency ratio in South Africa, for so many urban African households represent a spatially separate but functionally integrated part of a larger household. The following figures are therefore presented for comparative purposes rather than meaningful interpretation. The dependency ratio for greater Durban (Durban, Inanda and Pinetown) in 1990 was 2,0, as compared with 3,2 for South Africa.[18] Due to the support rendered by urban households to family in rural areas, the latter is probably the more meaningful statistic. It points to considerable pressure on employed household members.

Women-headed households

Rodgers (1989) holds that poverty is notably higher in households with a high proportion of women among active household members, and especially so when the household head is female. Lipton (1988) counters that women are not over-represented among the poor, and finds poverty primarily in large families and among children. In his view there is in fact little wage discrimination against women, within given job categories (p. 23). Rather, he argues that wage differences are mostly explained by the length of the workday and type of job. He maintains that discrimination arises from women having to accept inferior standards of health, education, mobility and job entry, and so being pushed into lower-wage jobs. Mazumdar (1988: 60) agrees that women are 'crowded' into a narrow band of the market which pays low wages, but suggests that in order to escape this crowding, women are prepared to accept lower wages than men in traditionally male jobs.

Chant (1991) approaches this debate from a very different perspective, arguing that women-headed households may fare better than conventional nuclear households because the internal distribution of income is more equitable. She points out that a large number of women-headed households may inevitably come about where the local economy provides more jobs for women than men. Textiles and service industries, for example, employ more women than men. But women-headed households can also occur where the economy is structured around migrant labour, or where men are needed at certain times of the year for farming activities. In a context where urban liaisons are fragile, women-headed households may also result. Since men tend to distribute their incomes unequally within the family, Chant maintains that in a women-headed household, in which income is distributed more evenly among household members, everyone may end up better off – even where that income is relatively small.

Chant's position is appealing in principle, especially if one agrees with Lipton. But there are flaws in her logic. If women earn less than men – regardless of whether this is the result of crowding or discrimination within job categories – then a household with more female than male earners will have a lower total income than one where all the earners are men. This effect is reinforced if the head of household is a woman. Unless income distribution within a male-dominated household is especially unfair, it would seem that women-headed households would generally be worse off financially, as they would have a smaller pool of resources which no amount of equitable internal distribution could enlarge. In the light of this, it is alarming to note that the 'proportion of incomplete [sic] female-headed households in the townships of the PWV has risen to over 55 per cent ...' (Schlemmer and Humphries 1989: 10).

Hofmeyr (1990) found that wage differences between men and women are narrowing. Budlender (1992) has concluded that the opposite is true! Either way, the differences are still marked. A number of factors explain these differences.[19]

i.   Women are crowded into low-wage sectors: domestic service, community and personal services, clothing, textiles, and shoe manufacture. Only 25 per cent of those employed in manufacturing are women. There are very few women in mining, construction and electricity.

ii.   Women are under-represented in unionised employment. Maggie Magubane, Women's Co-ordinator of the National Union of Metal Workers of South Africa, says that this is due to the traditional practice of women staying in the homelands in order to take care of the house and children; employer bias against women because of the belief that there are jobs only a man can do; and the anticipation that women will take maternity leave.[20]

iii. 'In South Africa in 1987, one per cent of all African male workers were artisans as opposed to 0,2 per cent of African women; 51,2 per cent of African male workers were semi-skilled compared to 33,2 per cent of women; 42,3 per cent of men were unskilled compared to 28,3 per cent of women; and 5,4 per cent of men did menial work compared to 38,3 per cent of women' (Budlender 1992: 355).

To throw the cat among the pigeons, I might also observe that while girls have higher levels of enrolment in South African schools, their exam results are not as good as those of the boys.[21] They consequently do not have equal access to jobs.

iv. Only 30 per cent of economically active urban African women are employed in the formal sector. Within the informal sector men predominate in larger and/or more lucrative businesses. The exceptions are women who run shebeens, trade in drugs and engage in prostitution. More typical women's activities are retailing and services: vegetable selling, dressmaking, selling second-hand clothing, selling new clothing purchased from outside the area, running shack shops, and hawking cold drinks, paraffin and household items.

Nutritional status

Kahnert (1987) has indicated that in low-income countries commonly a half or more of their population cannot afford to feed themselves adequately. In a middle-income country the statistic usually lies between 20 and 33 per cent. Calculations of this sort, based on household income, mask even sharper actual discontinuities between poor and ultra-poor in respect of nutrition (Lipton 1988). The nutritional status of the destitute jeopardises their health and affects their capacity to supply labour; this means that in order to involve the destitute in development projects, one may first have to assist them to achieve a reasonable nutritional or health status (Mohan 1985). Lipton (1988: 7) holds that

> it is wrong to see the poorest 10-15 percent in developing countries as an 'underclass', accessible, if at all, only at very high unit cost. That may apply to many of the poorest in developed countries; measures to raise 'the productivity of the poorest' may be unpromising where most such people are very old and alone, or addicted to alcohol or other drugs, or severely ill or handicapped in mind or body. This is not the case for most ultra-poor in the developing world. They are mainly young, members of big families, and able if properly nourished to participate fully in school and work.

Somewhat surprisingly, the South African comparison is not as bad as the 20 to 30 per cent norm would lead one to expect. Ina Perlman[22] says that Operation Hunger is feeding almost 2,5 million persons. The figure of 2,5 million is up sharply from less than 2 million at the beginning of

1991 and is blamed on both the drought and economic decline. Perlman says that unlike much of Africa, we now have a 'pre-famine situation' – not because of a shortage of food, but because of affordability. The implications are tragic since 25 000 people a year already die from hunger-related diseases, and a quarter of all deaths in the African community are malnourished children under the age of five.

One should note that 70 per cent of Operation Hunger's assistance is rendered in rural and peri-urban areas. The implication might seem to be that nutritional deprivation is not much of an issue in urban areas. But, because of growing unemployment and the rapidly increasing cost of food, greater involvement in urban areas is anticipated. As to who actually receives assistance, Perlman points out that targeting is decided in consultation with the community concerned; most often they favour the children.

CONCLUSION

The above material suggests that South Africa's urban poor comprise mainly the youth and households without male income-earners. The primary vehicle for escaping this poverty is an increase in employment opportunities. Is it likely?

Fallon (1992) is pessimistic. He concludes that the ever-slower growth in employment is due to:

- upward pressure on African wages;
- the tendency to greater capital intensity;
- a scarcity of skilled labour and management; and
- the recession since the early 1980s.

Of these factors, only the recessionary forces may be quickly reversed. In the interim, pressure for minimum wages and job security will further curtail hiring.

What does this mean for South Africa? Does it make sense to assist the poor through development planning? On the one hand, if urban labour markets work, and earnings are determined by supply and demand, yet remain low, then 'one must act on the supply and demand for labour in order to raise employment, productivity and incomes' (Kahnert 1987: 8). In World Bank parlance, this implies efforts to overcome market imperfections and distortions that retard human capital formation and reduce demand for labour. In addition to enhancing human resource development, the World Bank recommends that the public sector should play an indirect role in development through removing distortions in access to or prices of complementary factors of production or public services, and also those which raise the cost of doing business. For the foreseeable future, however, it seems unlikely that the government will facilitate a decline in real African wages.

On the other hand, if economic trends leave the economy with a great imbalance between the supply of and demand for urban labour, and if one should not in any case be sanguine about the functioning of the labour market, what potential is there for government to play a more direct role in promoting development? And what chance is there that the poor will be able to act in a co-ordinated fashion, to levy demands on government and on business, and to undertake development activities themselves? A preliminary assessment may be made here, based on the interests of the state, business and the unions.

The future state is likely to represent a compromise between the ANC and the National Party (NP). The constitution, economic policies and obstacles posed by an entrenched civil service will themselves create severe difficulties for any desire to engage in far-reaching redistribution. Is it too cynical to wonder whether such an inclination might ever arise? For one thing, the NP will obviously be concerned to safeguard property rights. It has little regard for the urban poor and historically has attempted to exploit their poverty to minimise the impetus for migration from rural areas. For another, the ANC has powerful constituencies in petit-bourgeois groups and organised labour (Freund 1986) and, in the light of limited resources, will find it difficult to serve less well-organised constituencies. The point is that it is unclear whether urban poverty will be a priority issue for the likely future government or coalition.

With regard to business, South Africa is renowned for concentration of ownership. In itself, this does not prevent subcontracting to small-scale, inherently more labour-intensive enterprises, as is common for example with Japan's highly agglomerated *keiretsu*.[23] But, what with the limited capacity of small-scale enterprises to deliver differentiated products, on the one hand, and the corporations' tradition of internalised sourcing, on the other, it seems neither has much to contribute to employment creation. South Africa's major corporations are much more concerned with productivity and industrial peace than with enhancing employment creation. Increasing productivity in a static market suggests little likelihood of employment creation.

With respect to labour, 2,4 million workers were unionised in 1990, half of those by COSATU (SAIRR 1991/92: 269). Since unionised workers earn 21 per cent more than non-unionised workers (Fallon 1992), in a declining economy COSATU's primary interest must be one of protecting the jobs of its members. Further, while COSATU has talked of forming a union for the unemployed, this is somewhat unlikely. COSATU has certainly evinced a concern for community affairs and has proved to be a powerful ally for civics, but its self-interest is to assist communities, not to change the terms under which members of those communities gain access to employment. We should remember Castells's description (1983: 268) of the struggle in Madrid: 'Labour and neighbourhoods fought different battles, even if often they clashed with the same police and exchanged messages of solidarity inspired by a common political matrix: they were allies, not comrades.'

This leaves us with little choice but to view the mobilisation of the poor as central to the amelioration of poverty. In this regard, civics seem 'heaven-sent', since, as Dan Sandi notes, 'it is amongst the poor and oppressed that developmental projects must start ...'.[24] There are, however, a few disconcerting points about the way civics perceive their role.

First, Moses Mayekiso, President of the South African National Civic Organisation (SANCO), equates the interests and indeed also the membership of civics and unions (*Reconstruct* 1992, 3: 2). This is unfortunate and, often enough, inaccurate. It is important to note that the interests of workers and community organisations are not identical and they confront different issues. Any attempt to conflate their membership and interests will mask the interests of unionised workers, the unemployed, and members of the community concerned by, say, the absence of crèches, trash collection, and other such issues.

Secondly, domestic and international foundations and aid agencies are prepared to make money available to legitimate organisations with development capacity. One effect of this is to accentuate competition for hegemony within the townships. This compounds the civics' tendency to monopolise claims to be representative and to deny a role for other bodies. This in turn gives rise to several other problems. Some civics appear to be stuck in an oppositional relationship with the state, and residents suffer from a lack of development initiatives. In addition, certain church or women's groups may have a better capacity than the local civic to address the development needs of the urban poor.

Civics, moreover, serve specific constituencies which may be poorly aligned with local needs. Hostel-dwellers, residents of informal settlements and women, for example, can all legitimately claim to be poorly represented.

Despite these problems, the following material continues to use the convenient shorthand of referring to civics as the vehicle for organising from the bottom up. This usage is not intended to exclude other institutions of civil society from taking on this role.

There are four reasons for supporting institutions such as civics. Firstly, governments have not proven adept at targeting policy and project benefits to the poor. Inevitably, the benefits are siphoned off by intervening groups and institutions. Secondly, as a matter of practicality it seems advisable to seek collaboration with already legitimate institutions which come closest to representing the interests of the mass of South Africa's low-income population. Thirdly, civics provide a vehicle for the empowerment of communities. They do this at varying levels and in diverse ways. For example, civics can be the vehicle through which the inhabitants of a town can themselves claim the space for, lay out and maintain a sports field. Or a civic itself may become a business unit, subcontracting to the municipality for garbage collection. Or the civic may be the vehicle through which deficiencies in municipal services are brought to the attention of the city engineer and, correspondingly, the civic may constitute the political pressure point for demands for a greater share of the municipal budget. Civics can enable people to take command of their lives. Lastly, civics can act as a restraint on the arbitrary exercise of power, can pressure bureaucracies to provide information and make their decisions consistent, using transparent criteria, and can provide a vehicle for community participation in decision-making.

NOTES

1. Reference to 'homelands' is problematical. First, depending on one's location on the political spectrum they are called bantustans or reserves, homelands, or self-governing or independent national states. Second, one has of course to disavow any perception that the designated area represents the appropriate territory or basis for citizenship for the relevant ethnic group.
2. $1 equals approximately R3.65.
3. In respect of the household share of personal income, note that black households might share income but be split between rural and urban areas. This means there is a tendency to count functionally integrated but geographically divided households as separate households. This overstates the number of poor households and exaggerates the level of poverty.
4. For example, see Hindson (1987), Lemon (1992), Swilling and Shubane (1991), Tomlinson (1990), and Western (1987).

5. There were 3,5 million instances of population removal. Some people were moved more than once.

6. Black local authorities have been widely rejected as illegitimate and have been a focus of sustained opposition. Where they exist in a township, they were 'elected' by a small percentage of potential voters. Their participation in negotiations is resisted by more authentic community groups and often brings the negotiations to a standstill. On the other hand, both Africans and whites view white local authorities as representative of white opinion within the given jurisdiction.

7. The status of Africans as temporary sojourners in urban areas affected entrepreneurs who were expected to move their businesses to the homelands. Southall (1980) describes the various restrictions. For example, in 1963 the government decreed that trading rights would only be conferred on Africans who had a permit to live in urban areas, Africans would be denied the right to form companies or partnerships, African trading was restricted to buildings constructed by local authorities, Africans could not carry on more than one business ... In 1968 Africans were even barred from selling products to other race groups. In contrast, the homeland development corporations did much to assist small enterprises in the homelands. Only since the late 1970s has the government progressively relented on the various restrictions. To a significant degree it appears that this was motivated by their sense that future political stability required the existence of an African middle class.

8. Eighty per cent of African workers spend an average of two and a half hours a day commuting; the balance spend four and a half hours commuting (McCaul 1987).

9. Anecdotal evidence has it that the rise is about ten times faster. However Fallon (1992), although showing instances when in certain sectors the rise was twenty times faster, restrains us with a demonstration of how the differential increase in incomes varies among sectors, cannot be calculated for the economy as a whole, and anyway started to slow down in the second half of the 1980s due, largely, to the country's economic woes.

10. The labour force is defined as all men and half of all women between the ages of 19 and 64 years. The annual average absorption capacity divides the average annual increase in the labour force by the average annual growth in formal employment. The 1986-1990 figure was provided to the author after further research by Ligthelm and Kritzinger-Van Niekerk. Note, however, that the Table is a bit misleading as it appears to indicate that in the early 1990s less than 9 per cent of all new entrants to the labour force will gain formal employment. If we assume that the average working life is 40 years, this means that 2,5 per cent of the labour force stops working every year. In addition, the effects of AIDS should be considered. The result is that the figure of 9 per cent is an underestimate by several percentage points.

11. Personal communication, Lolette Kritzinger-Van Niekerk, Development Bank of Southern Africa, 8 September 1992.

12. Personal communication, Johannesburg, 17 July 1991.

13. Personal communication, Johannesburg, 9 July 1991.

14. The one major exception was 'The Second Carnegie Inquiry into Poverty and Development in Southern Africa', but its upshot was a book which employs dated data (Wilson and Ramphele 1989). The book represents a compendium of many individual research efforts and its relative emphasis is on rural poverty.

15. This section is culled from a number of authors but owes an especial debt to Rodgers (1989).

16. See Chant (1991: 6, 7).
17. In 1989 migrant workers constituted 11 per cent of the economically active population. This figure was supplied by David Viljoen of the Development Bank of Southern Africa.
18. The statistics were supplied by David Viljoen of the Development Bank of Southern Africa.
19. This explanation is largely based on Budlender (1992).
20. Conversation on 16 February 1993.
21. This observation has produced some vitriolic responses. It reflects data supplied to me in respect of the pass rate in Soweto's schools. But it is surely not all that surprising given that the phenomenon is reported in many countries in the world. Explanations centre on teacher bias, assumptions regarding the subjects girls are likely to excel in, and social pressures on girls not to perform better than the boys. My daughters go to an all-girls school!
22. Interview in Braamfontein on 2 June 1992. Operation Hunger is the major source of nutritional assistance in South Africa.
23. 'The keiretsu system links already powerful companies, banks and insurance firms into even more powerful groups that can dominate markets in good times, drive out competition in bad times, and provide protection from ... hostile takeovers and stockholder demands for quick profits ...' (*Washington Post* 6 October 1991) For example, the Mitsui keiretsu incorporates, amongst others, the Mitsui Bank, the Mitsui Mutual Life Insurance, Japan Steel Works, Toshiba and Toyota.
24. Sandi is the General Secretary of the South African National Civic Organization. The quote is taken from his reply to a letter from Noel Ndhlovu of *Learn and Teach*.

Chapter 3
The Origins of Development Planning

The purpose of development planning is to facilitate economic growth and employment creation within an urban area, and contribute to the area's tax base. Many would add that it is also intended to enhance a community's ability to assume greater control over its economic destiny.

The origins of development planning lie in the ineffectiveness of regional planning and the structural transformation which has created economic problems in many American and European cities. While there is consensus on the relationship of development planning to structural transformation, its relationship to regional planning is often debated. When I suggested to colleagues that development planning is replacing regional planning as the vehicle for determining where economic growth should occur, I often received a sceptical response. My first undertaking, therefore, is to vindicate this position.

FROM REGIONAL PLANNING TO DEVELOPMENT PLANNING

There are two ways of demonstrating that there is a shift from regional planning to development planning. One indicator is that the institutional location of responsibility for development planning has shifted downwards. The other is that, regardless of which level of government is responsible for regional planning, the nature of regional strategies has changed. For example, where previously strategies attempted to attract industries to peripheral regions or declining cities, there is now a shift to fostering indigenous enterprise within those locales and targeting benefits to, say, run-down areas within those cities. I argue that in high-income countries, both trends are substantially true. The two notable exceptions are the United Kingdom and the European Economic Community. Both are addressed below.

The situation is rather different in low- and middle-income countries. They appear to be rethinking their high degree of centralisation, and are being encouraged to do so by the World Bank. As regards regional planning, though, they are being urged either to forego such planning or to adopt secondary city strategies.[1]

Regarding the locus of responsibility, Goldsmith and Newton (1988) point out that decentralisation is generally equated with democratisation and that few dare speak out against it. They agree with Sharpe (1988) that there is 'compelling evidence' for the growth of subnational government and add that this has also strengthened community or neighbourhood level government. Wolman (1988) notes though that we should go beyond simply looking at the location of responsibility within government; we should examine what functions are served by changes to this location. A few examples demonstrate his point.

i. The United Kingdom under Thatcher was the one high-income country that experienced a high degree of centralisation. Wolman argues that this enabled Thatcher to reduce local budgets and expenditure on welfare and redistributive services, and also to oppose the socialist development strategies of certain Labour Party-controlled local governments.

ii. In contrast, decentralisation in terms of Reagan's New Federalist policy, and his disavowal of responsibility for social services, enabled him to cut back social spending. In other words, 'given different political structures, different means are required to achieve essentially the same needs in two countries' (Wolman 1988: 429).

iii. When Sweden's Social Democratic Party regained power in 1982, it redirected responsibility for industrial policy to the counties and, in particular, to the municipalities. The background to this is that Swedish regional policy has shifted from a goal of inter-regional equity toward self-reliant intra-regional development programmes. However, Krauss and Pierre (1991) explain that an additional motivation for the change was that the central government's industrial policy had proven unsuccessful and that it was politically expedient to relocate responsibility. The municipalities now seek to lead economic and employment planning for their area, and become directly involved in project negotiation with public and private actors.

iv. On coming to power in France in 1981, Mitterrand supported decentralisation both to regions (groupings of departments) and to departements. Pickvance (1991) argues that the decentralisation reflects a growth in trust between central and local governments.[2] The region's involvement in development planning consists of negotiation with central government and the preparation of five-year contracts which list the investments and actions the region intends to undertake. Both the region and central government are then committed to financing, or co-financing, these investments. Typical contracts attempt to improve research and training, improve infrastructure in the region, and assist small and medium enterprises to become more efficient through providing finance for consulting services and technological advice. Local involvement in this planning is illustrated by the city of Rennes (Le Gales 1990). When the Left won the election for Rennes in 1983 the new mayor formed CODESPAR,[3] which comprised business people, the unions and the local authorities. The body is responsible for strategic economic and social planning, which in large part means working out a programme that will be included in the regional plan and so ensure access to finance from central government.

v. With the advent of the European Economic Community, there has been a progressive shift of responsibility from national governments to the Community; the Community in turn is increasingly liaising directly with regional and local governments. The Community's regional policy is intended to counter the negative effects of integration, and overcome inequalities between regions: some remain fairly backward because of their dependence on agriculture, while others have fared poorly as a result of structural change. Countries like Italy and England, which have serious regional problems and limited agricultural subsidies, aim to use the Regional Fund to counterbalance the agricultural subsidies. (The resources allocated to regional policy have never come close to matching the agricultural subsidy.) Even with this upward shift in responsibility, changes in the substance of regional policy reflect the move to local, indigenous development.

Evidence of this trend towards decentralisation in low- and middle-income countries is provided by Silverman (1990). He provides a list of 116 low- and middle-income countries that are decentralising, or are decentralised! But, like Goldsmith and Newton, he points out that decentralisation is an intricate concept and, in particular, that effective government requires both a strong central government and strong local government. It is not a zero-sum game, with more power for one level representing less power for another. Instead, while central government functions have grown, local and neighbourhood functions have grown more.

The World Bank (1991a) argues the case for decentralisation on economic grounds. It is worth noting why the Bank views decentralisation as desirable. In its view, the financial and technical weaknesses of municipal institutions are a constraint on urban productivity and therefore on national economic development. Bank analysts argue that this results, at least in part, from central government controls over the investment process: central agencies decide on specific investments, undertake technical planning and implementation, and then leave the outcome to the local authority to operate and maintain. But local authorities frequently lack the motivation and capacity to fulfil this function. The Bank envisages a shift in central functions away from providing infrastructure and services directly, towards creating an enabling regulatory and financial environment. Local governments will partly replace central government in providing and managing urban infrastructure and services, but not completely. Instead, a greater role is envisaged for the private sector, individuals and communities.

More relevant for this study is the second trend: the shift in how government attempts – whether at regional or local level – to promote growth in specific locales. To demonstrate the trend, I delve into history and explain differences among countries.

The USA's 'modern phase' of regional planning occurred from the 1950s to the 1970s.[4] Presidents Kennedy and Johnson funded programmes intended to relieve unemployment and improve incomes. Principal agencies involved were the Economic Development Agency and federal-interstate institutions such as the Appalachia Regional Commission. (The Appalachian Programme arose out of Kennedy's campaign pledge to address the newly discovered poverty in the area. The movie *Deliverance* depicted the poverty in this region.) The programmes generally stressed investment in infrastructure such as highways, and industrial parks and growth centres that were intended to attract manufacturing investment. In effect, the programmes were intended to integrate backward economies into the national economy.

According to Alonso (1989: 223), the demise of these programmes arose out of 'disillusionment with [their] effectiveness, fiscal crisis, ideological shifts, and a gradual recognition that changes in the economic structure of the United States and its position in the world economy negate the position of manufacturing as the principal sector for development for most regions'. He also observes that 'there is general dissatisfaction with the style of regional development planning which prevailed a generation ago, and yet there is no new clear-cut set of strategies to replace it' (p. 221).

The smaller scale of regional planning in the USA, compared with European and other countries, is due to the spatial integration of America's market economy, high rates of population mobility, rapid economic growth and an antipathy to planning, long-term income convergence, cultural uniformity and a federal system of government.[5] The last point became particularly significant with the move from a strong presidency associated with Roosevelt to a weak presidency ushered in by Nixon in 1969. Under a weak presidency, it is more difficult to build consensus among different localities and states. This is especially damaging if the goal is a policy which favours some locales over others. Americans have therefore had to make do with competition between the states and between cities to attract or retain investment. I refer to this later as the traditional approach to development planning.

The companion to the traditional approach in most countries in the first three or four decades after World War II involved regional planning by the central government. This was as true for France and Italy as it was for South Korea, Kenya and South Africa. At a formal level, regional polices are neutral. The European Economic Community, for example, supports intervention to promote efficiency and equality. Yet Alonso (1991) claims the European Regional Commission has responded to estimates that about 100 million people live in areas of relatively low income and/or high unemployment with a proposal that $10 billion be spent every year in programmes whose underlying purpose is to restrain migration to the main centres. The desire to restrain urban growth is especially apparent in middle- and low-income countries where the growth of large cities is viewed as 'explosive' and potentially destabilising, and as imposing an intolerable burden on government budgets.

A further reason for regional policy is that persistent regional differences in income and unemployment levels threaten costs at the ballot box, especially for high-income countries that have a higher incidence of elections!

During the 1960s and the 1970s the vehicle for diverting growth to other regions, cities and towns was commonly a growth centre strategy, accompanied by development controls in the large cities. A number of countries also attempted controls on urban migration, but these failed.

Growth centre policies are seldom viewed as effective. In an evaluation at the end of the seventies, Stohr and Todtling (1978) concluded that while growth centres may reduce inter-urban disparities, they tend to accentuate disparities within peripheral regions.

Growth centre policy encountered problems in Europe because, as Molle (1988) puts it, it is premised on the decentralisation of industry. This was problematical given that a declining proportion of the labour force was located in the manufacturing sector. There were other problems too, including structural changes, which saw increasing inter- and intra-regional specialisation, and the reconcentration of (especially financial) services in core cities, which negated growth centre policy. Molle notes that the European Economic Community is now looking to assist small and medium companies to develop new products, distribute products and process information, and evaluate the technical feasibility and marketing prospects of new products and production processes. These activities are later referred to as typical of the entrepreneurial approach to development planning in high-income countries.

In the case of middle-income countries, as noted, they are urged to reduce the emphasis given to policies that attempt to influence the location of employment and population (World Bank 1991a; Peterson *et al.* 1991; Rondinelli 1991). The reason offered is that the more successful these policies are, the more they introduce economic distortions and so slow economic development. However, summarising an expert review of Third World urban problems sponsored by the United Nations, Rodwin and Sanyal (1987: 5) comment that 'the [UN] group is sceptical about the benefits of unfettered urbanisation which has resulted in the demand – impossible to satisfy – for employment, housing, transportation, and other services'. It is difficult not to be sympathetic to the predicament of governments which are experiencing rapid urbanisation.

In effect, the reasons underlying the need for regional policies still abound. The popular alternative strategy proposed nowadays is that middle-income countries should adopt secondary city strategies, reduce the perceived biases towards large cities in taxation and the location of public spending, and back economic policies that alter the terms of trade in favour of secondary cities. An example of the last suggestion is the belief that if countries shift their industrial policies away from import substitution – which steers manufacturing investment to the largest cities – and towards export promotion, they will experience a reorientation in the location of investment. Thus, in South Africa, it has been held that export promotion would provide a relative locational advantage for the coastal cities, rather than for the larger inland market in Pretoria and Johannesburg (Van der Berg and Lotter 1990).

Even if secondary city strategies did succeed, their impact would be small. This is because urban growth in most middle-income countries is more a consequence of the growth of the already urbanised population than of urban migration. Thus, if a secondary city does capture a share of future urban migration, this will only constitute a small proportion of the overall urban population increase. In addition, attempts to redirect the location of public expenditure would be confronted with budgetary deficits and consequent constraints on public spending, and often also with structural adjustment programmes. Furthermore, it remains to be seen whether countries which switch to industrial policies that favour export promotion do in fact experience a relocation of investment. This certainly did not prove true for Seoul (Rondinelli 1991).

Regional planning suffers from a barren policy repertoire. Successes have been claimed even where there has been no net employment creation. Development planning, on the other hand, changes the terms of reference. The purpose is still to promote development within given locales, but to do so in a way that adds to the net growth of employment and incomes. High-income countries are looking to development planning as a substitute for regional planning. Arguably the same trend will appear in middle-income countries.

STRUCTURAL TRANSFORMATION

The structural transformation of the American and European economies both explain why regional policies were impotent and lends further insight into the motives of local authorities in those countries for undertaking development planning.

Manufacturing and services

Studies of structural change in high-income countries generally equate deindustrialisation with the loss of manufacturing jobs and the growth of the service sector, and assume that the process is ongoing. Neither is necessarily correct.

Much depends on how deindustrialisation is measured. For example, while certain regions of America and Europe might lose manufacturing employment, this does not mean that they will also experience a drop in manufacturing output. Cheshire (1991) observes that in Europe there is no correlation between change in industrial employment and change in industrial output (between 1983 and 1987). Thus, among European countries, Ireland did worst on the former measure and best on the latter: it lost jobs while producing more. Alternatively, even though manufacturing output may increase, it might increase more slowly than output in the service sector, and so again lead to the impression of deindustrialisation. When we combine relative and absolute trends in respect of manufacturing and services output and employment, the picture can shift focus.[6]

The furore surrounding deindustrialisation should therefore alert us to other interpretations: a change to alternative growth industries which benefit different regions; deindustrialisation in certain cities and regions and structural decline; structural transformation in prosperous regions and the move to a post-industrial economy; the OECD's declining dominance of the world's manufacturing output;[7] and the move towards flexible specialisation (which is explained below).

Ordinarily we would think that a point of difference between high- and middle-income countries is whether or not it makes sense to view manufacturing as a major source of growth. For example, we might take it for granted that in high-income countries the service sector will replace the manufacturing sector. This appears to be true in some areas, but not in others. In France, where the manufacturing sector did well, so too did the service sector. De Guademar and Prudhomme (1991) argue that the service sector is not a substitute for the manufacturing sector; rather, employment there complements employment in the manufacturing sector. They also hold that the distinction between the two sectors is less and less meaningful. While manufacturing is becoming information-intensive, functions previously performed within manufacturing enterprises and classified as manufacturing are now often supplied by consultants and classified as a service.

Will the output of the service sector continue to grow more rapidly than that of the manufacturing sector? Thurow (1989: 186) suggests that instead of being 'the wave of the future', the service sector is 'the wave of the immediate past'. He demonstrates that in the USA over two-thirds of new service jobs were located in three sub-sectors: trade, hotels and restaurants; real estate and business services; and financial and insurance activities. The growth of the first reflects the late-night and weekend services required by women as they moved into the labour force; this move is now complete. The growth of the second can to some extent be traced to the commercial real estate industry, but the real estate boom of the 1970s is over, and office and warehouse space stands unrented. He finds the expansion of business services puzzling, as the rate of growth exceeded that of output, it occurred during a period of office automation, and was much faster than in the rest of the world. Lastly, financial services increased rapidly due to deregulation and the expansion of world capital markets, but this too was a one-time phenomenon. In contrast, the success of American manufactured exports and the need for policy initiatives to reduce the trade deficit may well lead to a revival in manufacturing output and, to a lesser extent, in manufacturing employment.

The geography of transformation

Structural transformation has specific implications for the future location of investment and growth. The case of services is easily addressed and we will deal with it first. Trade and business services locate where the market is and do not themselves initiate locational change. The caveat here is that technological improvements facilitate the decoupling of front and back office functions and the decentralisation of the latter. Thus Fainstein and Fainstein (1989: 26) write that 'whereas the spatial deconcentration of manufacturing was facilitated by the development of telephone and transport technology, allowing communication between headquarters and production sites and the movement of goods to far-flung markets, the decentralisation of office work awaited breakthroughs in telecommunications and technology for data transmission'. Thus one finds the Jamaican government investing in a teleport to transmit and receive data by satellite in Montego Bay, so that it can compete for data entry and processing services such as credit card and airline accounts. Thurow (1989) raises a very interesting question: why has there been so little decentralisation of back office functions?

Financial services are rather different. There has been a concentration of financial services into three 'world cities' – New York, London and Tokyo – with less pronounced concentration in secondary financial cities like Chicago and Los Angeles. But, on the whole, there have been bank mergers, and staff lay-offs among banks and on Wall Street; and, throughout the financial service industry, the concentration of fewer jobs into fewer centres.

In the case of the manufacturing sector, structural transformation has produced stark adjustments. Many manufacturing- and resource-dependent cities have been devastated. Pittsburgh lost 100 000 jobs in 10 years, while Hamburg, Glasgow and many other cities have also shown marked decreases in manufacturing employment.[8] Thurow (1989: 182) makes the point that 'prosperous areas that have had a comparative advantage in the growing industry lose it, not because they have changed for the worse, but because different industries have taken the lead ... and the characteristics that are most conducive to the growth of these new industries are different from those needed by the old leading industries'. The older regions which might continue to do well are those whose strength lay in the productivity and skill of the labour force, and their willingness to innovate and adopt flexible labour practices.

Fainstein (1990b: 553, 554) provides a pithy summary. Restructuring refers to

> the transformation of the economic base of cities in the advanced capitalist world from manufacturing to services; the rapid growth of the producers' services sector within cities at the top of the global hierarchy; the simultaneous concentration of economic control within multinational firms and financial institutions, and deconcentration of their manufacturing and routine office functions; the development of manufacturing in the third world; and the rise of new economic powers in the Pacific Rim.

Income inequality

The economic restructuring in the Western World has accentuated income inequality. This may be attributed to:

- lower wages in services than in manufacturing;
- relatively higher levels of wage inequality within the fastest growing manufacturing and service industries;
- the downgrading of manufacturing jobs due to the preponderance of low-wage work in new manufacturing industries like electronics;
- the reorganisation of production, the repression of unions and the rise of sweatshops and homework; and
- technological change within the manufacturing sector leading to fewer semi-skilled and skilled better-paid jobs.

The lower incomes common to the various branches of the service sector, relative to the manufacturing sector, are evident in Table 3.1. This suggests that when the growth of a country or city becomes based on services, its incomes decline. Pittsburgh exemplifies this: by 1991, its annual wage income had dropped by $10 billion in 10 years, as relatively high-paid manufacturing jobs were replaced by relatively low-paid service jobs. Its major non-governmental employers are now banks, universities and medical services.[9]

Table 3.1 *Compensation in service industries in relation to manufacturing, 1983 (manufacturing = 1,00)*

	USA	Japan	Germany
Wholesale trade	0,56	0,83	0,78
Finance	0,84	1,34	1,22
Social community	0,57	0,79	-
Private services	0,67	0,93	0,85

Source: OECD National Accounts 1972-84, Vol. II, Table 13; cited in Thurow 1989: 181.

Fordism versus flexible specialisation

There is some faddishness when it comes to explaining these trends, how production is organised, and where it is located. Explanations nowadays often centre on flexible specialisation; my response to this is somewhat sceptical.

Since the 1970s we have seen a shift from what Trachte and Ross (1985) call monopoly capitalism to global capitalism. In the decades immediately following World War II, American and, to a lesser extent, European capital were hegemonic, market shares were static and there was little price competition. The change towards global capitalism represents significant contestation of markets through product differentiation, quality and prices. This change has been associated with the rise of the Pacific Rim countries and the decline of old manufacturing areas and resource-dependent regions in high-income countries.

The competitiveness of many Asian and a few South American countries was attributed initially to lower labour costs. The difference in costs is often dramatic, but it is also easy to overemphasise this. For example, labour costs amount to only 18 per cent of total direct production costs of British manufacturers (Williams *et al.* 1987). In addition, many countries which have succeeded in export manufacturing, have done so despite rapidly rising labour costs. It seems that arguments surrounding labour costs should be qualified. They are a significant factor for labour-intensive industries such as textiles and electronics, and these industries have led the decentralisation to low-income countries.

The most commonly held view is that the sharp increase in the decentralisation of manufacturing plant, which dates to 1973 and the OPEC oil boycott, represents a new stage in the development of capitalism. However, Fainstein and Fainstein (1989: 22) argue that 'decentralisation tendencies have existed throughout the history of capitalism', and that what we are seeing now is the effect of competition from the Pacific Rim countries. The tendency of the locus of production to shift is long-established under capitalism; what is new are the particular countries which are becoming dominant.

Much of the blame for the deindustrialisation of Western countries – or rather, their lack of a competitive posture – has been ascribed to their reliance on Fordist methods of production. Fordism has been defined in various ways; combining the formulations of Scott (1988) and Storper (1990), one can say that Fordism refers to large and highly capitalised enterprises which engage in continuous-flow processes (petrol or steel) or assembly-line processes (cars, capital equipment and consumer durables). They are distinguished by a search for internal economies of scale based on technical divisions of labour, the standardisation of outputs, routine production processes and dedicated, expensive, capital equipment.

On the international stage, the more successful competitors now adopt more flexible methods of production. Their advantage is found in high-technology manufactured goods and associated services, craft-based production (which is usually labour-intensive and organised in batches), producer and financial services, and restructured consumer durables and capital goods. The importance of flexibility is that the suppliers are able to differentiate their product and serve market niches of varying sizes. Thus the *New York Times* (24 October 1991) makes the point that 'using their great advantage in making very short production runs of specific models, the Japanese appear intent on filling scores of niche markets. They are betting, in other words, that the traditional mainstream auto market, on which Detroit has long depended, has become forever fragmented.' A General Motors executive comments that the new Japanese cars are not aimed at 'the kind of family-car markets that we focus on. I don't think these cars are built with the bulk of American users in mind.'

The flexibility achieved by Japanese car manufacturers is based on their ability to shift from one product or process configuration to another (the dynamic component); and their ability to rapidly adjust quantities of output (the static component) (Storper 1990). The static component is made possible by vertical disintegration, which means the formation of networks of specialised suppliers who contribute to the final product. The use of a network of suppliers enables a firm to change product specifications rapidly – and oblige suppliers to bear the brunt of cut-backs in production.[10]

The difference between American and Japanese car manufacturers in this regard is illustrated by General Motors, which internalises 70 per cent of the value of the automobile production process, and Toyota, which internalises 30 per cent (Hill 1989). This is a crucial distinction because labourers producing for suppliers to Toyota do not earn the same wages as Toyota employees and have less job security. In other words, a much higher proportion of an American car is produced by workers earning primary wages. Secondly, the average Japanese automobile manufacturer deals directly with 171 primary suppliers, who in turn assume responsibility for the product quality, delivery time, and so on of 4 700 secondary suppliers, who themselves are accountable for the products of another 31 600 suppliers (Hill 1989). The existence of these layers locates labour-intensive, small-batch, low-value-added production among Toyota's suppliers, while Toyota is able to concentrate on scale economies.[11] In contrast, General Motors co-ordinates many more than 171 suppliers who, historically, have often been located far from the point of assembly. The implication is that orders arrive some time in advance of assembly and inventories have to be stored and financed.

Williams *et al.* (1987) summarise the differences between mass production and flexible specialisation on the following scale.

Flexible specialisation		Mass production
low	dedicated equipment	high
high	product differentiation	low
short	length of production run	long

They challenge several features of the supposed distinction between Fordism and flexible specialisation, and provide a 'cold shower' for enthusiasts of flexible specialisation. They argue, for example, that:

i. Industries cannot be situated entirely at one pole of the above scale or the other.
ii. Japanese car manufacturers employ assembly lines and dedicated equipment. They differ from Western car manufacturers in their use of 'mixed lines', producing two or more models on the same line.

This is possible because of the way Japanese producers use networks of suppliers and the just-in-time inventory system, which in turn reduce change-over and set-up times.

iii. Japanese dedicated equipment is not flexible in the sense that equipment can be readily reprogrammed to produce a new product range. The commissioning cost for this change-over is about 60 per cent of the cost of the total system. In other words, the notion that robots can easily be reprogrammed is a 'myth'.

iv. The dedicated equipment the Japanese employ is as expensive as that of Western car manufacturers, and they too are dependent on scale economies.

Williams *et al.* hold that Fordism only provides a marked cost advantage in the case of complex consumer durables with numerous components, such as cars. They cite a survey of British manufacturers which showed that only 31 per cent used assembly lines – and only half of these were automated. Furthermore, only 3,4 per cent of the United Kingdom's labour force is engaged in assembly line production. Fordism is not so prevalent that it can be said to describe 'the trajectory of manufacturing history' (p. 421).

Life would be easier if we could attribute the rise of the Pacific Rim countries, the relative demise of manufacturing in the West, and the regional restructuring of the economies of Western countries to the respective reliance on flexible specialisation and mass production. The foregoing material precludes such a generalisation. Indeed, it seems clear that certain countries such as South Korea have depended on scale economies to such an extent that they are unable to adapt to flexible specialisation. Korean companies have to go offshore to realise these advantages.

Yet rather than dismiss the topic, we should none the less be alert to the implications that a commitment to flexible specialisation has for a middle-income country's industrial strategy. Storper (1990) holds that the conditions under which competition now occurs have changed. That is, markets are considerably more contested and congested than before. This competition sometimes renews price competition based on attempts to exploit scale economies, but more often it spurs 'new forms of nonprice competition in the form of increased and more rapid product differentiation and product changeovers' (p. 430). These forms of competition are inherently risky, causing producers to intensify their contest for market share by exploiting ever-smaller niches. However, 'the "background"

investment in equipment, product planning, and marketing are, if anything, greater than ever, especially in technology-intensive production
processes ...' (p. 432). Since 'these investments require amortisation over a
large quantity of output of one good, or over a range of differentiated
goods ... [it is] unlikely that specialised producers will find their markets
exclusively within the borders of one country ... and so increasingly
require that products be geared towards both domestic and international
markets' (p. 432).

In sum, if middle-income countries are to develop their manufacturing
capacity, they have to identify market niches which, ideally, serve both
domestic and export demand. The initial period of production can serve
the domestic market while manufacturers gear up for international standards of price, design and quality, after which they compete to enter the
export market. But for this purpose they will have to engage in product
differentiation and specialisation.

The basis for development planning?

Arguments around flexible specialisation are often associated with the
claim that the restructuring of national economies leads to the 're-
emergence of regions as meaningful economic units', that the regions are
based on 'industrial districts', and also that the political disintegration of
the welfare state is leading to the 'devolution of industrial policy to local
authorities' (Hirst and Zeitlin 1989: 9). In this way the stage is set for
regional or metropolitan development planning.

While I obviously support the view that old-style regional planning is
giving way to development planning, we should beware of assuming
that this trend is based solely on flexible specialisation, as this suggests a
fair amount of spatial determinism. Many advocates of flexible specialisation believe that where static and dynamic flexibility and just-in-time
inventory systems are in place, it is imperative that production should
be located within industrial agglomerations based on networks of
specialised suppliers. The advantages of industrial agglomerations are
described by Hill (1989), who notes that proximity to the parent company
is desirable for subcontractors who sell a large proportion of their output
to one company, or who sell high-value or bulky items. Proximity also
facilitates interaction with subcontractors and mutual responsibility for
product design, reduces transaction costs, and allows for changes in
delivery schedules.

Perhaps the extreme example of industrial agglomeration is that of

Toyota City in Japan, but one should note immediately that Nissan has a much more dispersed arrangement. Other industrial agglomerations include Silicon Valley in California, Scientific City south of Paris, and the Cambridge-Bristol axis in England. But these spatial patterns are 'so modest as to be dwarfed by longer-established patterns' (Lovering 1990: 168). Lovering (1990: 169) suggests that flexible specialisation and the pattern of industrial districts 'should be viewed as a contingent local outcome, not an inexorable process of contemporary capitalist development'. Thus Fainstein and Fainstein (1989) note a variety of different urban forms in Italy, the United Kingdom and the USA which show marked differences in the spatial relation of one enterprise to another.

However, warnings against interpreting flexible specialisation in a deterministic fashion do not obscure the fact that flexibility does enhance a city's competitive posture. Clarke (1989) points out that companies search for cities that enhance their flexibility and competitiveness. He holds that

> the current competition between communities for jobs and income is more subtle than before. It is no longer a matter of the costs of production; the social relations of production, even the local history of labor-management relations are the terms of competition. While it is tempting to reduce the aspects of community life to wages and prices, to do so would do significant conceptual harm to the difference between simple cost accounting and the complexity of social and local attitudes to innovation and flexibility. (p. 208)

The result is that 'flexible specialisation' and conferences such as the 'Dialogue on flexible manufacturing networks'[12] are 'all the rage'. Intellectuals, who do not bear material costs when their analyses prove wrong, are especially susceptible to viruses. Cerebral antidotes may be timely. But, having cautioned the reader, the arguments from which one derives a role for development planning are worth rehearsing.

Sabel (1989) argues that five developments are contributing to such a role:

- the emergence of successful industrial districts in numerous countries around the world;
- the reorganisation of large corporations such that responsibility for product lines is decentralised to units that engage in subcontracting and sales;

- the convergence of large and small firms into subcontracting relationships;
- the transformation of local government into job-creating agencies; and
- the co-operation of trade unions in development strategies.

Co-operation within and between large and small firms can include sharing knowledge about markets and industrial processes; aiding, investing in and upgrading subcontractors; and sharing market opportunities where firms have an excess of orders. These activities are all part of the new lexicon, a 'new orthodoxy of endogenous local development'.

CONCLUSION

The move to development planning was a reaction to the economic crisis prompted by global restructuring and the inability of old-style regional planning to address the resultant problems. The trend is apparent as cities throughout the world assume responsibility for attracting investment, supporting indigenous enterprise, and sustaining community efforts. The second section of this chapter dignified the trend by providing a theoretical surround. Of particular significance is the perception that metropolitan areas are coming to represent coherent economic regions for planning purposes.

NOTES

1. Respectively, see Silverman (1990) and the World Bank (1991a); Peterson *et al.* (1991), the World Bank (1991a), and Rondinelli (1991). A secondary city strategy is a revised growth centre strategy. A growth centre strategy combines investment in infrastructure and perhaps social services in the centre, and provides incentives to enterprises to locate themselves in the centre. A secondary city strategy differs from a growth centre strategy in that fewer centres are designated and the centres chosen are already relatively large and successful cities outside the country's core.
2. Pickvance advances a model where, when central and local government share the same values, responsibility for implementation is decentralised; whereas, if there are few shared values, central government appropriates the power and related responsibilities.
3. Comite de Developpement Economique et Social du Pays de Rennes.
4. See Sundquist (1975) for a detailed history and Alonso (1989) for a contemporary review.
5. This paragraph is based on Friedman and Bloch (1990).
6. De Guademar and Prudhomme (1991) demonstrate the changing focus in relation to France. In the United States it appears that manufacturing employment and manufac-

turing output have declined, but neither in a marked fashion (Rodwin 1989).

7. The Organisation of Economic Cooperation and Development includes Australia, Austria, Belgium, Canada, Denmark, Finland, France, Germany, Greece, Iceland, Ireland, Italy, Japan, Luxembourg, the Netherlands, New Zealand, Norway, Portugal, Spain, Sweden, Turkey, the United Kingdom and the United States.

8. The examples are taken from Judd and Parkinson 1990.

9. The figure was supplied by Bob Gleeson of Carnegie-Mellon University during an interview on 27 September 1991.

10. Sayer (1989) observes that the suppliers need not come from other firms, although this is how it is most commonly perceived. The suppliers could equally well come from within the same firm, provided that the relations between the branches of the firm are governed by market forces and that these are strongly embedded in their non-market relations. This clarification regarding the meaning of vertical disintegration is important since the obvious objection to the relevance of the flexible specialisation material in this book is that it does not allow for the concentration of ownership typical of manufacturing capacity in South Africa.

11. This is a point which should not be lost on the reader. Despite their reputation for flexible specialisation, the Japanese have also pursued scale economies. Thus, Alan Webber and William Taylor contend in an article in the *International Herald Tribune* (28 April 1992) that 'the economic model with which Japan scored so many victories in the 1980s – a model premised on cheap capital and fabulously disciplined mass manufacturing – is giving way to a new logic of competition that emphasises creativity and speed. A world in which the nimble power of innovation surpasses the brute force of economies of scale and massive capital spending is a world in which the United States will flourish.'

12. See the *Proceedings*, a conference organised by the Consortium for Manufacturing Competitiveness, Southern Technology Council, 16 January 1990, Fort Walton Beach, Florida.

Chapter 4

Development Planning and the Formation of Urban Coalitions

There is no single guide which shows how to achieve the goals of development planning. A number of articles and books have been written on development planning; they often differ quite markedly. The multiplicity of approaches to development planning complicates any attempt to summarise the 'discipline'. To simplify matters I have:

- grouped the approaches in terms of their origins in local government, the community and the private sector;

- asked what benefits the participants seek from engaging in development planning; and

- described their past and present approaches to the process.

This chapter goes on to suggest how the foremost interest groups in a city – politicians, officials, business people, community organisations, and unions – can best co-operate to promote development. Even if one takes as given that each group has its own motives for participating in the planning process, American and European examples of 'urban coalitions' suggest that development planning is most effective when undertaken in a collaborative manner. In particular, urban coalitions facilitate strategic responses to overall processes of structural change and, if there is broad representation on the coalition, increase the probability of a fair distribution of the benefits of growth.[1]

The last part of this chapter explores probable differences in the way these strategies might be applied in South Africa. It seems that the presence of local governments with demonstrable capacity, a powerful private sector, and strong unions and civics, offers a potential balance of forces conducive to an effective urban coalition.

PUBLIC SECTOR APPROACHES
TO LOCAL DEVELOPMENT PLANNING

Why engage?

There are five rationales for public initiation of local development planning. Two of these are the economic explanations we would anticipate. A third centres on the role of community organisations in extending the effectiveness of local governments. The fourth describes the self-interest of politicians: where there is poverty or inequality, political leaders will often feel it necessary to be seen to be trying to promote development. The last rationale is based on the progressive mode, and argues that in addition to promoting economic growth, development planning is used to encourage participation in planning and ensure that the allocation of public resources is fair.

The economic rationales are provided by Eisinger (1988: Chapter 3). Public assistance is used to promote increased private investment. On the one hand, it is hoped that increased private investment will lead to new jobs, lower unemployment, reduced poverty and higher personal incomes; and that the greater demand for goods and services will lead to further private investment, and so create income and employment multipliers. On the other hand, it is hoped that increased private investment will create a larger tax base through additions to the capital stock, jobs and personal incomes. This could permit either a lower tax rate, which enhances the investment climate, or higher tax revenue, which makes possible improved public services and amenities. Eisinger reports that where there is increased private investment, private benefits typically follow, that is, more jobs and better incomes. However, he continues, one should bear in mind that when this occurs it can prompt migration into the area. In this case, the anticipated public benefits would not be realised. Taxes are not reduced, and are more likely to be absorbed by the greater number of business establishments and workers.

The role of Community Development Corporations (CDCs) in expanding the reach of local authorities is explained by Evan Stoddard, Director of the Urban Redevelopment Authority of Pittsburgh.[2] He states that Pittsburgh lacks the resources to reach all the city's neighbourhoods. Instead, where community organisations take the lead, the Authority can assist these organisations and so reach more people. Avis Vidal[3] endorses this approach, noting simply that there are certain types of services which community organisations are best equipped to deliver.

The motivations of political self-interest for initiating development planning are fairly obvious. Politicians at local level cannot afford to disregard unemployment. Even if their initiatives are undertaken largely for show, or with the aim of channelling the benefits to select groups, politicians must be seen to be trying to promote development.

Finally, a good illustration of the progressive approach is the 1984 Chicago Development Plan, which strove for equality between neighbourhoods, races and income groups. The Plan focused on job creation and balanced development between downtown and the neighbourhoods. Neighbourhood development was to be implemented through community organisations. City resources and public-private ventures were to be targeted and increased citizen participation encouraged (Bennett *et al.* 1987).

Approaches

The public sector has generally adopted a combination of traditional, entrepreneurial, urban efficiency, and human resource development approaches to promoting development. The agencies involved often represent different levels of government.[4] The progressive model is less common, but not unknown.[5]

The traditional approach consists of trying to attract investment from established, potentially mobile industries through concessions of one sort or another. This competition is vigorous among nations, and between regions and cities.

A more recent innovation involves regional or local governments acting as entrepreneurs. In this role they attempt to identify growth industries (typically deemed to be small, high-technology industries), lend money to or invest in new or expanding local firms within these industries, and strive to promote exports by firms falling within their jurisdiction.

The urban efficiency approach favours free markets, the removal of price controls, and the removal of state ownership (that is, privatisation). The role of the state is limited. For example, even if the public sector is responsible for the provision of a good or service, and perhaps determines the conditions under which charges are levied, responsibility for provision is separated from the actual production and financial administration. The private sector is favoured for the latter functions.

In addition to these approaches, which are targeted at capital that has anticipated trickle-down benefits for the urban poor, there are various other approaches which aim to benefit labour and/or the urban poor more directly and which can be taken as strategies for local development. The most common are human resource programmes, but there are other more radical approaches, such as the attempt by the Labour Party-controlled Greater London Council to implement an industrial strategy which would enhance the position of labour. The initiative proved unrealistic, but is interesting historically; I describe it in the section on progressive approaches. A more realistic alternative is provided by Chicago under the administration of Mayor Harold Washington. In some respects the orientation and policies of his administration are what one would hope for in South Africa.

Traditional

In the United States the traditional approach has primarily involved competition between states (without regard to where the investment is located within the state) and municipalities to attract investment from large, established industries. Since employment creation is nowadays most rapid in the service sector, competition to attract investment now includes this sector. However, the competition is segmented between 'central, information processing, professional jobs' and 'back-office, data processing jobs'. An example of competition in the former is the struggle that occurred between New York and Jersey City over attracting the commodities exchange.[6] Competition in the latter is exemplified by functions such as the processing of credit card accounts. Such functions are amenable to decentralised locations, and this prompts competition between, say, India, Jamaica and smaller towns in the American hinterland.

Underlying the traditional approach is the assumption that growth is stimulated through capital relocation, and decline prevented through capital retention. Competition consists primarily of marketing a location by offering low taxes or tax abatements, cheap land, and measures such as low-interest loans or loan guarantees which lower the cost of capital. Southern states have also used right-to-work laws to deter unions, and require smaller business contributions to unemployment and medical insurance to reduce the cost of labour.

In the USA, traditional competition originated in the southern states and has been ongoing since the 1930s. But it is only since the 1970s that this competition has became widespread throughout the USA. This was due to structural changes within the US economy and the consequent loss of manufacturing employment, together with a real decline in federal aid to the states.

In the United Kingdom, Liverpool and Jarrow initiated traditional competition during the Depression when they advertised the benefits of locating in their cities, built factories and industrial estates, and made loans to industrialists. These activities became progressively more widespread over the following decades. In particular, increased unemployment and reduced regional incentives in the 1970s prompted local authorities to pursue industrial development with greater vigour.[7]

The traditional approach is generally regarded as having failed. One reason for this is that when many localities are competing for investment by offering location concessions, the concessions blur the advantages of alternative locations. Furthermore, 'policy-makers gradually realised ... that all through the period in which state legislatures and city councils of declining regions were passing lavish economic blandishments, businesses continued to move out, and the toll of job losses mounted. At the same time the pace of capital flight abroad accelerated' (Eisinger 1988: 89).

Similar local competition has been evident in Brazil where local governments offered firms free land, tax rebates and below-market financing for investment (Ferguson 1990a). The effort succeeded in urban areas adjacent to São Paulo, but here relocation was probably inevitable, given the worldwide trend towards larger sites and access to national transportation networks. In contrast, Chile's national government, fearing 'beggar thy neighbour' competition, prevented local governments from setting their own local tax rates.

An important insight into traditional planning is offered by Wells and Wint (1990) in their research into efforts to attract investment to a country *without* at the same time offering concessions. They sought to explain which factors promote direct foreign investment, and looked at per capita GNP (+), GNP growth rate (+), balance of payments current account balance (-), annual rate of inflation (-), political stability (+) and investment promotion (+).[8] (The signs in brackets represent the hypothesised direction of the relationship.) In their model, which combined high- and middle-income countries, the statistically significant variables were political stability and investment promotion, at the one per cent level, and GNP per capita, at the five per cent level. When the same model was run for developing countries, GNP per capita and political stability were statistically significant at the one per cent level and investment promotion at the five per cent level.

The United Nations Industrial Development Organisation (1980) provides a comparison for middle- and low-income countries when it reports that there are three variables which affect willingness to invest in export processing zones in such countries. These are the wage/productivity trade-off, political stability, and a predisposition to favour foreign investment and private enterprise.

Both UNIDO's views and Wells and Wint's findings reinforce the conclusion that material concessions are not critical if foreign investment is to be attracted. What is important is the management of a nation's economy and its politics, and how these are *perceived* by the investment community. It is significant that Wells and Wint (1990) detect a strong relation between attempts to market a country and inflows of foreign investment. Given South Africa's history of discord and the nature of the debate around its future economic policies – on nationalisation in particular – it is likely that investment promotion will prove a necessary and ongoing function of government.

Entrepreneurial state

The origins of the entrepreneurial approach lie in the economic malaise of the 1970s. Instead of regulating development (primarily through designating land uses), many planners and other professionals became oriented towards promoting urban economic development. This shift was also prompted by increasing recognition of the shortcomings of regional planning.

This change in focus was aided by the ideological shift of the 1980s which redefined the respective contributions of the public and private sectors to development. Responsibility has shifted to the private sector, with an emphasis on market solutions to development problems. In high-income countries, the role of planners came to be directed at working with the private sector to promote urban development; in middle- and low-income countries this move is still underway.

These changes in thinking affected high- and middle-income countries equally, but arguably the impact has been more pronounced in middle-income countries. This is because local governments in high-income countries are more resilient – they generally have better administrative and technical capacity and stronger finances. Further, the nature of their relationship with local business people often obliges these local governments to adopt a proactive development path.

The reverse is true for local governments in middle-income countries. In the first place, local business people may be overshadowed by transnational corporations who are unconcerned about specifically local development issues, and deal with central government in their transactions over import licences, access to foreign currency and so on. Further, local governments in these countries have less administrative capacity, experience greater difficulty in supplying services, and are less adept at exploiting local sources of revenue. These governments are thus more dependent on their national government. But this national government might itself be in the throes of a structural adjustment programme, and its options for new urban policies, alternative budgets or a different role for the various levels of government might well be limited. It is not surprising, then, that Eisinger (1988) assigns the role of 'entrepreneurial state' to local and state governments in the United States, while the pursuit of 'urban efficiency' is the role the World Bank accords local governments in middle-income countries.

The entrepreneurial approach differs from the traditional approach in almost every respect. In terms of Eisinger's summary, the assumption is that growth is promoted by discovering, expanding, developing or creating new markets for local goods or services. The goal is to facilitate new business formation and small business expansion in the given jurisdiction, as opposed to competing to attract investment from large firms located outside the jurisdiction.

The reason for calling this kind of state 'entrepreneurial' is that the public sector may offer low-interest finance or assume an equity position in selected high-risk enterprises. The selection process will be based on presumed growth industries, identified through a strategic plan undertaken with the private sector. The enterprises might be high-risk because they include opportunities that the private sector may either have overlooked or be reluctant to pursue, including opportunities in new markets, new products and new industries.

Urban efficiency

Urban efficiency prescriptions represent an emerging consensus among many scholars and the United Nations family of organisations.[9] The World Bank (1991a) urban policy paper has four foci: the promotion of urban productivity, the relief of urban poverty, environmentally sustainable urban environments,[10] and related urban research. The first two issues are central. (The Bank's urban missions to South Africa also use research to build consensus and promote local ownership.)

In effect, the Bank is shifting the urban agenda away from neighbourhood interventions, such as low-income shelter projects. One reason for this is that a project-by-project approach can never deliver the scale of intervention necessary to solve the problem. For example, while we might embark on a number of squatter upgrading projects, the number of sites involved is invariably less than the growth in demand. Thus the Bank is exploring alternative approaches which create a policy and regulatory environment that enables large and small enterprises, NGOs and consumers themselves to provide shelter and services. The Bank is investigating how national and local government might implement the new agenda through its Urban Management Program, and so there is still an exploratory element to their initiatives.

When addressing urban productivity, the Bank (1991a: 9) stresses:

- Strengthening the management of urban infrastructure ...
- Improving the city wide regulatory framework to improve market efficiency and to enhance the private sector's provision of shelter and infrastructure.
- Improving the financial and technical capacity of municipal institutions through more effective division of resources and responsibilities between central and local governments.
- Strengthening financial services for urban development.

In respect of urban poverty, the Bank (1991a: 10 and 11) differentiates between managing the economic and social aspects of poverty and creating a safety net for the ultra-poor. The economic dimension involves:

- Increasing the demand for the labor of the poor through government policies to encourage labor-intensive productive activities.
- Alleviating the structural constraints inhibiting the productivity and growth of the informal sector ...
- Increasing the labor productivity of the poor by reducing constraints preventing labor-force participation ...

The social dimension entails:

- ... expenditure for human-resource development ...
- Increasing the access of the poor to infrastructure and housing ...
- ... supporting ... community initiatives and local, nongovernmental organisations.

Lastly, safety-net assistance to the ultra-poor would comprise food assistance, health care, employment, and other measures to moderate a decline in income. The presumed context is one of short-term economic setbacks due to, say, structural adjustment programmes.

Many of the above propositions are well-known, but the Bank's policy paper has managed to combine them in a clear and comprehensive manner and to do so within an ideological framework appropriate to the era. Ultimately, however, the paper presents a pessimistic assessment of what local governments and communities can do. Perhaps the Bank's experience of working with communities has led them to lower their sights, but I find it difficult to accept that one should be so constrained. I hope, in the following pages, to demonstrate a broader view.

Human resource development

The traditional, entrepreneurial and urban efficiency approaches assume that development is rightfully promoted by the private sector and that benefits trickle down in the form of jobs and improved services made possible by higher taxes. But it is now apparent that the urban poor will have to wait a long time if they are to rely on trickle-down processes. As the earlier discussion of economic restructuring showed, manufacturing employment in high-income countries has declined. Those manufacturing jobs which are increasing rely more on low-wage labour, and less on the semi-skilled and skilled. The service sector, which has grown in many places, is divided between high-paid professionals and low-wage, often part-time workers. The overall outcome has been greater inequality (especially in the USA – Peterson 1991: 8) and greater unemployment (less so in the USA).

The focus of human resource programmes in high-income countries is on enabling the poor and the structurally unemployed to become productive participants in the capitalist economy. There are two goals. The first is to increase their access to jobs; the second is to improve the productivity of those who have jobs. Ultimately, the concern is with jobs which offer access to the disadvantaged, which are likely to last, and which offer potential for advancement.

Questions of access arise since unemployment is generally concentrated among certain groups. An obvious example is African-American youths in the USA, especially those living in the central city, among whom unemployment rates are approximately 10 per cent higher than the rates for youths in general. On the one hand, industries have left the central cities, poor levels of schooling make other kinds of employment inaccessible, and hiring policies are often discriminatory. On the other hand, poverty has persisted, despite numerous programmes intended to relieve it. The fact that this is especially true among African-Americans has given rise to a literature – all too often with a hidden agenda – on the 'urban underclass'. However, close analysis of this apparent underclass reveals a diversity of characteristics and causes, and in the end one seems to be talking simply of those who live in the ghetto and are poor (Peterson 1991). The explanatory power of such a formulation is rather poor.

The situation in South Africa is different in that while the civics emphasise education, they do not always have the same objectives in mind. That is, they certainly hope that additional training will make their members more competitive on the job market, but they also seek to improve their ability to manage city government and to act as councillors. The latter goals are important, but not central to this book. The former goal is what human resource development strategies are all about. However, as Blakely (1989) points out, training serves little purpose when the jobs do not exist. Indeed, training in those circumstances serves more to raise the entry standards than to improve the lot of individuals. This fact has prompted me to shift the focus on human resource development. Rather than discuss human resource development as a development planning strategy, I instead deal at length, in Chapter 6, with community economic development. For us, therefore, the issue is less the training of individuals than it is discerning whether civics have the capacity to promote economic development and then, on the assumption that a number do, debating what they might accomplish.

Progressive

The Left offers a vigorous critique of most efforts at development planning, but cannot put forward a noticeably different approach to local economic development (Fainstein 1990a). Progressive development planning is therefore forged in ideological compromise.

In general, progressive government has three defining characteristics. First, perhaps the one feature common to activists in progressive government is their willingness to question whether market-determined outcomes are necessarily better than distributional judgements made by government. Thus progressive planners disparage development programmes which hope for 'trickle-down' effects and strive for programmes characterised by growth with equity. Many progressive planners go further and are prepared to challenge property rights, impose rent controls, support co-operative housing, and assume responsibility for or regulate the supply of services.

Secondly, a characteristic of activists working in a progressive administration is their desire to supplement contact with the council and the direction of bureaucratic policy with participatory decision-making. The organisational base of a new progressive administration will usually be community organisations whose tactical strength lay in mass action, and the activists will view such action as a counter to the quieter but more pervasive lobbying of business.

Thirdly, the development policies favoured by progressive administrations include indigenous business development, housing subsidies and alternative forms of housing supply, linkage between neighbourhood and downtown development so that the expansion of offices downtown – often with public support – creates benefits for the neighbourhoods, and a bias towards the development of low-income areas and small enterprises. These policies have much in common with a community-based approach to economic development.

Mier and Moe (1991) warn that progressive administration holds two dangers. Community groups might be co-opted by government; for example, community organisations were restrained in their criticism of Mayor Washington for fear of embarrassing his administration. In addition, progressives in government need a broader base than community organisations in order to govern, to be confident of re-election, and to foster private investment, and may well be drawn into a series of compromises which cause them to lose sight of their principles and their mandate. Both government, and through it the community, may end up being exploited by business. As a counter to this, Fainstein (1990b) warns that community groups should continue to organise and remain vocal on critical issues. Failing this, a progressive government will be hostage to private interests. Indeed, it is reported that Mayor Washington rather enjoyed pickets outside City Hall as they strengthened his hand (Hollander 1991).

COMMUNITY APPROACHES TO LOCAL DEVELOPMENT PLANNING

So far it has been relatively easy and largely correct to maintain two distinctions which become questionable in the case of community organisations. The first distinction is that between local development planning which is oriented to economic development and that which is oriented to other community issues. The distinction becomes a bit artificial in the case of communities since community organisations often strive to achieve a variety of goals. While some organisations will have a relative focus on employment creation, others will share this goal with efforts at housing rehabilitation and improvements in the supply of social services. For example, in the United States 87 per cent of CDCs provide financial assistance for low-cost housing, 30 per cent are involved in commercial and industrial projects, and 35 per cent attempt to create and support small businesses (Wiewel and Weintraub 1990).

The second distinction is between community organisations which engage in projects, and those which prefer to remain advocacy organisations, influencing policy and budgetary allocations. There are solid reasons for the latter position: poverty problems are vast and only governments and the private sector dispose of sufficient resources to address them. Thus community organisations may think it preferable to influence the decisions and expenditure of the public and private sectors, with potentially significant ramifications, rather than undertake a few small projects. An additional concern is that when a CDC becomes dependent on its funding sources, it may lose sight of its principles, its leadership may be absorbed into establishment structures, and it may begin to articulate the problem in a different way and voice a different agenda (Fainstein 1987).

Because of this I have engaged in some sifting to isolate the economic role of community organisations and consider the advocacy role and its potential economic benefits.

Why engage?

The ensuing discussion focuses on American CDCs. One reason for this is that welfare systems in Europe do not propel low-income communities towards organisation to the same extent as in the USA, where there is minimal welfare support and considerable economic and social exclusion. In Germany, for example, members of social movements lived off the state and were characterised as utopian until most, it seems, were incorporated into the parliamentary tradition through the Greens Party (Meyer 1987). Another reason is that left-inclined political parties such as Britain's Labour Party felt that community organisations intruded on the responsibilities of the state – in contrast to the Conservative Party, which believes in individual self-help.[11] A third reason is that formerly dynamic urban social movements – such as those in France in the 1960s or the Citizens Movement in Spain under Franco – have withered away.

Indeed, it is questionable whether CDCs exist in any comparable form in Europe. CDCs are a product of American tax legislation which makes contributions to them tax deductible. This focus on American CDCs seems especially relevant because of their similarities with South Africa's community development trusts (CDTs), recently established to implement local development projects; like the American CDCs, they have also been granted tax-exempt status.

The histories of social movements written by Castells (1983) and Fisher (1984) warn against generalisations. Yet it does seem true to say that, in the advocacy mode, the mobilisation of communities occurs when there is a discrepancy between actual and expected conditions, and the likelihood of success is dependent on disarray among the elite (Fainstein 1987). For example, the mobilisation during the 1960s occurred in a context of economic growth; heightened, but unrealised expectations on the part of minorities due to the rhetoric of the Johnson administration; a turbulent social environment due to the Vietnam war; and co-operation from many Democratic elites.

Different conditions apply in the development corporation mode. These conditions burgeoned after the Johnson-era poverty programmes, which were largely viewed as a failure. Despite' spending '... over $10 billion in between the War on Poverty in 1964 and its reorientation in 1970, there was only a marginal decline in the absolute number of poor people. ... What is clear is that the notion of community- or locality-based economic development became strongly rooted in the national psyche at this time' (Blakely 1989: 21). This view, which still prevails, holds that community organisations are especially effective as development agencies and as a vehicle for delivering the benefits of federal programmes.

In respect of economic development,[12] CDCs commonly pursue one or more of the following objectives (Blakely 1989: 201):

- generating employment for particular groups;
- gaining control over the local/neighbourhood economy;
- inspiring self-help and co-operative group-oriented assistance;
- operating for the public benefit;
- providing an alternative or intermediate sector for economic activity; and
- promoting democratic management and control of enterprises.

Approaches

Advocacy

There is ongoing debate between those who believe that community organisations would serve their constituencies better if they became or started CDCs, and those who hold that an advocacy role garners more resources for the community. This debate is particularly pertinent to South Africa, as the civics are in a less advantageous position than their American counterparts – they have fewer resources and technical skills. Their comparative advantage may well lie in advocacy and pressure tactics.

With reference to the USA, McKnight and Kretzmann (1984) argue that an inherent weakness of advocacy organisations is that advocacy presumes a target which is visible, local and capable of making a difference. Such targets proliferated in the past, but they are less abundant nowadays. For example, banks, industries and commerce have left most low-income neighbourhoods; major plants are leaving the cities and often also the nation; and a large number of the enterprises which remain in a city have been acquired by larger corporations with head offices in one of the 'world cities' and are now less exposed to local pressures. Alternatively, if the target is to be local government, then the ongoing fiscal crisis and greater privatisation render them less able to fund revitalising programmes. In addition, the privatisation of services renders them less susceptible to political pressure. In other words, when capital is mobile and often controlled externally, and when local authorities are constrained fiscally and notoriously vulnerable to threats of relocation, times are hard for urban social movements.

This raises the question of why South African civics have so often been successful. Has it been because of disarray among the ruling elite? Has it been due to the financial impact of the various boycotts? Or is it that when a civic in South Africa seizes land, for example, this action is qualitatively different to political pressure from communities in high-income countries?

Community development corporations[13]

There have been three generations of CDCs. While CDCs had many different origins, the first generation had two critical stimuli. The first was the Ford Foundation's 'Grey Areas Program' which, in the mid-1960s, provided grants that were intended to build local development institutions for implementing social and economic programmes in poverty-stricken areas of America's cities. The second stimulus came from the federally-sponsored 'Special Impact Program' for CDCs (an amendment to the 1964 Economic Opportunities Act) which formed part of President Johnson's War on Poverty.

The context for these stimuli was a sense among a majority of middle-class Americans that reparations were due to minorities after centuries of discrimination. Their willingness to undertake such a war on poverty was, of course, further stimulated by the urban riots which began with Watts in 1965.

By 1970 there were fewer than 100 CDCs throughout the USA; some had failed and many were struggling. None the less, this number grew rapidly during the 1970s to about 1 000 by 1980. In large part this 'second wave grew out of nonprofit organisations that had formed to take advantage of federal support for low-income housing ... [or] evolved out of the social service organisations and community action agencies that the federal Office of Economic Opportunity' had inspired since 1960 (Peirce and Steinbach 1990: 26).[14] In addition, support from foundations had been growing since the 1960s and was now a major source of finance, again largely as a result of disillusionment with Johnson's war on poverty.

The Reagan administration dismantled these federal funding programmes. One could argue that many Americans felt that sufficient resources had been devoted to overcoming poverty and that, in so far as it was possible, the playing field had been levelled.

None the less, the number of third-generation CDCs is now in the order of 5 000. This increase was made possible by redirecting the energies of CDCs. While their goal remained the creation of stable, quality jobs, the means by which they pursued it changed. Whereas initially CDCs tended to own and manage their own businesses, a task for which they were ill-prepared, they shifted towards nurturing local enterprise by supplying equity capital, loans, incubator space and technical assistance. This was often done in partnership with the private sector, which was used to filter local businesses into the economic mainstream.

An inevitable associated change is that, as a result of becoming more dependent on private and local authority funding, CDCs tended to forego their advocacy role. Their style has become more technocratic and there is always the danger that a CDC will grow distant from the community, will become 'a development corporation in search of a neighborhood' (Graham Finney, cited by Peirce and Steinbach 1990: 32).

Small enterprise

The type of business development activity undertaken by CDCs includes establishing manufacturing incubators and filtering loan applications to formal financial institutions. A dominant theme in the literature on these efforts is that they should be directed at small and medium-sized rather than micro or informal enterprises. This focus is held to be more efficient and to lead to a more rapid rate of employment creation. However, we should be concerned about recommending such a focus in South Africa, because the people who have access to employment in small and medium-sized enterprises are family-members and others with an employment history and education. This excludes the mass of South Africa's poverty-stricken urban population.

    While the arguments surrounding the efficiency of targeting relatively larger enterprises may have value in America's ghettos, it is not clear that they are valid for South Africa. Probably the two main constraints on the growth of small enterprise in this country are the size of (or limited access to) the market; and access to capital. As regards the market, the archetypal small enterprise in America is the ubiquitous 'mom 'n pop' store which serves a low-income population with daily items and thus has limited growth potential. This contrasts with informal enterprises in a middle-income country which face fewer restrictions in moving to points throughout a city where demand is concentrated. (The informal markets on the streets of New York City suggest that this is not an entirely fair comparison!) As regards capital, case studies such as ACCION International (discussed in Chapter 6) suggest that enabling informal enterprises to gain access to capital is not necessarily less efficient than serving small and medium enterprises. Indeed, often the reverse seems true.

    What emerges from the last two sections is the view that:

* community organisations seldom run successful enterprises;
* such organisations can help with the creation and expansion of micro and small enterprises;
* the object is to increase incomes and employment; and
* this object is often best served in partnership with the private sector and government agencies.

Worker co-operatives

The notion of worker co-operatives is popular among South Africa's intellectual Left. It is less fashionable among the workers. While certain unions have attempted to establish a few small co-operatives, the workers apparently view them as a means of survival, having recently lost their jobs, rather than as an affirmative, worker-controlled, long-term endeavour. In one sense, this is 'realistic' in the light of the more conventional wisdom that co-operatives 'either fail or cease to be democracies of producers'.[15] But it is also generally the case that interest in co-operatives peaks when the economy is in recession.

Yet there are success stories, of which Spain's Mondragon co-operatives and industrial democracy in Yugoslavia are perhaps the best known.[16] I describe these examples in Chapter 6 and debate whether they are replicable in South Africa. Here our task is to define co-operatives. In general, there are three variations.

The first is the worker co-operative! By definition:

- each worker has one vote;
- the net income of the enterprise is allocated to workers on the basis of labour (hours worked/level of pay); and
- the net book value of the co-operative and its assets are owned by the workers and are not transferable.[17]

Workers gain access to the co-operative by paying a membership fee which contributes to the co-operative's capitalisation. (The fee may be deducted from future earnings.) This means, as well, that in case a worker later wants to leave the co-operative, each worker retains an account with the co-operative reflecting the net value of his or her share. The account may increase if the value of the co-operative's assets increase and if it retains a share of net earnings within worker accounts (in order, say, to undertake new investments); alternatively, it may decline if the co-operative deducts funds in years when it experiences losses. If a member leaves the co-operative, he or she receives the original membership fee and accumulated earnings.

Employee share ownership (ESOP) is a lesser form of worker ownership, especially as workers tend to hold a minority of shares – often non-voting shares. In South Africa ESOPs are generally limited to 10 per cent of a company's outstanding stock, including shares held by executives. In the case of some companies which disinvested from South Africa, employee share ownership increased to 24 per cent. In this instance 25 per cent was set as a maximum to prevent employees acquiring a blocking vote.[18] In other words, ESOPs have their place, but not in a discussion on co-operatives in South Africa.

Lastly, industrial democracy, such as that in Yugoslavia, illuminates the Mondragon experience and provides its own lessons. Because of uncertainty due to the present upheavals, I refer to the situation as it was. Yugoslav enterprises remain under 'social control', but the workers form a 'workers' council' which can make decisions in all areas of enterprise activity, including product lines, financial planning, technological innovation, salaries and investment. The council also elects, and may recall, the management board and plant director.

What about unions?

This book emphasises three negotiating partners: civics, local authorities and business. Is there not a role for unions?

In part the limited reference to unions reflects the author's greater access to American and English material than that of other countries. In England unions have a say, but it is via the Labour Party, which makes it indirect and unsatisfactory. In America, unions have been consulted when development planning is undertaken at the metropolitan scale. However, much development planning occurs within parts of a city and the issues addressed are not so much strategic – the direction of the metropolitan economy – as local. That is, union involvement in formulating industrial development strategy has little to do with local civic concerns such as services, the informal sector, subcontracting relationships, and access to capital. Moreover, since unions draw their membership from throughout a city, and since support given to an organisation in one neighbourhood may mean fewer resources for another, unions are at risk when acting locally.

It is probably safe to generalise that, in middle-income countries with high unemployment, unions and the mass of the urban population do not share common goals. This is especially true in South Africa where, according to COSATU, only 17 per cent of the country's workers are unionised (SAIRR 1991/92: 285). Since formal employment and membership of a trade union set one aside from the urban poor, unionised workers are inevitably defending their interests against the mass of the low-income population. The union's struggle is based in the workplace, not in the community.

It seems clear that union involvement is appropriate when the scale is metropolitan (and regional) and when the issues are of a strategic nature. The rationale for this is found in arguments raised in Chapter 2: certain industries concentrate in specific metropolitan areas and are not randomly spread throughout the nation. The implication is that the area constitutes an appropriate scale for studying the potential for co-ordinated action to promote future development.

It is in this light that South Africa's unions are interesting. For example, COSATU:

- is studying industrial policy options through its linkages with the Economic Trends group and the work it is undertaking in the Industrial Strategy Project;
- is active in the NEF;
- participates and makes proposals in regional economic forums whose purpose is to chart development strategies for the respective regions;
- participates in labour-management accords;
- engages in debate with industry representatives regarding the restructuring of specific industries;[19]and
- facilitates development at a local level through, for example, helping to broker peace in townships in Natal which previously were devastated by conflict, or through showing an interest in starting co-operatives.

In effect, COSATU's member unions are helping to plot the development trajectory of the country and its regions and cities. Yet their contribution is unlike that of the civics. For example, although COSATU has yet to indicate a formal opinion on the matter, it seems to be reluctant to join local and metropolitan initiatives. This is variously explained as being due to:

- the fear that development planning at the metropolitan scale would benefit certain union members at the expense of others elsewhere in the region;
- unequal power relationships between the major cities and their hinterlands;
- COSATU's limited ability to sustain negotiations at both the regional level and in a number of urban areas; and
- the view that rural development is also important to members and that rural development necessitates a larger scale of planning.

Were COSATU to engage at the metropolitan level, what might it recommend? An interesting bit of history, which is also a quaint example of an ill-conceived metropolitan industrial strategy intended to serve labour, is found in the efforts of the Greater London Council (GLC) under the leadership of the Labour Party in the 1980s. The story is worth repeating here as many in COSATU might well find similar strategies attractive.

'Quaint' is not used in a flattering sense; after a decade (1971-1981) in which the proportion of the city's labour force in manufacturing employment declined from 33 per cent to 19 per cent, the GLC adopted policies which accentuated economic decline. The London Industrial Strategy, together with the London Financial Strategy and the London Labour Plan, aimed to achieve a peaceful transition to socialism (Eisenschitz and North 1986). The objectives of the industrial strategy were to:

- prioritise the needs of the workers;
- bring resources (human potential, land, finance and technical expertise) which had lost their market value due to the restructuring process into production for socially useful ends;
- ensure that investment decisions were based on social criteria identified by workers and community groups rather than determined by profit; and
- enable the Council (in partnership with the above groups) to take the lead in industrial development through some degree of public ownership and control.

In effect, the capitalist mode of production was identified as the essential problem and the GLC strove to create a socialist alternative.

The GLC was never able to pursue these goals. Instead, it was obliged to implement a 'watered down' programme. Compromise was inevitable in a context of lost manufacturing plant, heightened competition and capital mobility, and opposition from Thatcher. Indeed, what could this strategy realistically hope to achieve, in an area limited to metropolitan London? If, 'in an integrated world economy, a single country [cannot] go it alone' (Judd and Parkinson 1990: 20) – as was the case with France's industrial strategy – how could a single city do so? The moral, for the purposes of this book, is that we should not be tempted by the 'go it alone' rhetoric current in some circles in South Africa (Bond 1991). The point is to enable the metropolitan economy to adapt to and exploit competitive pressures, not to oppose them.

In sum, unions can advance progressive interests which include both employment creation and higher incomes. It is not helpful to harp on the fact that they represent only a small proportion of the country's labour force.

PRIVATE SECTOR APPROACHES TO LOCAL DEVELOPMENT PLANNING

Why engage?

The classic depiction of why the private sector engages in development planning has been provided by Molotch (1976). He distinguished between immobile capital – people or companies whose fortunes are closely tied to an increasing local population, a growing market, and higher land prices; and mobile capital – enterprises that serve a larger market and are relatively immune to the state of the local economy. It is in the interests of mobile capital to contribute to local development, and this section concentrates on their activities. However, this does not mean that we can exclude mobile capital, for it is they who are targeted in the traditional approach to development planning. In relation to them, we have to ask to what extent they are affected by local initiatives to promote development.

Immobile capital

According to Molotch (1976), immobile capital behaves like a 'growth coalition' which propagates 'growth machine' politics. The participants include property developers, banks with exposed positions in property, commercial interests, utility companies, newspapers, linked service providers like lawyers, architects and real estate agents, and universities.

'Growth machine politics' refers to a situation where there is a contested terrain within an urban area, but where a commonality of interests emerges in the face of competition between urban areas. One example of this would be where a weak and decentralised local government combines with a wide diversity of property-owning groups, creating competition over the location of infrastructure, zoning, property taxes, urban redevelopment, and the like. Politicians are beholden to these interests, because, in the absence of a strong political party system, they depend on electoral contributions for their careers. Molotch and Vicari (1988: 190) are critical of property investors, and argue that they are 'betting not on their skills at choosing or developing products that have intrinsic merit but, rather, on their capacity as politically skilled actors to alter the spatial structure of the city'.

A second instance of growth machine politics might arise where localities are competing for investment through issues related to the 'business climate' – taxes, environmental legislation, expenditure on cultural facilities, urban redevelopment. Here Molotch suggests that formerly competing groups will now combine their efforts in order to promote growth. Again, Molotch is critical of growth coalitions. He argues that while their ideological foundation is the need to create jobs, in practice they attempt to distribute the costs of growth (for example, more services, public sector employees, congestion and pollution) while appropriating the benefits.

Clavel (1986) and Clavel and Wiewel (1991) have countered that one should periodise conceptions of growth coalitions. In their view the coalitions arose out of America's New Deal urban programmes in the 1930s which used federal subsidies for public works, housing and economic development. These policies helped transform the cities: suburban single-family housing, central offices, retailing and services in suburban malls, dispersed manufacturing, and inner-city slums became the norm. The transition gave rise to, and was abetted by, growth coalitions, which Clavel and Wiewel date from the 1940s to the 1960s, and also the 1970s in some cities.

They hold that growth coalitions served to build 'new owner housing in the suburbs while redlining the inner city ghettos and demolishing low-rent properties for offices and highways ... [all of which] created and exacerbated inequalities in the basic constituencies' (p. 5). They continue that the coalitions might have survived the resultant urban conflict in the 1960s, were it not for the structural changes which accelerated in the 1970s: the loss of manufacturing employment; a proportionate and usually an absolute increase in the number of service jobs which, on the whole, paid lower wages; and more pronounced urban income inequality. The upshot was that with the migration of the white working class to the suburbs, the creation of suburban shopping malls and office parks, and America's conservative backlash, there was no longer any motive for nor political interest in downtown growth strategies. Growth coalitions had served their purpose.

In my view, both arguments are flawed. First, Molotch's disregard for growth coalitions is premised on the assumption that they attempt to promote growth either through political intrigue or through traditional policies designed to attract investment – in which case there is no net employment creation and no overall gain.[20] Would one be equally critical if entrepreneurial approaches were applied or if development strategies were formulated with the participation of community groups? In the face of economic decline, coalitions whose *raison d'être* is economic growth within their cities now find greater favour. Secondly, 'private sector development organisations' (PSDOs) still abound, and they are often little different from the growth coalitions. This is especially true when the coalition is augmented by transnational companies looking to establish 'command centres' in urban downtowns. Thirdly, 'urban coalitions', which differ somewhat from growth coalitions, are resurgent. Judd and Parkinson (1990) write that many cities now strive to become 'intentional cities', which identify the constraints and opportunities arising from the process of structural change, and which adopt policies enabling them to identify and occupy new economic niches.

The book edited by Judd and Parkinson contains descriptions from North America and Europe of many different forms of urban coalitions whose goal is economic regeneration. These differ from growth coalitions in three respects: the extent of government entrepreneurship, the amount of planning, and the level of priority accorded to those in greatest need (Fainstein 1990a). Thus growth coalitions serve the interests of private participants and politicians, and may well disadvantage the poor whereas urban redevelopment, for example, leads to relocation. Urban coalitions, conversely, serve a wider array of interests, and often include community groups and the working class on planning bodies.

One should note, though, that most references are still to growth coalitions, even though Molotch and Vicari (1988) now accept that the American example is probably an exception. Several alternatives show that the extent and form of private engagement in development planning are about as varied as the context.

Hungary provides an interesting example of the spread of development planning.[21] Shortly after the collapse of communism in 1989, Hungarian local governments initiated development programmes modelled on the American experience. Debrecen, for example, adopted a programme which includes the following projects, initiated prior to completion of the city's strategic development planning process.

i.   Together with the Atomik Institute, a physics research laboratory, the city has established a small-business incubator. The incubator is located on the Institute's campus and provides entrepreneurs with access to its high-technology equipment and expertise.

ii. In partnership with the Lagos Kossuth University, the city has created a Small Business Development Centre that assists local entrepreneurs with business development and management.
iii. Debrecen has adopted traditional industrial recruiting techniques.
iv. The city is itself implementing large projects such as creating a lake and a tourist recreation centre.

This list would be familiar to development planners – with the exception of the fourth point, where the city itself has undertaken major investments; American cities, in contrast, would proceed by means of a public-private partnership.

In **Japan,** regional planning is undertaken by central government. In 1957 the Ministry of International Trade and Industry (MITI) became responsible for determining where future growth would occur when it assumed the prerogative for rationalising the country's transportation and industrial location structure. The government is attempting to divert growth from Tokyo to the adjacent cities of Osaka and Nagoya, and to 25 technopolises, stretched across Japan (Sazanami 1991). For those accustomed to the limited achievements of regional planning, the striking aspect of the technopolis programme is the detail: the specific functions of each technopolis are prescribed and the associated research and development capacity is specified.

This detail masks the fact that MITI cannot direct investment to the sites it deems optimal for investment. Indeed, MITI's influence waned when its role in guiding the allocation of capital to specific sectors and industries diminished due to Japan's becoming a capital surplus country. While it still attempts to convince major companies where to invest on the basis of, say, the shortage and high price of land in Tokyo, these attempts have seldom proved effective. The successes attributed to private-public partnerships in steering Japan's economy find no parallel in the country's attempts at regional planning.

The specifically American preconditions for the emergence of local growth machine politics are conspicuously absent in Japan.[22] There are strong political parties, government is centralised, and although there is intense speculation in property, this is undertaken from the centre where the *keiretsu* contribute to the Liberal Democratic Party and maintain close ties with the central bureaucracy.

Conditions are different again in the **United Kingdom**. Harding (1991) provides the most direct assessment, despite the fact that his paper is limited to property development. He writes that:

i. 'Business participation in the ... urban political process has been on the wane for over a century as the combined effects of the universal franchise, the political mobilisation of nonbusiness interests in urban areas, the suburbanisation of economic elites, the bureaucratisation of corporate enterprises and the internationalisation of capital have left the Labour Party and its constituency as the dominant urban player.' (p. 300)

ii. Historically, property speculation was heavily taxed and in addition to the local authority there were many non-private land-owners, for example, the church and the crown, all of which diluted attempts at redevelopment.

iii. Services were provided by relatively strong local authorities who obtained financial assistance from central government.

iv. The United Kingdom lacked the ideological predisposition for public-private partnerships and had a strong party system.

v. The structure of ownership of land was relatively centralised among large corporations.

The Conservative Party altered things somewhat. The Conservatives set out to change the basis of local authority intervention so that it would be compatible with their vision of the future economic order, to mobilise the private sector in urban regeneration, and to expand central government influence over public programmes. The last aim should be seen in the light of the control exerted at local authority level by the Labour Party. The Labour Party's economic policy focused on indigenous development, advice to small businesses, rejection of inter-urban competition, and targeted development so that the jobs created served the needs of the poorest. In response, the central government did away with institutions such as the Greater London Council and promoted urban development through, for example, the urban development corporations,[23] Urban Development Grants (City Grants) and the Derelict Land Grant. By the mid-1980s, these measures had begun to stimulate business interest.

At the same time, browbeaten Labour-aligned local authorities were themselves pounding the development drum. They formed a variety of 'enabling agencies' with varying degrees of private involvement.[24] Occasionally these agencies were motivated by a desire to pre-empt the formation of urban development corporations (UDCs) for their areas. Because of more extensive municipal property ownership in the United Kingdom, development often comprised joint development with the private sector or the sale of public assets.

Mobile capital

Of course, capital is largely mobile. Mobile capital takes many forms in countless locations, and the owners of capital are generally considered impervious to local economic development coalitions.[25] But do the owners of capital respond to location incentives?

These incentives are still predominantly in the traditional mould (Levy 1990). Yet it is clear that the reasons why firms locate where they do have little to do with the blandishments of the public sector. New firms prioritise access to customers, access to growing markets and access to raw materials. For expanding firms the critical factors are maintaining the current labour force and safeguarding access to markets. Managers of branch plants are particularly concerned about the quality of the labour supply and the absence of unions, but also mention market factors.

It is only when governments are prepared to pay a great deal that they can expect to influence location decisions. Thus, in South Africa, it was only when decentralising industrialists were paid a quarterly, tax-free cash grant per labourer – which exceeded the going wage – that industrialists attributed their moves to the concessions.[26] If one thinks of one of the foremost locational incentives in the USA, tax abatements, Bluestone and Harrison (1982) show that a 20 per cent tax abatement is typically equivalent to a 2 per cent wage differential and therefore argue that tax abatements are of little consequence. Kieschnick (1983, cited in Eisinger 1988:146) reports that his survey of ten states revealed that most firms in a state are unaware of the location concessions and still fewer make use of them.

Indigenous, high-technology industry

Three themes surface in Western Europe and the USA when an entrepreneurial style of planning is adopted. The first is that assistance is targeted to small, indigenous high-technology industries. The rationale behind this is the realisation that most manufacturing employment is located in small establishments, and that employment in such firms is growing more rapidly than in large corporations.[27] Further, small businesses have been viewed as better able to adapt to processes of structural change and the reorganisation of production. Finally, small indigenous businesses are less spatially mobile than large firms and, once they become the recipients of public support, are less likely to leave the area.

The second theme involves venture capital policies that subsidise private enterprise. These policies are based on the assessment that small businesses are vital to the future of an area's economy. In sum, the 'declining importance of economies of scale in the less capital-intensive industries dependent on advanced technology, the growing tendency to contract out the manufacturing of component parts to independent suppliers, and the need for more flexible production and management systems to respond to the challenge of rapid product innovation all suggested ... the necessity of a small business sector and a public policy matrix to support it' (Eisinger 1988: 241). Public support is held to be especially necessary for two types of firms thought to be poorly served by the private capital market: firms engaged in research and development with a long time-lag before production, and firms whose market is growing rapidly.

The last theme is that subsidies and investment are often directed at export industries, whether they export out of the region or out of the country. These industries often receive export loans and assistance with marketing. This emulates MITI in that the local or provincial government evaluates particular products, product cycles and the competitive posture of local entrepreneurs; it differs from MITI in that the organisation of Japanese industry is characterised by a competitive oligopoly with many backward-linked small suppliers and subcontractors. In Japan, therefore, MITI is dealing with a few major actors in each sector, from whom many other smaller enterprises take their lead. In the USA, by contrast, high-technology sectors might be populated by literally hundreds of competitors.

However, do small firms confront serious problems in gaining access to capital and does the public sector offer a significant source of capital? Are small firms keen to export, or is there local inertia? Eisinger (1988) argues that in general the entrepreneurial programmes are still too novel, and so the jury is still out. Yet he also describes a few small businesses which rely on financial institutions for their initial capitalisation – as is the case for informal sector activities in middle-income countries (Page and Steel 1984). Eisinger also reports a degree of private inertia which is retarding state export programmes.

The position to which I am heading is similar to the one I adopted on the traditional approach. There it was apparent that the private sector was largely unaware of the location concessions, and seldom used them. A counter-example was given in South Africa, where the location concessions became extraordinarily expensive to the state, yet beneficial to

individual firms. These concessions were credited with inducing significant relocations, but no net employment creation.

We are drawn to the rather obvious conclusion that the level of private
participation in local initiatives will reflect the extent to which public
expenditure and concessions enhance their profits. In direct proportion to
this, public influence over the project will reflect the extent to which its
supply of low-interest capital or its exercise of public powers to, say,
assemble land, build infrastructure or waive zoning restrictions affects the
project's profitability. The difference between traditional and entrepreneurial approaches – which seem most relevant to the evaluation of private sector approaches – is that the former disregards net employment creation
and unabashedly defines success when jobs are relocated to the area. The
latter measures success in terms of business expansion and additional jobs.

Approaches

Chapter 7 refers to various approaches in development planning: assistance from prominent business people, single projects with companies,
relations with development consortia, and private sector development
organisations (PSDOs). Instead of spending time with each here, it will be
more useful to examine what they all have in common: public-private
partnerships.[28]

The problem to which city governments responded in the 1970s has
changed. Initially they sought to incorporate minorities into the city's
mainstream. Then structural changes weakened city economies, diminished their tax bases, and created greater dependence on the private sector. With the advent of conservative economic policies, economic
development has become their top priority. The resultant development
programmes take the form of co-operation or partnership with business
leaders, and their objective has usually been taken as synonymous with
the expansion of private sector employment.

Most public-private partnerships take the form of offshoots of municipal government linked to private or not-for-profit firms such as CDCs.[29]
Public control is maintained by elected officials, but is generally limited
to instances where public funds are allocated. Thus, partnerships are generally insulated from day-to-day oversight. The actual role of the participants varies according to who initiates the project and how much public
intervention is necessary to implement it. The fact that government is to
some degree reliant on private resources means that these partnerships
limit the scope of action of public agencies. Indeed, from the point of

view of the government officials who actually manage public-private partnerships, they are little different from business ventures. Consequently the requirements for citizen participation are diminished. Less than 10 per cent of cities which use this type of partnership emphasise directing the economic benefits to poorer neighbourhoods.

Public-private partnerships have produced a turn-around in several cities. They have been synergetic because they combine government powers with private sector management and flexibility. The cities improved their performance relative to their regions and reversed the net loss of jobs. This reversal is attributable to capable local leadership and the willingness of government and the private sector to co-operate, as well as the ability of that leadership to identify a growth strategy which gives a city specific advantages.

The negative side to these partnerships stems from their inherent inequality. They exclude participation by community bodies, bypass democratic processes and bias a city's development strategy in favour of specific interest groups. The exception to this rule occurs when communities are well organised. Then the communities are often included in decision-making processes, win favourable budgetary allocations for their neighbourhoods, and obtain resources for development projects.

FROM PUBLIC-PRIVATE PARTNERSHIPS
TO URBAN COALITIONS

Development planning has commonly been introduced in reaction to unfavourable changes in the local economy. Plant closures and the apparent need to compete with other localities for mobile capital are common stimuli to local efforts. Another response is to oppose deindustrialisation, although these efforts have proved unable to withstand the competitive pressures inherent in global capitalism. Nowadays the goal is more modest: to enable a city to anticipate and to adapt to a process of change (Judd and Parkinson 1990). Even this is more easily prescribed than implemented. The fashionable suggestion at this juncture is that a city needs a strategic plan formulated by a public-private partnership.

We have seen that public-private partnerships, while useful, embody certain problems. The lesson for the mass of the urban population is that public-private partnerships need to be transformed into representative bodies which promote fair outcomes.

There can be no predetermination of the members of an urban coalition. Every urban area will have its own economic, political and community institutions and traditions which, in some way, will be unique to that area. Economic trends will also be important. As Markusen (1989) has shown, the type of regional politics is closely related to structural trends within the regional economy.[30]

The characteristics of a coalition can be depicted in the form of axes on a graph.[31] The vertical axis describes the willingness to be proactive and entrepreneurial and to formulate a differentiated development plan. This requires the targeting of specific industries or sectors, the commitment of public and private resources, collaboration by unions and community organisations, and the participation of small-scale enterprises. The horizontal axis describes the range from stable, united and democratic coalitions to divided, weak, public-private partnerships.

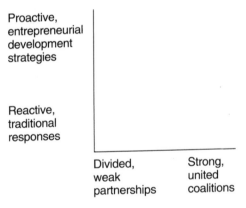

The coalition's immediate task would be to build trust through a fair assessment of development needs, problems and opportunities, and the resources available to deal with them. The vehicle for doing this and for charting the city's future generally takes the form of a strategic planning exercise. (I describe such an exercise in Chapter 7.)

APPLICATION IN SOUTH AFRICA

I initially thought the appropriate title for this section should be 'Relevance to South Africa?'. Yet at this stage the question seems a little redundant, as local coalitions are already a reality and are undertaking development planning. On reflection, the relevant issue appears to be what differences in application we should expect in a middle-income country with a blighted history.

For whom is development planning intended?

We have already noted two strands of thought in development planning. One emphasises the incorporation of minorities or poor and unemployed people into the urban mainstream. The other responds to urban decline and seeks more widespread economic renewal. How well do these strands accord with the middle-income context of mass unemployment and rapid population growth, and indeed, with the potential for industrial strategies which exploit the disadvantages of high-income countries?

The answer is that local development planning in middle-income countries does not focus on 'minorities', on those with marginal (low-paid, part-time) employment, or on 'inner cities'; but rather on the mass of the low-income population. Further, the economic structure and competitive posture of cities from high- and middle-income countries show marked differences. High-income countries have seen the flight of capital, and middle-income countries have often been the beneficiaries (although this is not true of South Africa). The upshot of global economic restructuring is that quite different employment strategies or sectoral foci are likely to emerge. In particular, middle-income countries are in a position to adopt labour-intensive industrial strategies and seek an economic structure which contrasts sharply with those in American and European cities.

Differences in application and perception

There are two further reasons why American-style local development planning might be inappropriate to South Africa. First, urban decline is accentuated in the USA by the structure of local government there. Allegheny County, for example, in which Pittsburgh is located, contains 139 municipalities. This constitutes a means of denying poor municipalities equitable access to the resources of the metropolitan area and reinforces the process of inner-city decline. While this crazy-quilt of local governments has parallels with local government under apartheid – the Durban Functional Region has sixty-six local authorities – it does not represent our future. South Africa looks forward to functionally-defined urban areas where resources are spread more reasonably.

Secondly, traditional competition between cities and states has not occurred in South Africa. In this, South Africa is like most other countries where central government exercises a strong hand in regional planning and prevents local authorities from competing with one another through tax and other concessions.

In South Africa those who are persistently unemployed are also not perceived in the same way as equivalent groups in high-income countries, as revealed in the literature on the 'urban underclass'. While there may well be some people who cannot hold a job due, say, to alcohol or drug dependence, psychiatric problems or age, the term is a little disquieting as it legitimises their detachment from larger social and economic problems (Gans 1990).

Does it make sense to talk of an underclass in South Africa? We should remember Lipton's argument (1988) that in developing countries, the poorest are commonly the youth and those from large families who may first need adequate nutrition and health services before it is reasonable to think of them participating successfully in the economy. In these circumstances, defeatist arguments about an unreachable underclass are not helpful. Nor are grand claims regarding the potential for development planning. We should acknowledge a distinction between economic development and welfare. The values underlying economic development are that it reaches out to the mass of the population, that it helps to empower them as economic (and political) actors, and that it articulates development options in which business – and often government – see little gain. This implies working with communities, the poor and the unemployed; but it is not a surrogate for welfare to the needy.

Can community organisations deliver?

Much of what I have written relies on civics to represent the urban poor. Can they deliver?

American CDCs have better funding and greater technical capacity than South Africa's civics, yet their record is mixed. If we look at the American experience and the history of the civics to date, the following seems plausible. If the issue is the mobilisation of an area's population to confront economic hardship, then many civics do appear to have the necessary legitimacy and organisational capacity. If the civic is required to hold its own during strategic planning and technologically and financially sophisticated bargaining within an urban coalition, then it will need help. If the civic undertakes to run an enterprise, then American experience suggests it will fail.

Civics need money. They need training. And they should be wary of attempting to run enterprises, especially where the private sector has been unable to make a profit. Civics have a comparative advantage, but not as entrepreneurs.

In conclusion, it is obvious that we cannot blindly transplant foreign experience with local development planning into our context. This book presents the good ideas of others. Our task is to apply a contextual sieve.

NOTES

1. In considering the notion of urban coalitions the question arises whether it makes economic sense to engage in development planning for an urban area. For example, Eisinger (1988) holds that the linkages of a modern economy are so dispersed that when American states undertake economic development planning, they do so because politicians are obliged to pursue such policies and not because the states represent self-contained economic regions. However, the recent literature on industrial agglomerations, noted in Chapter 2, suggests that there is an increasing likelihood that economic and political space will overlap. In this context, urban coalitions make even more sense.
2. The interview was conducted in Pittsburgh on 26 September 1991.
3. Professor Vidal is Director of the Center for Community Development of the New School for Social Research. The interview was conducted on 23 August 1991.
4. The expressions 'traditional' and 'entrepreneurial state' in relation to development planning were coined by Eisinger (1988). My treatment of these approaches is generally based on his exhaustive book.
5. See Clavel (1986).
6. *New York Times*, 7 October 1991.
7. However, after the defeat of the Labour Party in 1979, a number of Labour councils briefly employed local development strategies as a vehicle for demonstrating an alternative to government policies. Rather than 'restructuring for capital', they advocated 'restructuring for labour'. Their strategies included council procurement agreements which obliged firms to adopt certain hiring policies, designing 'socially useful' projects, and encouraging popular participation in policy formulation.
8. Investment promotion entails improving a country's image as a favourable location for investment, generating investments directly, and providing services to prospective and current investors.
9. See Clarke (1991), Peterson et al. (1991), Rondinelli (1991), the World Bank (1991a), and the Urban Management Program of the United Nations and the World Bank, which is premised on urban efficiency, cost recovery, and privatisation.
10. I do not return to this as it does not appear to be a priority of the World Bank's urban missions to South Africa.
11. The observations regarding the role of community organisations and the views of the Conservative and Labour Parties are those of Michael Parkinson. He argues that the only effective community organisation in the UK occurred in the area of housing. The interview was conducted on 30 April 1992.
12. The qualifiers 'in respect of economic development' and later 'inhabitants of low-income neighbourhoods' are important. Obviously, many community organisations will not lack resources. The gay community in San Francisco is one such example.
13. This history of CDCs is based on Peirce and Steinbach (1990).
14. This support came largely from the Community Services Administration (which replaced the Office of Economic Opportunity in 1964) and, late in the decade, from the Department of Housing and Urban Development's Office of Neighborhood Development.

15. The quote is from Beatrice and Sidney Webb, cited in Whyte (1988: 3).
16. I focus on these examples because they are so often mentioned in South Africa, but a more realistic form of co-operative is the small labour-intensive venture with simple technology. My recommendations in Chapter 5 consider how to promote the formation of this kind of co-operative.
17. Dickstein (1991) asserts that there is no one universally accepted definition of co-operatives. For example, she accepts that worker control suffices to distinguish a co-operative. This definition is taken from the University of Illinois at Chicago Center for Urban Economic Development (1987).
18. My thanks to Judy Maller for this information. Interview conducted on 18 May 1992.
19. The clothing and textile industry is likely to be an early example of restructuring. Such restructuring could have local implications where the industry is concentrated in one or a few centres.
20. It has been argued that business people are typically ill-informed about potential locations for investment and that, even if advertising and concessions do not lead to net employment creation but result in better-informed decisions and a more efficient space economy, then traditional development planning does produce an overall gain (Levy 1990).
21. This section is based on Buss (1991).
22. For an assessment of the interaction between central and local government, and between politicians, government and the private sector, in respect of the Tokyo Waterfront Development, see Machimura (1992).
23. The corporations have the power to acquire, clear and develop land. They undertake the provision or renewal of services, the reclamation of derelict land, the enhancement of access and the improvement of the environment. Since their boards are appointed from the centre and primarily consist of business people, they in effect usurp the development role of local authorities (Lawless 1988).
24. See Gore (1991).
25. While this seems logical, I point to contrary examples in Chapter 7.
26. A Taiwanese textile industrialist I interviewed said that he was considering locations in either Malaysia or Brazil, but then decided to come to South Africa when he heard that labour was free. In this instance, in the Ciskei 'homeland' around 1985, the monthly wage per male employee in the lowest wage category was R60, that for females was R45, whereas the cash grant per labourer was R110 per month.
27. See Chapter 5 for reservations about Birch's (1979) data, which underlie this discussion.
28. This discussion is taken from Fainstein and Fainstein (1991), Knox (1988), Shearer (1989) and Squires (1989).
29. Partnerships often act as private ventures to supply goods and services which previously were supplied by the state. This trend has become so prevalent that the partnerships have been taken as synonymous with privatisation (Knox 1988).
30. For example, an area experiencing rapid growth induced by endogenous enterprise will be likely to experience struggles over land use, infrastructure and the environment. These struggles will be fought out at the local level and there will be little potential for unity. On the other hand, an area experiencing the exit of manufacturing jobs will be united in the search for adjustment assistance and reinvestment.
31. The graph has been adapted from Judd and Parkinson (1990: 297).

Chapter 5

The Role of Local Government in Development Planning

Each of the following three chapters will proceed in essentially the same manner. I refer back to the related approaches identified in Chapter 4 and ask two questions: Is the approach relevant in general and does it make sense in the context of South Africa? In this chapter I examine the ability of local authorities to promote development within the traditional, entrepreneurial, urban efficiency, and progressive approaches to development planning.

The assumption is that local authorities, who are presently keen to promote economic development, will in the future be encouraged by central government to engage in development planning. This assumption is problematical, because there is no clarity as yet regarding the functions that will be devolved to local authorities. Rather than be put off by this uncertainty, let me rather assert that the dictates of a country's constitution and the nature of its economic system and governing coalition are poor predictors of what local authorities actually do. A disconcerting feature of the designated responsibilities of local governments is that the actual roles various local governments play often differ even when, formally, they appear the same; and vice versa. *The Alice in Wonderland* quality of this assertion needs clarification and an introductory section explores the issue. This discussion poses a challenge to constitutionally-prescribed roles of local government, and endorses the view that if local authorities are eager to undertake development planning, then they do so.

VARIABILITY IN THE DEVELOPMENT ROLE OF LOCAL AUTHORITIES

Variability in the development role of local authorities does not mean that they can decide upon that role independently. At least three factors have a bearing on the issue: the structure of inter-governmental relations, the relative balance of power between levels of government, and the process of economic restructuring.

With regard to the structure of inter-governmental relations, in his study of 116 middle- and low-income countries that are decentralised or are in the process of decentralising, Silverman (1990) found that only ten had federal constitutions. Even when federal constitutions entrench decentralisation, as in Mexico or Nigeria, the constitution often masks central domination of allocative decisions at the state level. Since local governments in federal systems commonly have the same relationship with state government as local and provincial governments in unitary systems have with central government, local authorities are always structurally dependent on higher levels of government. Yet differences in approach are apparent in federal systems such as America, since states have constitutional protections from central government that enable them to pursue independent development policies. They often do this in concert with local authorities, with the result that local variations may arise on the basis of the state in which the city is located.

The dynamics in the power relations between local and central government are exemplified by the tension between the Conservative Party under Thatcher and Labour Party-controlled metropolitan bodies in the United Kingdom. Thatcher was able to remove these bodies since the form and functions of local government are defined within a 'framework of laws passed by Parliament' (Pickvance 1991: 55) and are not protected by a constitution. A more sanguine outcome is provided by Rennes which benefited from both increased decentralisation of responsibility for planning and the fact that the same party was in power at both the central and the local level (Le Gales 1990). The result was a flow of central resources for projects which were prioritised within the community.

Ultimately, development policy, whether it emanates from the city or central government, is located within a context of economic restructuring which is global in scale. This imposes limitations on the available economic alternatives, with the result that 'dissimilar institutional structures ... can be the vehicle for quite similar substantive policies' (Fainstein 1990b: 568). Both New York and London, for example, experienced deindustrialisation, transformation into global financial centres, and increasing income inequality, accompanied by the onslaught of conservative social policies that accentuated the shortage in affordable housing and the supply of social services.

An illustration which nicely confuses our presuppositions is provided by Krauss and Pierre (1991). They explored the relationship between a country's political environment and its constitutional and economic systems, and in this light asked whether the presence of the same systems in different countries would lead to similar industrial strategies. They compared parliamentary systems within two homogeneous countries, Sweden and Japan, and contrasted this with the United States, where there are many dispersed points at which interest groups can have a bearing on policy. In the former countries, the parliamentary majority can direct policy. In the USA, regardless of the political origins of the President and the Congressional and Senate majorities, policy-making requires the formation of *ad hoc* coalitions built around specific issues. Consensus is obviously much more difficult to achieve in the USA and it is, to some extent, due to the inability of federal government to formulate an industrial policy that this responsibility has shifted to the states and local governments (Eisinger 1988). On its own, this would suggest that a country's constitution and system of government dictate the potential role of local governments in development planning. However, in Sweden counties and especially municipalities are responsible for industrial policy, whereas in Japan there is a significant centralisation of responsibility within MITI. Development planning is therefore of especial interest in Sweden and the USA, but less so in Japan. We therefore arrive at a wholly unpredictable outcome: there are similarities in the location of responsibility for development planning between Sweden, a country governed by a social democratic party which is dependent on the support of organised labour, and the USA under Reagan and Bush (and now Clinton).

The responsibilities of local authorities can vary within similar constitutional arrangements and yet be alike when the constitutions differ. If one were to venture two assessments of the trends, the first would be that there is an increasing tendency to decentralisation, including that of responsibility for development planning.[1] The second would be that in South Africa the inertia of the transition coupled with the dynamism of the local environment and struggles around 'bread and butter' issues has created a setting conducive to development planning. One might say that Americans started looking at local economic development in the late 1970s, that Europeans did the same thing during the 1980s, and that South Africans are being drawn into the arena in the 1990s.

DEVELOPMENT PLANNING

The South African tradition manifests an extraordinary level of interference in spatial affairs: in shaping the form of the apartheid city; in trying to control population movement; and in trying to direct the location of employment creation. What of the future? The ANC has indicated that it would adopt a regional policy intended to alleviate regional welfare differentials, with a special focus on the homelands (where it would be most inefficient to locate economic activity). I have argued previously that the ANC's stance is both understandable and problematic.[2] The reason has already been demonstrated, namely that the regional planner's policy repertoire is sterile. Regional planning has proved ineffective and it is for good reason that the trend is towards development planning.

Should we anticipate that the ANC will cede its prerogatives in regional planning to localities?[3] I imagine that a future government would initially be reluctant to do so, but that as unresolvable regional issues entail political costs, decentralisation might become desirable. It is notable that two of the most deprived regions, in terms of per capita income and unemployment, are the Eastern Cape and Natal, the traditional homes of the Xhosa and the Zulu. Policies which have a bearing on the spatial distribution of material well-being are extremely politicised. My hypothesis is that if presented with a credible alternative, a future central government might soon wish to jettison responsibility for development planning. The following material tries to present such an alternative.

Traditional planning

Concessions[4]

The traditional approach consists of concessions to attract investment, promotional activities, and other initiatives such as export processing and free enterprise zones. The focus is on the supply side of the economic equation, and government bodies attempt to reduce the costs of production as an incentive to locate within their jurisdiction.

Concessions may be intended to promote growth across the entire city (or state/province) or to target development in specific locations in the city. The concessions include:

• reduced taxes – tax exemptions, abatements and credits mostly designed to encourage investment in commerce and industry;

- cheap capital – debt financing where government makes or guarantees a loan, or tax-exempt bond financing, especially in the form of industrial revenue bonds and umbrella bonds;[5]
- cheap land – perhaps achieved through the sale of land owned by a local authority or land acquired by a development agency for the purpose;
- the development of infrastructure and industrial and commercial sites, financed by grants to a local authority or undertaken by a development agency created for the purpose;
- tax credits on job creation and job training (both less common);
- reducing the burden of regulations which affect the business environment;
- marketing the location through surveys, advertising, direct approaches and 'one-stop shops';
- land subsidies through tax increment financing;[6] and
- the creation of a variety of forms of development corporations or enabling agencies to implement the development process.

It is surely clear that when these concessions are offered by a development agency or subnational government body, government bodies elsewhere will feel obliged to enter the competitive fray. This form of competition serves little purpose since, when concessions become widely available, they fail to distinguish one location from another. The competition transfers capital from the community to corporations and may harm local industries through creating shortages in the supply of skilled labour, causing housing prices and land values to rise, requiring investment in infrastructure to overcome congestion, and exacerbating pollution. Indeed, were we to conclude that the concessions worked, we would in effect be claiming that they succeeded in promoting inefficiency in the space economy. There are important reasons why central government should circumscribe traditional forms of competition.

The more common problem is likely to be that central government itself, as in South Africa, employs concessions in its attempt to redistribute manufacturing jobs (in South Africa, a declining number of such jobs). Historically in this country there were controls on the supply of industrial land in the major cities in order to restrain job creation and migration, and increasingly excessive decentralisation concessions in the form of transport subsidies and tax-free, cash grants for labourers employed.

The present concessions are more modest. Due to its cost and inefficiency, the earlier decentralisation policy was revised with effect from

April 1991. The new policy was spatially uniform, in that a two-year establishment grant and a three-year profit-based incentive were made available throughout South Africa, excluding the PWV and the 'Durban Core Area'. The 'Durban Functional Area', the Cape Peninsula and portions of the PWV did, however, receive 60 per cent of the two-year establishment grant.

Such concessions may well be used by the next government, but regional policy will confront a major obstacle. COSATU has argued for and is increasingly achieving one wage per job throughout the country. If Bell (1983) is right that, aside from the concessions, it is Far Eastern competition which is forcing labour-intensive industrialists to decentralise in search of cheap labour, then one wage per job will contradict government efforts to promote decentralisation. This is especially so given lower levels of labour productivity in the periphery. A future government might well consider the willingness of Brazil and Mexico to set up regional zones with different minimum wages (Mazumdar 1988: 42).

Investment promotion[7]

As noted in Chapter 3, a disdain for concessions does not mean a rejection of marketing. Marketing an area or country involves improving its image as a favourable location for investment, generating investments directly, and providing services to prospective and current investors. While all activities may occur in parallel, there is typically a progression in focus from improving the area or country's image to generating investment.

Attempts to improve a country's image typically entail:

- advertising in the general financial media;
- participating in investment exhibitions;
- advertising in industry- or sector-specific media;
- conducting investment missions from source to host country and vice versa; and
- conducting general information seminars on investment opportunities.

Generating investment requires:

- direct mail or telemarketing campaigns;
- industry- or sector-specific missions;
- industry- or sector-specific information seminars; and
- firm-specific research followed by sales promotions.

Lastly, servicing investment involves:

- investment counselling;
- expediting the processing of applications and permits; and
- post-investment services.

Promotion, in the sense of marketing an area, is a standard tool of the traditional approach. It succeeds when an urban coalition undertakes a strategic planning exercise and strives to promote international business in sectors and industries which are potentially linked to domestic industries. Here it seems appropriate to view development planning efforts as more entrepreneurial in nature.

South African parallels

There are a number of South African examples of local attempts to market a city. Johannesburg established such a function in 1991 and the Greater Durban Marketing Authority was set up in 1992. However, the example I have selected is the one most highly praised by a representative of the South African Chamber of Business, namely Pretoria.[8] Pretoria is also interesting since it uses Memphis, Tennessee as a model!

Peet du Preez, Marketing Manager of the Pretoria City Council, believes that it is the city council's job to ensure that the city is well managed. More particularly, he argues that it is not the city council's job to market the city; rather the council should facilitate capitalist development – it should exploit the energy and knowledge in the private sector in order to promote private employment creation. To this end he has got the private sector to chair the twelve working groups which are to prepare Pretoria's marketing plan. The groups are tourism; culture; arts; commerce and industry; sports and recreation; agriculture; nature conservation; transport; property development, investment and construction; training, education, technology and research; mining; and security. The purpose of the working groups is to get the people of Pretoria committed to the marketing plans for the twelve sectors. The plans will subsequently be consolidated into a 'three-page' marketing document for Pretoria. The financial and practical know-how will be supplied by Deloitte Pim Goldby.

In addition to participating in working groups, business is also represented in five chambers of commerce and industry. In particular, the Northern Transvaal Chamber of Industries is trying to expand overseas trade and attract foreign investment.

There are two obvious problems with Pretoria's approach. The first is that the working groups do not involve the 'people of Pretoria'. Instead, development plans are being prepared through public-private liaison. Despite the enthusiasm of the business community for this liaison, it is clear that in today's environment little point is served when such plans are prepared independently of more representative groups. This is not to suggest that all is lost. The 'Growing the Cape' project survived its Establishment origins, but there the consultants and Wesgro, who provided administrative support, had links with mass-based organisations, and institutions such as the Cape Town City Council have a better history of political legitimacy than Pretoria's Council. Du Preez is alert to the need to involve such organisations, but uncertain how to proceed.

The second problem is that Du Preez's designation as 'Marketing Manager' and the preparation of a 'marketing plan' suggest a heavy emphasis on the traditional approach, which has proved ineffective elsewhere. Without actually having seen the marketing plans (at the time of writing they were still in preparation), it is difficult to make a more substantive critique. When questioned about his approach, Du Preez did say that assisting Pretoria's existing enterprises in the traditional entrepreneurial manner is a priority. It seems clear that while Pretoria is ahead of many cities in South Africa in actively undertaking development planning, the city's approach is rather dated.

Export processing and enterprise zones[9]

The rhetoric of enterprise zones claims they are intended to enhance the development of an entrepreneurial culture, to promote the creation and expansion of enterprises, and to create jobs. The idea of the enterprise zone was suggested in 1982 by Hall, who had been impressed by the achievements of small and medium-sized enterprises in Singapore and Hong Kong in promoting the development of those territories. He attributed their success to an entrepreneurial culture and wondered whether a similar culture could not be generated in the run-down areas of Western cities, in a milieu less obstructed by regulations, zoning restrictions, environmental legislation, and minimum wages. Enterprise zones were subsequently created in the United Kingdom, by states in America and by a number of other countries.[10]

Since they are intended to foster indigenous entrepreneurial development, enterprise zones are imperfectly described as a form of traditional planning. The reason for addressing them here is that they offer standard inducements: tax incentives, job creation grants, and cheaper land and buildings. The shift in focus from obstacles to entrepreneurialism seems purely pragmatic since it turns out that government regulations are deemed minor inconveniences by entrepreneurs, who are more attracted by tax incentives.

The popularity of enterprise zones among politicians is probably due to their symbolic value. In a context of economic decline and competition, enterprise zones are another means through which politicians and development officials can be seen to be doing something. Burnier (1992) suggests that large existing firms exploit this situation and often employ enterprise zones more or less as a bribe. She documents instances where the existing locations of large enterprises have been declared enterprise zones! More commonly, enterprise zones have prompted the relocation of commercial, retail and service concerns from one part of a city to another.

Dabney (1991) concludes that enterprise zones have a marginal impact on business location decisions, except in cases where the value of the incentive is large relative to the size of the investment. What is interesting about this conclusion is the loss of focus it suggests. Instead of being assessed as a vehicle for creating an entrepreneurial culture, the zones are assessed as a location inducement. Their value, it seems, is dictated by the fact that competing locations offer such zones. It is surely desirable that cities and states compete through creating an affirmative regulatory environment and an efficient administration, but not through tax and other give-aways.

Export processing zones (EPZs) do not fall within the repertoire of development planning strategies in high-income countries. They are premised on labour-intensive industrialisation based on a combination of low wages and high productivity. In a sense, EPZs are the middle- and low-income countries' equivalent of enterprise zones, and are included here for that reason.

The origin of EPZs lies in the remarkable success of export-led growth in newly industrialising countries. UNIDO (1980: 6) defined the EPZ as a 'relatively small, geographically separated area within a country, the purpose of which is to attract export-oriented industries, by offering them especially favourable investment and trade conditions as compared with the remainder of the host country. In particular, [the EPZs] provide for the importation of goods to be used on a bonded duty free basis.'

The attraction of an EPZ for many countries is that the area can be isolated from the more typical context of poor infrastructure and administrative inefficiency. The usual goal of an EPZ is to use foreign investment and the growth of exports to reduce the host country's unemployment. Other ancillary goals include the training of a skilled labour force, technology transfer, and access to international marketing skills.

A number of EPZs have achieved marked successes. Employment in electronics and textiles in Asian countries is often concentrated in the zones. (Of course the jobs would have been created anyway, but perhaps in a different area or country.) The employment created has largely been for women.

Would an EPZ constitute a useful strategy in South Africa?

I have argued previously that EPZs might well prove useful (Tomlinson and Addleson 1985, 1987b). On the one hand, certain coastal cities suffer from above-average unemployment and their economies are in decline; on the other, they have aggressive local leadership which seeks possibilities for economic development. If local coalitions identify opportunities for an EPZ, it would be churlish of central government to deny them the right to attempt such a strategy. Indeed, after many years, it appears that South Africa's Department of Trade and Industry is about to approve the creation of such zones. This involves a minimum five-year tax holiday, customs privileges, freer foreign exchange rules, relaxed immigration procedures and employment permit requirements, and exclusion from the Rand Monetary Area (*Star* 5 August 1992).

It is worth linking an EPZ strategy to Wells and Wint's finding that a country can be marketed without offering concessions. Yet Wells notes[11] that this finding notwithstanding, concessions of some sort are a nice ploy within a marketing strategy as they create the impression of a welcoming environment. He therefore suggests that some inexpensive but high-profile concession is worth considering. An export processing zone is such a concession.

What form might an EPZ take in South Africa? A problem is that EPZs are firmly opposed by COSATU which views them as a means of exploiting low-cost labour. Yet UNIDO (1980) found that wages were not lower inside than outside zones. My hope is that the major unions which form part of an urban coalition will negotiate the terms under which industries invest in EPZs. My assumption is that if EPZs form part of a negotiated industrial strategy which will spur a growth in employment, then the unions may prove willing to support them.

Finally, an interesting observation on the potential for EPZs in Durban: local businessmen enthuse about EPZs but worry that when wages and productivity are combined, the products of EPZs will not be internationally competitive. Instead, they speculate on the potential for an

EPZ which employs relatively high-skilled, high-wage Indian labour in the manufacture of technologically complex products.[12]

The entrepreneurial approach

The 1988 Annual Report of the Philadelphia Industrial Development Corporation (PIDC) contained the following statement from the city's Mayor, W. Wilson Goode:

> Over the last three decades, PIDC has been a shining example of the vibrant partnership between business and government in Philadelphia.
> During that time, PIDC has invested over $3 billion in more than 2 800 companies that sought its help. The agency has constantly adapted itself to the changing tides of the region's economy, continually developing new programs to accommodate the shifting needs of businesses.

The impression is one of a whimsical bride and an ardent suitor devising ever more devious strategies for entrapment. Yet that, in fact, is the style of entrepreneurial development planning: for every problem there is a programme.

The entrepreneurial approach involves a variety of government interventions intended to foster local development. In this approach, local government is willing to engage in the identification of growth opportunities and the allocation of capital and other forms of assistance to exploit the opportunities. Either local government avoids competition with the private sector, and focuses on investment opportunities that the private sector may either have overlooked or be reluctant to pursue, including opportunities in new markets, products, and industries; or it works in partnership with the private sector on selected projects.

In both cases, the work is directed in terms of goals established and industries and markets identified by a strategic planning exercise undertaken with the private sector. When the local economy is declining, the strategy generally seeks to spur investment and employment creation, and thereby expand the local tax base. When the local economy is growing, attention is paid to maintaining existing, and diversifying future patterns of investment. A common theme, though, is that the policies should be directed at small, high-technology firms which export. The preference for small firms follows research by Birch (1979), who demonstrated that:

- the majority of Americans are employed within small *establishments;*
- most employment growth or decline results not from the migration of jobs but from the birth or death of small establishments;
- different regions experience about the same rate of enterprise deaths; and
- variations in their growth rate are determined by the rate at which new firms are born.

Birch's data are problematical since they fail to distinguish between small firms and branch plants of larger enterprises whose headquarters may be located elsewhere. It is therefore unclear whether his data reflected on small enterprises or plants of large corporations, or both. Nevertheless, Birch has had a major influence over the targeting of small firms. Ironically, this is a policy which he rejects – 'Government's primary role is to clear the path. Its primary role is to provide access and knowledge, not direction' (Birch 1987: 205).

The preference for small, high-technology firms derives from the perception that their products are income-elastic and will often serve immature markets with considerable potential for growth. High-technology firms are also thought to be more likely to sustain a competitive posture in relation to foreign competition. If the firm exports a significant proportion of its output then it is especially favoured. This is because exports constitute one branch of American manufacturing which is doing well. Indeed, Eisinger (1988) reports that on average one new job is created by every $40 000 increase in the value of exports.

Promotion of indigenous enterprise

The government generally adopts some combination of the following policy instruments which are targeted at the identified industries:

i. Local or state government frequently offers low-interest finance or assumes an equity position in high-risk enterprises. The PIDC's assortment of potential loans is illustrative.
  (a) The PIDC-Financing Corporation participates in loans administered by the Pennsylvania Industrial Development Authority to assist enterprises that contribute to employment in the city and also to its tax base.
  (b) The PIDC helps businesses to apply for assistance from Pennsylvania's Machinery and Equipment Loan Fund.

(c) The PIDC-Local Development Corporation helps enterprises apply for loans from the Small Business Administration and participating financial institutions.

(d) The PIDC operates a 'pooled' bond programme for smaller enterprises. (This is the same as the umbrella bond explained above.)

(e) The PIDC administers Pennsylvania's Competitive Loan Program. These loans serve enterprises locating in Philadelphia's three enterprise zones.

(f) The PIDC-Financing Corporation also administers Pennsylvania's capital loan, intended for starting up and expanding small businesses.

There are other loans as well. The point is that there is such a multiplicity of programmes. In all, PIDC can provide up to 50 per cent of a project's total cost.

ii.   Government can also support venture capital programmes. Eisinger (1988) identified five such programmes:

(a) Development credit corporations, which are privately funded and privately managed, for profit funds whose investors obtain tax credits.

(b) Venture capital loan programmes, which in America are capitalised by state and federal funding.

(c) Product development corporations, where the government provides finance for the development of a product in exchange for a royalty. This support is typically supplied to existing firms in order to reduce the risk.

(d) Pension fund venture pools, where government designates a percentage of public employee pension funds to be made available as venture capital to local companies. This is the most common scheme in the USA.

(e) Venture capital corporations, which are either owned by government, or represent a combined investment of public and private funds. In the former case, the corporation may work in association with CDCs.

iii. University research parks, explained below, are extremely popular but seldom successful. Perhaps the two foremost examples are the research parks established by Princeton University and North Carolina's Research Triangle Park. Princeton opened the Forestal Center in 1977. Eight years later it had attracted more than 50 companies with more than 7 000 employees. The Center provided a major impetus to development in the Princeton corridor (between Trenton and New Brunswick) which is now littered with office, warehousing and manufacturing establishments.

In the case of North Carolina, the Research Triangle Park acquired its name from its location between Duke University, North Carolina State University and the University of North Carolina at Chapel Hill. The Park was intended to attract research to the area and to lead to the development of related industrial and production facilities. Central to the Park is the Research Triangle Institute, launched in 1959. Presently the Park has over 33 000 employees and it has given rise to many related developments dispersed throughout North Carolina.

Relatively spontaneous high-technology development has also been spurred through linkages with major research universities. The so-called 'Cambridge phenomenon' (Keeble 1989) falls into this category.

There is no successful South African equivalent of the university research park. The facilities at the University of Pretoria and the University of Stellenbosch initially prospered on government-sponsored research, particularly military research, but this largesse has since diminished. (Incidentally, American research designed to counter Russia's sputnik is credited with spurring investment in the Research Triangle Park.) In contrast, the University of the Witwatersrand's proposed Science Park was dependent on the private sector. Major investors were on the verge of committing themselves when reports were leaked that the area was to be expropriated and developed for informal housing as an extension of Alexandra township. Needless to say, the prospective investors withdrew. Given the remarkably small scale of R. & D. expenditure by local companies, it would be surprising if a venture of this sort were to take off in South Africa.

Flexible specialisation[13]

Flexible manufacturing networks (FMNs) are at the forefront of local and regional authorities' responses to the debate around flexible specialisation. The objective of FMNs is to increase the competitiveness of small and medium-sized firms. (We should note that FMNs do not refer solely to manufacturing. For example, there are eight seasons in the knitwear fashion market. Every six weeks, some 600 small firms in the Emilia-Romagna district of Italy share the cost of sophisticated market forecasts regarding fibres, colours, patterns and quantities.)

A network is a form of strategic alliance among firms, it is not necessarily a formal, contractual agreement. A firm can be a member of many networks at the same time. Horizontal networks arise, for example, when firms share a need for a common service or piece of equipment, or collaborate to fill an order for a final producer. Vertical networks occur when firms participate in a value-added chain.

Networks allow firms which produce for one or more steps in the value-added chain to achieve greater flexibility through:

- being able to specialise in and master rapidly-changing technology;
- linking with firms that have complementary skills;
- outsourcing for components in which the firm lacks a comparative advantage;
- employing production technology which facilitates short production runs; and
- serving more narrowly defined market niches.

Vertical networks also serve to bring about a change in attitude towards product innovation, product quality, market orientation, zero-defect programmes and just-in-time delivery. Whereas small firms are often suspicious of large firms and these new concepts, networking arrangements can produce relationships of trust that enhance the competitiveness of small firms.

The FMN model is based on the form of entrepreneurial organisation found in central north-eastern Italy, and other countries have enriched this model in their efforts to copy it. Why did FMNs first arise in Italy? Pezzini (1990) attributes their rise to several local features: a history of family farms that developed a tradition of co-operative alliances; small towns that some centuries ago began to produce items for foreign markets; and the demand for skilled labour by large firms and the diffusion of those skills. Indeed, there seems to be consensus that FMNs would not have developed in Italy without these specific conditions.

The many firms engaged in FMNs are highly competitive. The question is whether it is possible through alternative means to create conditions that might spur the formation of FMNs. Denmark is promoting FMNs in order to modernise its 12 000 small and medium-sized enterprises and enhance their competitiveness. The Ministry of Industry provides $11 000 for an initial feasibility study to any three or more firms considering establishing a production or service network. Thereafter, the Ministry provides matching grants on a fifty-fifty basis for the detailed planning and start-up costs of new networks. These costs might include the services of an engineer to integrate the process divisions of the firms forming the network, or the establishment of new outlet channels. In subsequent years the Ministry provides a declining subsidy to develop the skills and abilities of networks serving the international market. The government also invests in brokers whose job it is to link firms and enable them to solve common problems.

International business[14]

In America many states and cities attempt to promote international business. Public assistance is premised on the assumption that profit will motivate enterprises to participate, but that they may not be able to identify export opportunities due to cultural, language and other barriers. Public intervention is intended to minimise these obstacles and make the avenues for profit more apparent. The actual export strategy proposed will depend on the structure of the area's economy, its proximity to foreign markets, its location, population, infrastructure and so on. Table 5.1 summarises the typical export functions.

Table 5.1 *Subnational efforts to promote international business*

At home	Abroad
Holding seminars/conferences	Identifying sales agents
Individual counselling	Developing trade leads
Disseminating trade leads	through trade missions and
Studying foreign markets	participation in trade
Financing exports	fairs
Referral to local export services	
Publishing newsletters and handbooks	
Creating export trading companies	

From the point of view of an export promotion programme offering benefits to small enterprises, the efforts of the East Williamsburg Valley Industrial Development Corporation (EWIDCO) are interesting. The corporation works under contract to New York City's Public Development Corporation, which has overall responsibility for the In-Place Industrial Park Program. The areas served comprise 3 400 acres and about 100 000 jobs. The Program provides five basic services: area improvements, security, business services, employment,[15] and area marketing and promotion. In respect of business services,

> EWIDCO assists with applications for governmental assistance pro-
> grams (financing, energy tax credits, tax abatement, productivity
> studies etc.), provides introductions to banks, and provides experi-
> enced advice on expansion projects and strategic business planning.
> EWIDCO's newest service assists companies to export their products
> outside the USA. (Information flyer)

The vehicle for the last service is Brooklyn Queens Exports (BQE), a private, non-profit corporation.[16] BQE's goal is to increase exports from Brooklyn and Queens and to this end BQE provides a three-step trade service:

- evaluating products to determine whether they have export potential;
- actively marketing exportable products to foreign buyers; and
- handling all aspects of negotiating the transaction, shipping the
  order, and following up.

These services are provided for a negotiable commission.

Potential exporters are identified through the characteristics of the product and the company producing it. Potential interest in the product can be assessed through contacting overseas distributors and trade repre-sentatives, and through published trade leads. With respect to the com-pany, it is important that there is a management team in place with which BQE can work and which can be relied on to deliver a product in terms of specified quality, quantity and time. However, not all potential exporters are keen to export since doing so involves management time and the cost of shipping samples. BQE is an important example since the export programmes of most comparable organisations are oriented towards education rather than actually making sales.

An interesting variation on the theme of export promotion is shown in the activities of the Japanese Export Trade Organisation (JETRO) which, incidentally, works closely with BQE. JETRO is a non-profit, government-supported organisation which assists domestic entrepre-neurs in North America, Western Europe and Oceania to expand their exports to Japan. The services JETRO provides include information on the Japanese market, market trends and trade fairs, buying-missions from Japan, the 'Invitation to Japan' programme and so on. Japanese professionals staff 'internationalisation centres' and assist domestic entrepreneurs to identify Japanese distributors. While it is doubtful these services would have much value for most small South African entrepreneurs, they do provide important information for development planning purposes and would probably prove helpful to medium and larger enterprises.

The Greenhouse Compact[17]

There is increasing interest in implementing entrepreneurial development programmes on a regional scale. Past experience with Fordist production regimes suggested that sectoral targeting within regions was not feasible due to the spatially dispersed linkage and subcontracting networks of such regimes. The recent literature on flexible specialisation and industrial complexes indicates that regionally specific industrial strategies may well be more viable. The Greenhouse Compact provides a particularly interesting example of this.

The Compact refers to Rhode Island's attempt at strategic planning which identified niches in which the state's industries had a comparative advantage. The Compact aimed to build consensus among business and financial elites, labour, higher education, public officials and environmentalists on an industrial development strategy that would create 60 000 jobs and lead to higher wages. The governor of the state appointed nineteen representative members to a Strategic Development Commission, supported by a large technical staff.

The Commission's report emphasised five main policies.

i.   Classify industries according to their growth potential, and focus resources on industries in which the state has a comparative advantage.
ii. Emphasise industries whose products are sold outside the state. The Commission estimated that the creation of 25 000 jobs in such industries would lead to the creation of another 35 000 jobs.
iii. Support old and troubled industries and attract new industries.
iv. Propose research in high-wage industries which are, at the same time, industries in which the state has a comparative advantage.
v.   Suggest the state needs an improved business climate, including enhanced telecommunications, a more positive attitude on the part of state government, and cut-backs on the workers' social wage.

The Compact is highly pertinent to the present study because it proposes an industrial strategy at a subnational scale. In addition, the assumption that the state and private sector can identify target industries jointly is similar to the thinking which underlies the Industrial Strategy Project in South Africa.[18] The significance of targeting industries is apparent from the fact that the sectors within which growth is located will determine whether there is a significant reduction in unemployment and also whether value added will be equitably distributed. For example, Levy (1992) has shown that South Africa has export potential in both the capital-intensive petro-chemical and labour-intensive textile industries. This leaves the country with a choice as to how best to allocate its resources. It is just such a choice which the Greenhouse Compact proposed.

The Compact was rejected *in toto* by 80 per cent of the voters. On the Right there was a disregard for economic planning and doubts that a public-private partnership could pick 'winners'. On the Left there was a concern with the planning process itself: the Commission was portrayed as a corporatist body, bargaining among the leaders of functional interest groups. The Commission's members did not have a mandate, and were viewed as unrepresentative by the voters. In addition, the Commission ignored community organisations who, in functional terms, seemed barely relevant to an industrial strategy, but yet were politically important. These organisations evaluated the Compact and decided that the distribution of costs and benefits was not in their favour. Lastly, perhaps voters feared that the tax increase calculated as necessary to sustain the project had been underestimated.

The Compact offers two lessons. The first is that 'how planning and development activities are carried out and who benefits from them are as important as the details of the plans themselves if industrial policy or comprehensive economic development planning is to achieve the legitimacy and co-operation it requires to succeed' (Silver and Burton 1986: 277). The second is that corporatist planning – tripartite arrangements between business, government and labour leaders – threaten to 'result in pork barrel deals protecting vested interests' (Silver 1986-87: 360). This last concern has particular resonance in South Africa. Business and organised labour could gang up on government for subsidies and economic strategies which do not reach the mass of the low-income population.

The closest South African parallel is the 'Growing the Cape' sub-regional exercise in the Western Cape. As described by Bridgman *et al.* (1992: vi), this exercise seeks to identify a range of strategies to accelerate the development of the regional economy. It addresses issues which relate to both growth and restructuring. What makes this initiative different from previous attempts is the effort to involve the energies and skills of leaders from a wide range of interest groups – business, labour, local authorities, civic associations, government departments and para-statal services, company leaders, opposition political bodies and community groups, and experts with differing perspectives.

The project launched in November 1990 visualises three phases. In the first phase, information relating to the Cape economy was gathered to create a baseline of understanding. The second stage sought to identify existing trends and opportunities. The third phase – now under way – aims to assist local players, individually and in concert, to capitalise on these trends and opportunities.

In order to advance the third phase and to ensure that the process is ongoing the Western Cape Economic Development Forum has been established. Its membership is indeed as representative as the above claim. The Forum has been divided into seven commissions which are in the process of formulating proposals. The commissions are:

- Competitiveness: Manufacturing, exports;
- Competitiveness: Tourism, finance, services;
- Urban Development: Urban form, public transport, growth management;
- Urban Development: Housing process, finance, services;
- Black Economic Advancement;
- Poverty Alleviation; and
- Education and Training.

In contrast to the NEF, various regional forums and the DFR Metropolitan Development Forum, which are all organised on the basis of time periods(!) – long-term and short-term working groups – the Western Cape Economic Development Forum is sensibly organised around substantive policy concerns. This forum may be the first to test the potential of development planning in South Africa.

Critique[19]

Many programmes employed as a part of development planning are credited with 'marginal improvements', but they are never 'transformational enough'.[20] The problem, firstly, is one of scale. Development programmes generally use public funds to leverage private investment, but in a period of fiscal restraint, public funds are limited. Against a backdrop of national and international restructuring, underfunded programmes cannot hope to achieve a significant scale of intervention.

A second problem is that concurrent programmes are seldom well co-ordinated. For example, the National Council for Urban Economic Development (1991) provides the following abbreviated list of development activities occurring in most American metropolitan areas.

- City: grant-making, community development, planning, tax abatements, legislation, capital investment, business retention and expansion.
- County (adjacent suburbs): planning, job training, community development, business retention and expansion.
  Private sector development organisations: co-ordinating business attraction and retention.
- Chamber of commerce: marketing, small business development, minority procurement efforts, business retention and expansion.

Typically only the marketing of the area is co-ordinated. The other programmes overlap and are the subject of 'turf' wars. Indeed, the city and suburbs often compete for the same industry. As Ross and Friedman (1990: 6) put it, co-ordination 'remains an unnatural act between two non-consenting adults'.

A third problem is that the survival of programmes is only loosely connected to productivity. Indeed, programme evaluations are rare and, in any case, causation and success are very difficult to measure. Nobody is that sure whether individual programmes are effective or not. Hence the title of one article on development planning (Rubin 1988): 'Shoot anything that flies; claim anything that falls'! Programmes take on a life of their own. Politicians are seen to be doing something. Bureaucrats and consultants advocate development planning, and certain businesses benefit.

All this is characteristic of the public sector, and development planning is no exception. The market relationship, as it were, is between programme managers and the legislature, not programme managers and clients. Unless clients are expected to pay for the service, there will, in fact, be no measure of whether the service is worthwhile or whether taxes have been well spent.

To a considerable degree, the problem seems to lie in the nature of public sector 'technology'. Public programmes sufficed when the goal was an agency to attract investment to the state. But now the goal has changed and is more ambitious. It is to reach most of an area's businesses and community organisations with the capital and services they require to promote development. Once government is convinced there is a capacity constraint, technological backlog or skill shortage, a programme is created and civil servants are allocated. Budgetary allocations provide limited resources and require endless bureaucratic politics (not success in the marketplace) to ensure annual renewal. Programme overlaps and civil service procedures conspire to frustrate. This is a familiar story.

Thus Ross and Friedman (1990) and Fossler (1992) conclude that a 'Third Wave' in economic development strategies is emerging. The focus on indigenous development remains, but new organisational approaches are employed to pursue economic development. The following principles apply.

The programmes are **demand-driven** and **sector-specific**. In order to increase the scale of resources, they are often undertaken in partnership with the private sector. In effect, beneficiaries must be prepared to **contribute** time and resources to the programme.

The government sheds its former role as a monopoly supplier. **Partnerships,** privatisation and/or private competition in the supply of services are encouraged. The point is to move away from public programmes that advance public goals and to use markets to serve that end.

I believe these lessons will have a greater impact in South Africa than in America. While they will probably improve the effectiveness of development planning and programmes, they are unlikely to resolve problems in America with co-ordination and the strategic direction of the economy.

America's problems with co-ordination reflect the peculiar structure of cities there, where urban areas are broken into many municipal jurisdictions. The administrative borders of South Africa's cities are presently being integrated, and the definition of regions for the future constitution essentially reflects functional urban areas. Co-ordination will be much easier in South Africa.

The extent to which Americans are prepared to allow their economy to be directed through strategic planning is limited.[21] By contrast, Clark (1989: 206) observes that 'many nations have planned investment strategies around desired comparative advantage in the international economy; these same nations have also planned successive cycles of investment, disinvestment, and investment in other sectors'.

Unlike America, proactive economic planning is currently being practised in South Africa and this will continue in the future. If partnerships link into the deliberations of the NEF (see below) and then employ development planning at the local level, the impact of these lessons in South Africa will be far greater than in America.

Urban efficiency

Several years ago Kahnert (1987: 2) referred to experience with development planning in high-income countries and, in a paper written under the auspices of the World Bank, argued that the 'need and scope for effective intervention of this kind is even greater in developing country cities'. His paper represented a first attempt at assessing the experience of development planning within that institution, but seems to have been ignored.

Kahnert's paper has been overshadowed by the World Bank policy paper, *Urban Policy and Economic Development* (1991a). It is this document which must be the primary source for this section of the book. It repeats many of the issues Kahnert raised, but does not suggest that there are lessons which might be learned from comparative experience with development planning.

Complementing the policy paper are the first two 'Aide-Mémoire' of the World Bank urban missions to South Africa (World Bank 1991b, 1991c). These missions aimed to prepare the Bank for its eventual involvement in South Africa. Formal relations with central government were intended to begin once the country acquired a majority government. In the interim, the Bank missions were meeting numerous influential organisations and technical experts to gain a sense of local perceptions of policy and project priorities, as well as set up structures which would guide research and build consensus around those policies. The Bank's participation speeded up after Lewis Preston assured Nelson Mandela that the Bank would engage as soon as South Africa had an acceptable government; the money would begin flowing about eighteen months thereafter. Mandela was reportedly horrified by the delay (the time it takes the Bank to process project funding), and the Bank is now accelerating the process of project selection. The result is that the 'Aide-Mémoire', never intended to be more than preliminary documents, have to some extent been superseded. None the less, they provide an insight into the Bank's views of South Africa's urban problems.

The urban missions to South Africa

The Bank's 1991 missions found a situation rife with problems. They cite 'deficient service provision, deteriorating infrastructure, ... and distorted spatial settlement patterns and distribution of economic functions within the urban areas [that] constrained the productivity of the urban economy and its ability to generate increasing incomes, employment and services for the growing number of urban poor'. The attempt to remedy the form of the apartheid city has become a central focus of the Bank's urban mission.

The Bank also bemoans South Africa's over-regulated urban markets, and calls for regulatory reform at both the national and local levels to increase the supply and lower the cost of housing, finance, infrastructure and developable land, and increase business opportunities. It should be remembered that the country has a long history of prohibitions on African entrepreneurship, deliberate constraints on the supply of land for African housing and for industry (in order to constrain employment creation and the incentive to urbanise), government control of the African housing market, and so on, all of which have been regulated in minute detail.

The Bank's recommendations concerning the regulatory framework present few problems. When the Bank speaks to the authorities about reforming the system, increasing market efficiency, and privatisation, it is very much a case of speaking to the converted. Regulatory reform, which in many instances is intended to change the respective roles of the public and private sectors and enhance informal opportunities, is already being implemented. Importantly, though, these reforms are encountering serious opposition from the ANC, who justly claim that the government should no longer undertake unilateral change, and from unions, who fear that the privatisation of municipal infrastructure and services will lead to job losses.[22] We will return to this issue shortly.

On the positive side, the Bank was impressed by the administrative and financial capacity of the white local authorities and is optimistic that 'for most urban areas there appears to be a capacity for establishing viable, self-sufficient, self-financing local government on a sustainable basis, through integrating black and white cities, ... without dependence on fiscal transfers from the center'. The Bank also anticipates that unified local governments will be technically capable of delivering services.

However, one gets the feeling that the Bank blames the problems all on apartheid rather too quickly and too easily envisages the future rearrangement. South Africa is, after all, a labour-surplus middle-income country with a GNP per capita of $2 470 (in 1989) and limited technical and financial resources. Planact (1992b), for one, has demonstrated the non-viability of one-tax-base solutions; that is, 'analyses of this sort make it perfectly clear that with the present distribution of functions and revenue sources, most new local authorities will not be viable' (p. 101). Planact maintains that these analyses take no account, for example, of the capital expenditure required to upgrade services in predominantly African parts of town, and the extent to which the financial viability of white local authorities is dependent on on-selling electricity to African local authorities.

The Bank's tendency to 'blame it on apartheid' probably explains the focus on inequality. Despite the high proportion of the population living in poverty, the Bank prefers to look at inequality. It might be argued that a decline in poverty requires a decline in inequality. This may be so, but when the wealthy are few, the economy is declining, and the 'ultra-poor' will be with us for generations to come, one cannot but wonder whether the focus is politically motivated.

When the Bank examines what can be done at the level of the cities to alleviate poverty, it points to the obstacles faced by small-scale entrepreneurs in gaining access to capital, infrastructure and markets. This is no doubt true, but we earlier raised doubts about the extent to which the informal sector can provide a significant alternative for the urban poor.

The Bank refers to community groups in the context of the social dimensions of urban poverty.

> All cities in developing countries have active community groups that have sought to meet household and community needs in the face of ineffective government policy and scarce public resources. These activities include (i) encouraging the formation of community leadership … to represent and inform communities and to intermediate between communities and government; (ii) performing technical roles in shelter provision such as the purchase of building materials or finance of shelter; (iii) training communities for self-reliance; and (iv) maintaining infrastructure and social services.

This stance is both benign and unambitious. In the first instance, civics in South Africa have a decidedly more radical conception of their role as advocacy organisations than the Bank acknowledges. Secondly, CDCs, as an example of what civics could evolve into, often play a role in employment creation and influencing a city's economic strategy. Indeed, civics should promote urban policies which more directly serve their constituents, and should themselves wish to intervene as development agents.

Privatisation[23]

Privatisation is a hotly debated subject in South Africa and not one which can be avoided. I focus on privatisation in the urban arena, but first I want to clarify my starting-point. Popular wisdom favours privatisation, despite the fact that

> the claims of privatisation have been overstated and unsubstantiated. [Yet this] is not to suggest that the solution is the public sector either. To do so would be to make the same mistake as privatisation proponents when they claim that, in finding negative relationships between public sector spending and economic growth, the solution must be the private sector. The empirical findings to date are inconclusive. Apparently, the size of neither the private nor the public sector makes a difference in and of itself. This being the case, there must be some additional factors, unique to neither the public nor the private sector, that can provide a more credible explanation of development. (Yoder et al. 1991: 432)

According to Yoder et al. (1991) Germany and France have equally large public sectors, yet France experiences a much greater level of government intervention in the economy. Similarly, government spending in India is less than in South Korea, and the latter country has a much higher growth rate. Instead, fiscal, monetary, regulatory, and trade policy appear more relevant to growth than the mere size of the public or private sector.

As regards municipal goods and services, privatisation can assume different forms. Privatisation is generally taken to involve the sale of public assets and the replacement of public management by private profit-seeking. There are a number of variations on this:

- the sale of public enterprises and assets;
- partnership agreements which enable the public sector to benefit from private capital and management capacity;
- the leasing of business rights for goods and services traditionally supplied by the public sector (such as toll roads);

- contracting out the production of goods and supply of services, which enables the public sector to dictate the terms of provision (who benefits, who pays, how much) and to gain access to private capital and management;
- privatisation without deregulation, which means that the public sector retains the right to determine rates of return, prices and quality levels;[24]
- 'commercialisation', which means that capital has to be raised in the private sector, and the public agency is managed as a private enterprise;
- competition, where both public and private sectors supply the good or service; and
- discontinuing the service.

Arguments for privatisation and/or public-private partnerships centre on gains in management efficiency, the reduction of direct municipal outlays, the spreading of risks on joint undertakings, a cut-back in costs to taxpayers (if the service is supplied more cheaply by the private sector), and a maintenance of service levels without tax increases. If these benefits are realised, they are not to be sneered at.

Opponents of municipal privatisation, especially the unions, argue that privatisation leads to further unemployment. Others are concerned that the effect of privatising the supply of municipal services will be to exclude the poor since their incomes do not constitute effective demand.

Yet we should not be naïve. Governments have limited resources and distribute them among many competing constituencies. Since the poor are seldom a significant constituency and are unable to pressure government, the public delivery of services often fails to reach them. For the poor, the issue may well be less one of whether the public or the private sector delivers services, than of organising to ensure that they receive services at all.

In my view, the debate is not so much about whether there should be privatisation, but what form public-private partnerships should take. Partnerships enable municipalities to extend their financial and technical resources, and with community oversight can be enjoined to provide services fairly. It is encouraging to note that there has already been a willingness to compromise in this area. A good example is provided by the negotiations between Eskom (a state-controlled electricity supply corporation) and the Soweto People's Delegation, in which it was agreed to create a jointly held co-operative. This was not done in the end, apparently because the service area would have entrenched apartheid municipal borders. Maybe now that circumstances are changing, unified cities will allow collaborative agreements of this sort.

Critique[25]

The Bank's urban agenda is of considerable significance: when the next government comes to power, presumably with the ANC playing a leading role, it will be desperately short of resources and in urgent need of visible projects. The Bank, obviously, has the capacity to offer such resources and will be influential, but its likely influence extends beyond simply being a source of capital. This is because the Bank has an intellectual rapport with a prominent 'reform group' in South Africa. The group includes the Urban Foundation, the Development Bank of Southern Africa and the Independent Development Trust, and overlaps with both the government and the ANC. On the one hand, the group serves the government as a source of policy advice, and certain institutions within the group assist the government to implement its partial reforms. On the other hand, the group also serves as a policy forum for the ANC, while the Development Bank is assisting with the training of civics. The World Bank will probably adopt the lead within this group since its intellectual resources and comparative experience are convincing to those similarly inclined – if a little daunting to critics.

Will the future government be able to withstand the policy recommendations emanating from such a formidable group? As the ANC is nominally still a movement and not a political party, it is best regarded as still debating the issues and considering its options. It debates options both with allies from its political past; and with the government, the Urban Foundation, the Development Bank, and the World Bank. Clearly, there is potential for the ANC to be swayed by those with both good arguments and substantial resources.

This last point is critical for the democratic formulation of urban policy, and has an especial bearing on the involvement of civics in that process.

My pessimistic apprehensions are premised on the belief that (i) the policy recommendations of the World Bank and the reform group will have considerable similarities; (ii) the next government will be significantly influenced by both the intellectual dexterity and the resources of the Bank and the reform group; and (iii) civics and service organisations will not be influenced to the same extent.

There are three reasons for asserting the relative independence of the civics. First, the World Bank, and indeed to a large degree also the domestic groups, presently discourse with numerous institutions due to the absence of a legitimate central government. Ordinarily, the World Bank's style is to deal directly with central governments and, even though some Bank officials may wish to engage others in policy debate, their ability to do so is circumscribed by the host government. Will South Africa's future central government happily accommodate what will often be the dissenting views of the civics?

Secondly, the civics have engaged in a long fight to get where they are as participants in numerous local initiatives in cities around the country. Remember that the initiatives are intended to rationalise the racial borders of the apartheid city, determine policy in respect of the provision of housing and services, and promote economic development. Other participants in these initiatives include the private sector, political parties, major utility companies, and local authorities. In effect, the civics have achieved a position of considerable prominence and their influence will suffer if these initiatives wane. If urban policy is directed from the centre, and more especially if it is influenced by the current World Bank urban policy agenda, then these local initiatives may well decline in significance.

Thirdly, if divisions such as those mentioned do surface, they will exacerbate existing tensions between the ANC and the civics. These tensions could take the form of a struggle for intellectual hegemony between service organisations and, principally, the World Bank.

Many within the civic movement and in service organisations and other progressive groups are suspicious of the Bank's agenda in South Africa. Bank staff protest that there is no fixed 'World Bank view' and that there is flexibility, depending on the context. They cite two examples which illustrate this. Whereas the Bank would ordinarily favour a leading role for the private sector, its urban mission recommends exploiting the capacity of the (soon to be integrated) white local authorities so as to execute projects more rapidly. Moreover, the Bank proposes forming Technical Committees, with wide representation including the civics, to guide research on urban development problems and formulate policies.

One should, I believe, concede the point that there is no fixed view and that the Bank prefers to foster local consensus and ownership; but one should not forget that the Bank is oriented to free markets, the removal of price controls, and the removal of state ownership (privatisation). None the less, it should not be assumed that the contributions of the Bank and like-minded institutions in South Africa are 'bad'. Comparative material and an understanding of what has 'worked' elsewhere should inform domestic policy. In this respect, while the Bank's urban missions have identified urban problems which were already known to liberal and leftist urban scholars, its comparative perspective helped define the problems more clearly and had the effect of giving them a wider hearing and also legitimacy among establishment figures.

At the same time the Bank's preliminary discussions of potential remedies are less well-known among liberals and leftists, who are often unfamiliar with comparative material, frequently make do with the lazy assumption that South Africa is unique, or are simply predisposed to believe that recommendations emanating from the World Bank must inevitably reflect not 'what works', but 'what works in the interests of capital'.

It appears that invitations to participate with the Bank in, say, Technical Committees, are being treated with suspicion by civics and service organisations in particular. They have long endured the vicissitudes of South African politics, in which appearing to be co-opted can be extremely damaging. In addition, the service organisations have rather tended to monopolise the credibility stakes among civics and the ANC when it comes to technical assessments of urban problems, and there may be an element of 'turfism' in their position. For them, exceptionally difficult strategic choices are at hand. While they might well develop profound contrary analyses of South Africa's urban problems, they do not have the Bank's material resources or influence.

The progressive approach

Progressive planning has links with entrepreneurial planning and community economic development, and there is not always a clear line dividing the various approaches. What follows points to nuances and tendencies as much as to features which can clearly be labelled 'progressive'.

Perhaps the definitive characteristic of progressive development planning concerns process issues. In this approach communities are involved in decision-making, and mass action intended to mobilise opinion behind specific strategies is viewed as legitimate, even desirable, as a counter to the lobbying of other groups. And, where possible, community organisations are used as vehicles for implementing development strategies. Examples of this would be job training or the supply of capital to neighbourhood businesses.

The progressive approach shifts the relative emphasis. Whereas previous development strategies all too often focused on real estate ventures downtown, the focus is now on employment creation for defined target groups. The goal is now to achieve balanced development between downtown and the neighbourhoods.

The actual strategies reflect a difference in perception over the efficacy of market mechanisms and privatisation. Progressives are quickly convinced that the market may need a nudge in order to serve the interests of the poor and, ultimately, are not averse to the public supply of goods and services. In addition, progressives get excited when the conversation turns to worker buy-outs and co-operatives.

So what do progressives actually recommend? Minority hiring is common, but hardly seems relevant in South Africa where labourers are invariably African. Perhaps the South African equivalent is affirmative action on management positions, but this is not a strategy which has much to do with the relief of urban poverty. Government and corporate procurement set-asides for goods and services from African-owned firms are another strategy which may have greater application.

Related to the procurement set-asides are two additional themes in economic development. The first reacts against a focus on downtown real estate deals, and claims instead that 'manufacturing matters'. This focus is informed by:

- the difficulties encountered by the oversupplied office and commercial markets;
- the fact that the beneficiaries of these deals seldom include the urban poor;
- the point that manufacturing has innate attractions given that it pays higher wages than many service jobs; and
- surveys which find that, contrary to presumptions about the decline of manufacturing, there is often still a bustling small-scale manufacturing economy (Forrant 1990).

A second related theme is that the entrepreneurial assistance made available to small-scale enterprise should have a clearer focus on the needs of minority enterprises. For example, it is not assumed that the goal should be high-technology enterprises. Capital is set aside for small business lending. Entrepreneurial training programmes are established. Programmes to assist with business planning and marketing, even exporting, are put in place.

In my view we would miss the point if these processes, policies and strategies were viewed as the primary contribution of progressive development planning. The goal of progressives must be to articulate development issues in a different light, to change the conventional wisdom, and create a new development agenda. This sounds rather ambitious, but in important respects it is a service already being provided by service organisations in South Africa. When Planact became involved in the Soweto negotiations, it released a report which revealed, for example, how Sowetans subsidised the tax base of Johannesburg (Planact 1989). This fundamentally rearranged common perceptions of the issue and initiated a new agenda. The service progressives provide is to empower the mass of the population through articulating an alternative vision. Even though the resultant strategies will inevitably be forged in compromise with government and with business, the outcome is liable to be much more fair.

Thus we can hope for participatory planning, a redirection of municipal resources towards low-income neighbourhoods and community involvement in implementation. But we should also understand that this in itself is not enough. We are still talking about the politics of consumption, whereas the point is to change the agenda towards one of community engagement in production. It does not need repeating that the country will be caught between heightened expectations and ever more limited resources. Production activities including the provision of services, savings schemes, co-operatives, and assistance to small entrepreneurs should all become part of the agenda.

NOTES

1. This issue was discussed in Chapter 3. In addition, see Goldsmith and Newton (1988) and Silverman (1990).
2. See Tomlinson (1990).
3. Of course, central or regional planning agencies might employ the tools of development planning as a new means of influencing the location of development, but unless there is a decentralisation of responsibility the necessary local participation is unlikely to be forthcoming.
4. This section is based on Eisinger (1988), Harding (1991) and Sellgren (1991).
5. Bonds were popular among cities and states, since interest on them has historically been exempt from federal taxation. This means that government has been able to make capital available for plant and equipment at rates below those of the commercial banks. Industrial revenue bonds are different in that government bears no liability for the bond. Instead the bonds are backed by the revenue and collateral of the beneficiary firm. However, small and new enterprises typically lack collateral, and industrial

revenue bonds are unavailable to them. Umbrella bonds address this problem. An umbrella bond is a single tax-exempt bond which serves several enterprises. The enterprises share the administrative costs of the bond issue, and for investors there is less risk since the bond is backed by several enterprises.

6.   Tax increment financing requires that a city first calculate the value of property taxes which are generated by a district. This value is juxtaposed with the increase in property taxes which will arise from a project. The addition to the anticipated tax revenue is estimated prior to the project and this sum is used to back tax increment bonds issued by the local authority, the bonds being intended to pay for the project.

7.   This section is based on Wells and Wint (1990: 9 and 10).

8.   This section is primarily based on a remarkably inaccurate *Business Day* article (26 June 1992) and a follow-up interview with Peet du Preez.

9.   For an earlier, more detailed assessment of export processing zones and free enterprize zones, their origins and comparative practice, see Tomlinson and Addleson (1985, 1987b).

10.   Some might argue that the free port policies of a number of European countries preceded the enterprise zone concept.

11.   He expressed this view in a meeting on 16 January 1992.

12.   Interestingly, COSATU also worries about whether there are any potential new growth industries that are internationally competitive. COSATU claims that in contrast to the 'world's major trading nations [where] skilled labour and new technology have become the base for the manufacture and trade of low cost, high quality and design flexible products', South Africa's 'manufacturing ... sector ... is high cost, based on a very narrow market, poorly equipped with skills and in general with a very poor technological capacity'. In this respect see the Report of the COSATU Economic Policy Conference, 27-29 March 1992, *Economic Policy in COSATU*. This is the official policy document, although it 'represents a step in an ongoing process' of policy-making within the trade union federation.

13.   This section is based on the 'Dialogue on flexible manufacturing networks', the proceedings of a conference organised by the Consortium for Manufacturing Competitiveness published by the Southern Technology Council, 16 January 1990, Ramada Beach Resort, Fort Walton Beach, Florida. In particular, reference is made to the papers by Styers, Carlisle, Hatch and Pezzini.

14.   This section is based on Kudrle and Kite (1989) and Archer and Maser (1989).

15.   The corporation offers employers free recruiting and pre-screening of potential employees.

16.   The following information was supplied by Eric Bove, BQE's Export Programme Manager.

17.   This section is based on Silver and Burton (1986) and Silver (1986-87).

18.   The project is being undertaken by the Economic Trends Research Group in liaison with COSATU and the Department of Economic Policy of the ANC. The project intends to 'contribute to the regeneration of South African manufacturing by devising a set of policy proposals'. For a quick summary of the project see Joffe and Lewis (1992).

19.   This critique is based on Eisinger (1988), Fainstein and Fainstein (1991), Fossler (1992), and Ross and Friedman (1990).

20.   Of course, the Greenhouse Compact might have been.

21.   The failure of Rhode Island's 'Greenhouse Compact', which attempted to plot a com-

prehensive industrial strategy, is a clear demonstration of this (Silver 1986-87, Silver and Burton 1986).

22. For example, union fears on this score were heightened when the integration of the municipal administrations in Port Elizabeth led to many workers losing their jobs.

23. This section is based on Heymans (1991) and Knox (1988).

24. This differs from the above in that the decision to supply the good is made by a private enterprise but, because it is a natural monopoly, government regulates the conditions of provision.

25. This section is culled from Tomlinson (1992).

Chapter 6
Community Economic Development

In this chapter I consider how communities become engaged in economic development. Four topics stand out: initiatives intended to empower community organisations; the contribution of intermediary organisations; co-operatives; and attempts to assist small entrepreneurs.

EMPOWERING COMMUNITY ORGANISATIONS

It is usually assumed that civics, church groups, women's groups and other members of civil society will be the vehicle for community development strategies. This projects the past into the future; yet the nature and form of these institutions were shaped by a specific economic and social milieu, and that milieu is changing. Thus, is it valid to assume that the civics, in particular, will be the prime movers in community development strategies?

The future of the civics

Friedman (1991b) maintains that arguments for a continuing role for the civics and for the role of civil society in general are, to a considerable degree, a reflection of tensions within the ANC. There has been competition between the older, exiled leaders of the 1950s who incline towards a somewhat autocratic style of decision-making, and the activists of the 1980s who have developed – and are accountable to – local constituencies. The latter fear that decisions will be made in a rather top-down fashion, and demand consultation. In particular, activists fear compromises with the present government and business that would dilute both their power base and the relative strength of the masses.

Friedman is concerned that demands by activists for a distinct civil society may extend only as far as those institutions which are in the Charterist camp[1] and have their origins in the days of the United Democratic Front. He challenges Swilling's assertion that trade unions, civics, the churches, NGOs, organised progressive professionals, the Kagiso Trust, the service organisations and educational institutions are 'pillars of civil society' (Swilling 1991); instead he argues that 'civil society' properly refers to all institutions that are voluntary, market regulated or privately controlled, and exist outside government. Shubane (1991) comments that the institutions Swilling mentions are those which form part of a broad alliance against apartheid – rather than an open list. In other words, the issue may be less one of democratisation than one of hegemony and, therefore, it is possible that SANCO will circumscribe access to civil society. In the light of these arguments one is not reassured by examples of civics attempting to exclude or dominate other institutions when engaged in negotiations with government.

Indeed, some alarm is justified when Dan Sandi, General Secretary of SANCO, writes that

> I think it should be emphasised that civics today are volunteer organisations in the sense that all residents join their structures voluntarily (freedom of association), *although one belongs to a civic whether he/she is registered or not. This is because the civic is the residents, and the residents the civic* (emphasis added).[2]

Seekings (1992) makes the point that the civics conceive of 'the community' as all those within an area who have been oppressed by apartheid. This all-embracing conception precludes dissenting voices, who by definition are thought to be speaking against 'the people'.

The other side of this coin is the feeling among many that civics will be necessary under a majority government to ensure both that decision-making is democratic and that bureaucracies remain accessible to the masses. According to Pat Lephunya, General Secretary of the SCA, this feeling is informed by experiences elsewhere in Africa where liberation movements all too quickly became undemocratic governments (Collinge 1991). SANCO brings together about 2 000 civics that are united within thirteen regional structures. SANCO specifically rejects the possibility of civics becoming branches of the ANC. The goal is that they should be autonomous, mass-based structures.

However, it would be easy to become disingenuous. The leadership of the civics typically includes members of the ANC. Thus, one is not surprised when the Southern Free State Civics Congress says it feels free to endorse politicians with 'appropriate' policies and programmes.

This is not to deny that the civics have been prepared to adopt positions contrary to those of the ANC. The willingness of the SCA to negotiate with a delegation that included black local authorities is a case in point. The subsequent election of Cyril Ramaphosa, an SCA member, to the position of General Secretary of the ANC also reveals an acceptance of such differences.

A further complication is that there are regional differences in the civics' level of organisation, independence, and preparedness to adopt a development role. For example, few have the potential of the Wattville Concerned Residents Committee, which launched a land invasion and upgrading strategy that led to the creation of Tamboville on the East Rand. Alternatively, civics in the Pietermaritzburg area of Natal are more likely to be closely linked to ANC branches than to assert their independence, as in the Transvaal.

On the one hand, sceptics complain that the civics will invariably represent the ANC. On the other hand, Nzimande and Sikhosana (1991) worry that if civics monopolise local issues pertaining to, say, housing and services, they will separate the ANC from the concerns of the masses and weaken it. In sum, the picture is complicated and one makes generalisations at one's peril. There is potential for civics to adopt a range of roles, or even to succumb to a complete loss of autonomy.

It is in this regard that Robert Fisher's history of neighbourhood organising in America is informative (Fisher 1984). He points to distinct cycles in the character and form of neighbourhood organisations, cycles which reflect the political and economic context of the time. We should also note the experience of Madrid's Citizen Movement, which collapsed with the advent of democracy, and wonder whether the same will not happen to the civics. In the case of Madrid, Castells (1983) points to the 'contradiction' between the movement's political origins, its desire for autonomy, and its unwillingness to submit to the rules of the institutionalised political system.

The fact that the circumstances in which civics in South Africa achieved prominence are changing surely heralds the start of a new cycle. Seekings (1992), for one, attributes their importance to conditions beyond their control! In his view, credible political parties at first were banned and later were preoccupied with national political issues. In addition, black local authorities were illegitimate and the government, in its search for credible township representatives, lighted upon the civics. Yet with the exception of a few civics like the SCA and some others in the Eastern Cape, doubts have been raised about their popularity. The representativeness of civics is nowadays seldom taken for granted. Moreover, even the SCA has been unable to deliver on negotiated agreements such as bringing an end to the rent boycott in Soweto.

When one starts to examine the role of the civics under majority rule, their prominence seems likely to decline. The urban areas are being restructured – one city, one tax base, one government. Will the civics retain a role?

Will the civics retain a role?

Several contradictory positions can be ventured. Circumstances favouring continued prominence for the civics can be found in the changing political situation, in combination with the ongoing economic crisis. Heightened expectations will be juxtaposed with material deprivation – the 'bread and butter issues' which historically buoyed the civics.

The significance of this conjunction is evident in Fisher's assessment that

> the efforts of working-class and poor people's organisations develop best in periods of profound social dislocation when (1) the regulatory power of social institutions breaks down and (2) sharp economic change occurs producing depressed *or* improved conditions, the former encouraging people to defend themselves, the latter raising their expectations. It is not so much prosperity or depression at the national and local levels that leads to radical neighborhood organising, but rather external pressures on traditional communities and a breakdown of the routines of daily life that make people more receptive to activism and alternative organisations. Disturbances in the larger political economy, however, are necessary to create the conditions in which the powerless move to mass political insurgency. (1984: 159)

It should be remembered that the high points of insurgent organising in the USA occurred during the Depression and in the 1960s when there was rapid economic growth. In South Africa, of course, one foresees both raised expectations and economic dislocation. In Fisher's terms, the preconditions exist for a prominent role for the civics.

According to Planact (1992a: 205), the objective of the civics is 'to dictate the agenda, control development, organise the community, negotiate effectively while avoiding co-option, and determine development priorities from below'.

How would a majority government respond to such a hard line? Firstly, it would no doubt attempt to cross-subsidise services through redistributing resources from rich to poor. But this can go just so far. The disparity between the scale of resources available and the inadequacies in respect of shelter, infrastructure and services cannot be resolved in the short term. Secondly, the government could engage in co-option and offer civic leaders positions within the ANC and the bureaucracy. This alternative may well prove effective since most of the civic leadership are already ANC members. Moreover, like anyone else, civic leaders aspire to better housing, cars and improved schooling for their children, and it may well be that the leadership is decimated. Indeed, in a memo summarising SANCO's first meeting, Shubane attributes the disarray evident there to the civics' loss of skilled leaders to the now unbanned political parties. Thirdly, the classic response of governments to leaders who resist co-option is, of course, repression. The strategy adopted by a new government would probably be a combination of all three approaches.

The alternative position, that civics will succumb and lose their autonomy entirely, can be anticipated through reference to:

- the changing social and economic milieu;
- tensions within SANCO and between SANCO and the ANC;
- the history and origins of many civics, especially as a number do not appear solidly grounded;
- the motives of civic leadership and whether they will use their positions to realise political ambitions outside the civic movement; and
- the question of whether civics can evolve into development agencies of some sort (which offer jobs).

Several points advance this argument. One cannot ignore Seekings's claim that civics rose to prominence in a specific era, when black local authorities were virtually the only other partner for negotiations. The next government might disregard the civics, especially if they carp over the allocation of resources. Nor can one easily disregard Friedman's cynical observation that civics are often used as a launching pad for political careers. Indeed, it appears that in Natal a number of people are engaged in civic organising as a result of their failure to obtain positions of leadership within the ANC, and employ their civic positions to oppose local ANC leaders.

Secondly, SANCO appears to be developing a style which shows little regard for consultation. SANCO leadership have been accused of adopting positions which lack a mandate from membership and which contradict those of the ANC. This creates tensions with the ANC.[3]

Thirdly, few civics constitute social movements in the sense that they have achieved lasting and widespread support within their communities. The SCA and the Port Elizabeth Black Civic Organisation (PEBCO) have achieved such a status, but how many other civics could make this claim?

Fourthly, in a context of mass unemployment, who would blame civic leaders if they accept offers of employment with the ANC and government?

When one speculates on such matters, the more cynical path appears more realistic. Yet enervating conclusions are premature and the future of community organisations remains open. This book, encouraged by the democratic intent and longevity of many civic organisations, will proceed as if a number of them will survive.

Civic roles – organisation and advocacy

It can be argued that the 'comparative advantage' of civics lies in acting as advocacy organisations. The reason is that for civics to act as development agencies, they would need organisational skills, organisational capacity, resources (offices, staff, telephones, money), and technical skills.

In respect of organisational capacity and resources, in a few instances these shortages are being addressed by service organisations, donors, and by partnerships formed through community development trusts (CDTs) and section 21 non-profit companies. These needs could also perhaps be addressed by civics acting as delegate agencies supported by and acting on behalf of local authorities. None the less, there is little prospect that the majority of civics could make up for these shortcomings.

As regards technical skills, community organisations seldom pay well (if at all) and few offer any prospect of advancement. The notion of a personnel policy seems far-fetched. And the environment – working within low-income communities and scrounging for resources – does not lead to a sympathetic appreciation of individual material ambitions. Nor are the problems confined to South Africa. Writing of the American experience Peirce and Steinbach (1990: 67) observe that 'many bright young people in low-income neighborhoods have become expert community economic development operators. But there is concern that many of the smartest indigenous leaders, especially those who are black, Hispanic, or Asian, are lured to greener pastures in the business world or city government.'

My conversations with civic members suggest they do not appreciate that their shortage of skills cannot be remedied by a few short courses. The problem lies in the history of apartheid education and the inequalities Africans have endured, and there is no short-term solution. If a civic receives funding from an external source it can buy professional expertise, but since only the most visible civics attract funding and have the ability to pay wages at market rates, the large majority will forever be weak in this area. Not surprisingly, a prime motivation among the less prominent civics in forming SANCO was the possibility of centralised fund-raising and an equitable distribution of resources.

Lastly, a point repeatedly emphasised in the literature is that CDCs in America are successful now because they have had twenty years of experience. This experience is the key.

One can argue that the CDC route is not an option available to most civics. Simply stated, civics in South Africa do not have twenty years in which to develop skills. However, this need not be a damning conclusion, since many hold that advocacy organisations are more effective than development agencies anyway.

Advocacy organisations generally struggle for, and participate in, decision-making on improved supplies of goods, services and infrastructure. This broad frame of reference requires organisation in the community and a preparedness to engage in mass action; it also calls for a close analysis of the issues (a function often provided by service organisations).

Organised protest often produces greater development benefits than those a CDC can hope to achieve through its own projects. This is because the goal of protest is to influence the actions of government bodies, utility companies, and private companies. And the resources these groups might potentially allocate to a community are so much in excess of those which a CDC can ordinarily expect to obtain for a few small development projects of its own, that mass action often appears to be the better course to follow. One can argue, then, that the most appropriate goal for civics might be to participate in decision-making that affects their area and yet retain their ability to call for protest if their voice is not heard.

Three reservations have been expressed about such a role. First, Friedman[4] has objected that in a post-apartheid environment, mobilisation will be more difficult as there will no longer be such obvious mobilising symbols as apartheid and the black local authorities. In this he is obviously correct, but one could counter that mobilisation essentially occurs in response to material deprivation relative to the expectations of the people.

Secondly, Seekings (1992) and Friedman raise concerns that civics can seldom be taken as representative of their communities and that they are poorly organised. Friedman adds that civic leaders often seek positions in political parties or in government and that civics are a vehicle for achieving career ambitions. I have already noted Shubane's suggestion that the separation of civics and their leadership is a process already underway.

Thirdly, civic organisation and advocacy is an indirect strategy. Decisions are left in the hands of others and the community may well lose force if it engages in a series of unsuccessful power plays. A more direct approach has its attractions.

Civic roles – development agencies

Insurgent community organisations tend to evolve naturally into development agencies. For example, Fisher (1984) suggests that in America, the period of insurgency lasts for about six years, until the critical issues which brought the organisation into being have been resolved. Resolution often leads to the organisation fading away, but sometimes its core organisers persist in the form of a development agency. A famous example is the Woodlawn Organisation, started by Saul Alinsky, perhaps America's foremost community organiser, who was renowned for his abrasive, antagonistic style. The Woodlawn Organisation now comprises a number of paid professionals who implement projects, apparently without community control, and who are wary of community organisation lest it alienate potential funders.

The notion of insurgent organisations transforming themselves into development agencies is relevant to South Africa because of anticipated majority rule. Civics nowadays are not fighting the state for majority rule so much as struggling for projects and resources that will satisfy basic needs and promote economic development. A number of civics are contemplating parallel strategies, namely to act as both advocacy organisations and development agencies that become directly involved in the delivery of infrastructure, shelter and services.

The requirements necessary for civics to function as development agencies are found in Planact's discussion of the meaning of empowerment (Planact 1992a). Planact views empowerment as having four dimensions: planning, control, capacity building, and finance.

Planning refers to the maximisation of choice, as opposed to the mystification of decision-making by technical experts. This requires clarification of a range of options and the capacity to make choices on the basis of criteria determined by community interests. For example, Planact often uses community workshops to challenge technocratic, top-down assumptions and to determine new criteria.

Control is distinct from community participation and, in Planact's view (1992a: 210-211), requires an articulation of what institutions are available to promote development from below. Thus, with a view to empowerment,

> Community participation is a complex process of building the capacity of the most powerless and poorest communities to take greater control of the decisions, knowledge, resources and power that govern their daily lives. Many civics distinguish between community participation and community control: the former refers to participation in projects and programmes designed by *someone else*; the latter to strategies initiated and implemented *by the community*.
>
> Community control can only be achieved by building up from below an array of local development organisations and institutions that are different from civics and service organisations that have hitherto been involved in the development process. Civics will remain broadly-based community representatives articulating demands relating to the full range of community problems. Service organisations will continue to provide much-needed technical, training and 'organisational development' back-up.
>
> Specialised development institutions will be required to manage the resource flows, decision making and planning that lie at the heart of the development process. Structures under consideration in this regard are community development trusts and section 21 (non-profit) companies.

This lengthy quote is especially interesting as it reveals a specific vision of how civics are to deal with their organisational, technical and financial weaknesses. On the one hand, civics will continue to organise and be able to operate in an advocacy mode. On the other hand, they will create arm's-length development institutions which they control and use for planning and project implementation.

Community development trusts and section 21 (non-profit) companies[5]

The development institutions Planact has in mind are CDTs and section 21 (non-profit) companies. A number of CDTs and section 21 companies are presently being established. Both constitute vehicles for the provision of shelter and community facilities, the implementation of programmes intended to improve a community's quality of life, and the promotion of employment creation.

CDTs often comprise 50 per cent civic membership and 50 per cent membership by white local authorities, township administrators and local business persons. The Trusts are often presented as providing communities with control over local development but, failing agreement within the Trust, the best they offer is a veto. This is because membership of the Trusts represents a form of partnership and compromise which cannot easily be equated with community control. A major impetus behind many CDTs is the Independent Development Trust, which wants to use CDTs to manage projects it funds.

However, the Trusts are often regarded as relatively inept vehicles for development. Their members have other jobs, meet occasionally, and are often ill-informed on the decisions that need to be made. For this reason, section 21 companies may be better as they are companies in the true sense of the word, with directors and employees paid by the company itself.

Section 21 companies differ from ordinary companies in two crucial respects. First, the income and property of the company cannot be distributed to its members. Secondly, the members, who appoint the company's board of directors, can include a specified number of representatives elected by the company, and also other figures distinguished by their community service.

Even so, it is questionable whether a community that forms a company will retain control over it. The obvious analogy is the difficulty shareholders have in controlling the activities of their company's directors. But the American experience of non-profit companies is probably more relevant. When community activities become professionalised – to access funds and implement projects – the vehicles for project implementation become progressively more distant from the community.

Civics in South Africa are alert to this problem. There have been suggestions that a civic, or adjoining civics, should retain a focus on community organisation and, by creating separate CDTs or companies, avoid the compromises associated with professionalism. If adjoining civics share a CDT, this also reduces their requirements in respect of administrative resources.

A separate CDT or company also allows a degree of 'money laundering', in that the civic can remain politically untouched while the Trust accepts funds from sources that might otherwise prompt a squeamish response from community-based bodies. Having witnessed debates about whether to accept aid from certain bilateral and multilateral aid agencies, I can testify that this is not a matter to be taken lightly.

Finally, there is the prospect that once integrated local authorities are in place, they may take over the functions of CDTs and section 21 companies. It is therefore unclear whether CDTs and section 21 companies are intermediary institutions, or whether they will evolve into powerful organisations in their own right. American examples, such as the Pittsburgh Partnership for Neighborhood Development, suggest that if Trusts or companies become effective, they can become long-lived development agencies.[6]

INTERMEDIARY ORGANISATIONS

Intermediary organisations in both America and South Africa provide critical support to community organisations through financial and technical assistance and training.[7] They help to create and nurture those organisations, and share information and experience. I will describe prominent American organisations first and then look at service organisations and the Kagiso Trust.

The Local Initiatives Support Corporation[8]

The Local Initiatives Support Corporation (LISC) is perhaps the best-known financial intermediary in the USA. LISC was formed in 1979. Its formation was prompted by the recognition that fund-raising was difficult and time-consuming, that it detracted from the time available for development work, and that shortages of funds prevented the employment of skilled staff. Describing itself as a non-profit, social-investment banker, it provides communities with operating funds, project support, technical assistance and capacity-building programmes. By 1990 LISC and its subsidiaries had raised over $460 million. It provides an important service to funders (donors and investors – the latter through the National Equity Fund) since it evaluates potential projects critically and helps to leverage and package funds from various sources in a manner which spreads individual risk. The point about leverage is important. LISC is not the sole source of funds; rather, it lends credibility to projects and helps them raise additional funding which might well be ten times the contribution from LISC.

The technical assistance and capacity-building programmes are also worth noting. LISC helps with the building of organisations, for example, where there is no CDC in an area in which it wants to be active; assists with organisational maintenance, such as operating procedures, election of boards, and keeping the books; facilitates the development of technical expertise; and provides money for core operations.

LISC also shows how one can orchestrate corporate and bank support to community organisations and low-income areas. An illustration of this is the recent LIMAC[9] initiative, which includes the Rockerfeller Foundation and the Prudential Insurance Company. LIMAC buys low-income mortgages from banks. It packages these together and swaps them for AAA-rated bonds from Fannie Mae or Freddie Mac. These are financial institutions that operate in the secondary mortgage market in order to ensure its liquidity. LIMAC then sells these bonds through Wall Street. In effect, it is opening up the secondary mortgage market for low-income housing lenders. The banks replace the capital they allocated for the mortgage and are in a position to make further loans. The Community Reinvestment Act (explained below) motivates them to make the loans. The banks, LIMAC and Fannie Mae all bear a portion of the risk. For the banks, the retention of risk keeps them honest and the reduction of risk reduces their obligatory capital retention ratios and enables them to do additional business.

The Pratt Institute

The Center for Community and Environmental Development of the Pratt Institute in Brooklyn, New York City, provides technical assistance, training, and capacity building for community organisations and engages in related research. The Institute is of special interest because of the way in which its services are incorporated in a proposal for building capacity in South African civics by Ronald Shiffman (1990), the director of the Center. He urged the development of 'self-sustaining community-based, democratically run organisations capable of undertaking locally-initiated development activity' (p. 35). To this end his recommendations include:[10]

• bilateral support for technical assistance activities;

- the training of civic staff;
- an education and training programme designed to develop the capacity of blacks[11] to participate in civics and intermediary organisations;
- research to help inform the debate;
- networking between civics, intermediaries and donors;
- in-service training and staff retreats;
- a donor research centre; and
- a community development bank.

The Pratt Institute is available to provide courses, co-ordinate exchanges between the staff of American CDCs and South African civics and service organisations, and organise an exchange 'where a selected group of South African, U.S. and community-based practitioners from other countries would jointly participate in a multi-country community development tour and seminar' (p. 43). (Count me in for this option!) At Pratt, visiting participants would join their American counterparts 'in an experiential education program specifically designed to develop the capacity of community development and community economic development practitioners' (p. 38).

Shiffman's proposals betray two phenomena which I found common in the USA. First, South Africa is the 'hot issue' and, whether in Boston, Chicago, New York, Pittsburgh or Los Angeles, academics, community development practitioners and foundations are eager to get involved. Secondly, community development has 'salespersons' who market the approach. The above shopping list, for example, rather exceeds the capacity of a middle-income country with limited expertise, and exaggerates the extent to which local initiatives can address mass poverty. A touch of moderation would be appropriate.

The Pittsburgh Partnership for Neighborhood Development

The Pittsburgh Partnership for Neighborhood Development co-ordinates the efforts of CDCs in Pittsburgh, screens projects, provides technical assistance, and organises both operating funds and project capital.

The Partnership links sources of capital, management and technical expertise with the development efforts of communities through providing CDCs with funds, information, management, and technical assistance; and through providing funders with ideas, good investments, and a revitalised city. A critical service implicit in the Partnership's role is that it brings community organisations and sponsors together at a single point of contact. For example, for CDCs it provides a fund-raising service and offers sophisticated financial services; for funders it screens applicants and recasts proposals in a more practical vein, and then provides the management back-up that enhances their prospects for success. The Partnership's activities include housing, entrepreneurial training, business franchising, job placement, and community services. A measure of the Partnership's success is that LISC has ceased operating in Pittsburgh.

The closest South African parallel with the Partnership is the Kagiso Trust, but there is no metropolitan equivalent. It would seem natural for South Africa's service organisations to evolve into partnerships of this sort, were it not for their politicisation, functioning as they do in the Charterist camp.

Service organisations

Service organisations in South Africa assume a variety of forms. I have already described what is probably the best-known organisation in the urban arena: Planact.

> Planact is a funded, non-profit organisation working in the field of housing, local government and urban development. It provides technical, professional and organisational skills and assistance to communities adversely affected by state planning, apartheid policies and economic inequality.
>
> Planact works only on request to mass-based democratic organisations committed to urban development. Planact accepts projects on the undertaking that there is a clear mandate from the organisation making the request and in turn undertakes to be accountable to that organisation. (Planact 1990/91: 1)

Planact is guided by a specific conception of development as:

- above all else, a **process** rather than the delivery of a set of products to individual consumers;
- about **empowering** people and communities with the skills, knowledge and capacity to act effectively;
- aimed at gaining greater **control** for communities over resources, especially at local level;

- about **sustainable production** of needed goods and the **just distribution** of these goods; and
- about meeting **basic needs** and continuously improving the lives of as many people as possible.

Of especial interest to us is that a 'number of Planact's clients are beginning to explore economic development strategies, with the result that in some negotiating forums local economic development has been included in their terms of reference as an issue for negotiation' (p. 4). The result is that Planact has been drawn into the forums and is gearing up to serve this need.

A striking feature of Planact's client base is that it has primarily consisted of civics. We earlier cast doubt on the longevity of the civics. If doubt is warranted, then Planact and other service organisations must themselves be threatened. Speculation within Planact centres on income-generating activities such as serving local governments – once they have become democratic, of course. Income-generating activities are favoured given Planact's experience with the Kagiso Trust. Planact used to be solely funded by the Trust, but then the Trust suddenly withdrew its support (along with support for a number of other organisations).[12]

The Kagiso Trust

The Kagiso Trust was founded in May 1986 as a vehicle to assist with the European Community Special Programme for Victims of Apartheid, itself established in 1985.

The Trust was soon criticised for certain of its practices: for instance, without notice it ceased supporting a number of organisations. Often the Trust did not seem to know what these organisations actually did. These problems were explained as being due to the Trust's limited development capacity. It was said in some quarters that the Trust was predisposed to funding projects that were 'politically correct', yet the Trust was one of the first bodies to relinquish its ideological purity and to urge organisations to seek funding from domestic institutions hitherto regarded as politically unacceptable.

These criticisms stemmed, in a sense, from the fact that the Commission of the European Community initially focused more on ameliorating the consequences of apartheid than on development. The Commission found that in addition to supporting critical programmes that, for example, protected human rights and helped maintain a free press, it was engendering a dependency mentality and a welfarist approach. To overcome this problem, as the political situation in South Africa improved, the Kagiso Trust was recast as a development agency. The Trust was now to focus on the most disadvantaged and assist communities to change their own circumstances. In particular, the Trust recognised the resource constraints that a majority government would face, and so began to direct its funding to NGOs.

The Trust's current strategy is

i.   to identify existing genuine and potentially successful NGO and community networks as the basis for supporting local level development initiatives.

ii. to strengthen and expand the capacity of community structures, such as civic organisations, in urban and rural areas, to develop a policy for participating in development planning at the local and regional level.

iii. to increase the capacity of civic organisations to manage income generating projects. (Kagiso Trust n.d.: 3)

Along lines reminiscent of the Pittsburgh Partnership, the Kagiso Trust will

i.   become a facilitator that would locate internal and external resources when needed.

ii. help build resources available for local initiatives, including the creation of an 'alternative' capital development fund.

iii. provide management support.

iv. evaluate and advise on the viability of projects and enterprises.

v.   co-ordinate training needs and training resources.

vi. assist in project and programme design, etc. (Kagiso Trust n.d.: 4)

CO-OPERATIVES

Co-operatives that operate worker-owned enterprises are generally included under the rubric of community economic development. Such co-operatives are different to community or civic enterprises in that ownership is formally vested in the workers or members. Moreover, the workers can come from different communities. But co-operatives have an appeal for those who support community initiatives and can comfortably be regarded as a community strategy.

The concept of a co-operative is flexible. For example, the South African Clothing and Textile Workers' Union (SACTWU) started what it terms a co-operative, but the enterprise, known as Zenzeleni, is owned and run by SACTWU, which also appointed the general manager.[13] If we remember that one of the defining characteristics of a co-operative is that each worker has one vote which entitles him or her to elect a manager, it is apparent that SACTWU's Zenzeleni scheme is closer to a conventional business. It might be that if unemployed workers are to produce anything other than technologically simple products for a limited market, then a co-operative will need the assistance of a union, but co-operatives require a greater level of worker control than is evident in the case of Zenzeleni. Even so, Zenzeleni has struggled, and its workforce of 300 persons has been reduced by half.

The National Union of Mineworkers (NUM) has also helped to create twenty co-operatives that employ approximately 400 persons. NUM's goal is to 'assist dismissed workers in developing survival strategies, and [to] make a broader political and developmental impact in the impoverished rural areas through developing local economies in ways that empower those living there' (Jaffee 1992: 370). In this instance the assistance is geared to technical needs and sometimes also to start-up funds. NUM's co-operatives are intended to become self-governing and self-sufficient and so the notion of co-operatives is more apt here.

In all, South Africa has 100 producer co-operatives with about 2 000 members. The co-operatives commonly engage in sewing, knitting and weaving (39 per cent); building, brick-making, fencing and housing (19 per cent); and crafts, beadwork, grasswork and sisal products (11 per cent). Two features stand out. First, there is a division of labour along gender lines. Secondly, the two largest categories are predominantly found in rural areas.

Both in their numbers and in their products local co-operatives contrast sharply with the Mondragon co-operatives which, altogether, employ in the order of 20 000 people, and produce a variety of goods. For example, one co-operative group, FAGOR, produces consumer goods, industrial components, and engineering and capital equipment. Mondragon is a worthwhile case study, since it is often used locally as an example to gain support for the co-operative movement. The question is whether Mondragon has more than rhetorical significance. Is it an example South Africa's co-operatives can reasonably aspire to?

The Mondragon co-operatives[14]

Mondragon is actually the name of the town where the first co-operatives that now form part of the FAGOR[15] group were established. The history of this group is interesting in itself, but our concern must be with the extent to which it is replicable in South Africa.

An immediate difficulty with the Mondragon experience is the leading role played by Don Jose Maria Arizmendiarrieta, a priest in Mondragon.[16] Arizmendi taught a complex philosophy and his writings and sermons have been collected in a sixteen-volume text! Suffice it to say that he sought 'a new and more humane social order' and co-operatives were a means to this end. He inspired others to start the first and subsequent co-operatives. Arizmendi was a visionary, in that he foresaw and persistently urged the need to establish secondary co-operatives – a polytechnic,[17] a co-operative bank, an industrial research facility – which would serve the other co-operatives. Arizmendi did not sit on the boards of the co-operatives and was not involved in production and marketing decisions. None the less, when a successful project is initiated by one person, and then extended by his own efforts, often in the face of stubborn resistance, one immediately has to question whether the experience is replicable elsewhere.[18]

In Mondragon workers pay a fee to become a member of a co-operative. Each member has a capital account with the co-operative and his or her share of the profits is paid into that account. Membership gives each individual one vote and these votes are exercised at the General Assembly, during elections for the Governing Council, and in various other committees.

Decisions about salaries are based on three principles. The first is solidarity with fellow Basques, which means the starting wage for unskilled labour is much the same as that in the private sector. Secondly, the desire for internal solidarity leads to a balance between minimising differences in earnings and the need to reward performance and responsibility. The third principle is that everyone should know what others earn. In practice, the wage ratio in the past between starting unskilled workers and top management was 1:3. This ratio was later extended to 1:4,5 in exceptional circumstances. None the less, this remains a remarkably small differential, especially when contrasted with the differential between the American chief executive and the average factory worker of 1:93 (Reich 1991).

The form of the first co-operative, ULGOR, started in 1956, became the model for all subsequent worker co-operatives.

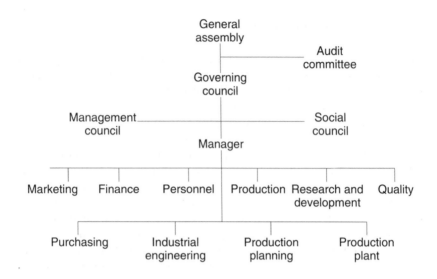

General assembly: Ultimate power resides in the assembly and all members are obliged to vote. The assembly meets at least once a year. In addition, the governing council or a petition from a third or more of the workers can call a meeting.

Governing council: The council is the top policy-making body. It is elected by the members of the co-operative, each member having one vote.

Manager: The manager is appointed by the governing council for a four-year term. He or she may be reappointed or deposed at any stage.

Audit committee: The committee is elected by members of the council. It performs an internal audit of the co-operative's financial operations and monitors its adherence to policies and procedures.

Social council: Council members, drawn from the different departments in which they work, are elected for two-year periods. Generally re-election for a second term is avoided. The role of this council has never been fully clarified and has changed over time. In general, it provides a vehicle for communication and addresses health and safety on the job, social security, systems of compensation, and community projects.

New co-operatives are initiated in various ways. A foremost player in this respect is the co-operative bank, the Caja Laboral Popular (People's Savings Bank), which is required by its constitution to assist in the creation of jobs through co-operatives. The bank assists people who are thinking about starting a co-operative, regardless of whether they come from existing co-operatives or not, and makes financial provisions for the inevitable losses in the first few years until the co-operative breaks even. The bank also subsidises an Entrepreneurial Division which initiates co-operatives, undertaking research and information-gathering on potential markets and feasible projects.

Existing co-operatives also start new enterprises. The role of these co-operatives is especially noteworthy: if they think a proposal worthwhile, they bear the costs of employing the leaders of the new co-operative, and rotate them between positions while they learn the job and prepare a business plan.

Interestingly, taking over failing firms is viewed in a negative light. While it is done occasionally, there seem to be severe problems in respect of restructuring the management system and 'socialising' the workforce.

At Mondragon there are many co-operatives and indeed several co-operative groups. FAGOR comprises thirteen co-operatives and about 6 000 employees. The bulk of its products are sold in Spain, but the group has an international marketing campaign and anticipates further growth due to European integration. The outcome of this scale of operation has been the creation of an administrative overlay able to undertake strategic planning and co-ordinate the movement of staff between declining and growing co-operatives. All in all, FAGOR represents a sophisticated enterprise.

Does it make sense to refer to Mondragon when searching for models appropriate to South Africa? We are looking at the product of nearly 40 years of growth and experience, of course, and it would be unreasonable to compare current South African circumstances with Mondragon as it is now. But do the preconditions exist?

i.   The role of Arizmendi is disconcerting. Perhaps the inauguration of a co-operative movement in South Africa requires a similarly dedicated and convincing person? If that is the case, then it is a matter of chance whether the right person will arise.
ii. Basque culture is renowned for its democracy and solidarity. Unfortunately South Africa's fractious society is not similarly distinguished.
iii. The Mondragon co-operatives were preceded by a polytechnic created under Arizmendi's direction. The graduates acquired the skills necessary to develop an enterprise, were imbued with the

social consciousness required to do this in a co-operative structure and through a sense of solidarity were themselves prepared to forego the higher incomes they could make as managers in the private sector. Education, ethnicity and social consciousness combined in a way one does not anticipate finding in South Africa.

iv. The co-operative movement was started as Spain entered a period of sustained growth in the 1960s. Later, during the 1970s and early 1980s, a number of co-operatives confronted crises and, indeed, the role of Caja Laboral Popular shifted towards helping co-operatives to survive. This contrasts poorly with the present sorry state of South Africa's economy.

v. Spain's economy during the 1960s was characterised by substantial import protections. The co-operatives were not competing with Sony and Toshiba. The world economy today is defined by competition on a global scale.

vi. Caja Laboral Popular provided a ready source of capital and, together with other co-operatives, also provided sustained technical assistance to potential new co-operatives. This support is unavailable in South Africa.

Yugoslavia[19]

Obviously, with the current mayhem in what was Yugoslavia, we can only guess how the situation there will have changed. In the past, Yugoslav enterprises were considered social property temporarily in the care of their workers. There were three management institutions: plant director, managing board and workers' council. Every enterprise with more than ten employees had to elect a council responsible for policy guidelines on, for example, product lines, financial planning, technological innovation, and marketing. The council elected – and could remove – the management board and plant director. The director and board oversaw the day-to-day operation of the plant. The actual locus of power lay with the plant director and technical staff. The relative power of the workers was evident in the frequency with which members of the councils and managing boards joined the workers during strikes.

While strikes within the Mondragon system and in Yugoslavia have been rare, the mere existence of strikes reflects the fact that ownership (in the case of the Mondragon co-operatives) or participation in decision-making do not necessarily translate into actual control. For example, in Mondragon the management controls job design, job evaluation and pay standards, and sets the agenda of the annual meeting. Moreover, the Social Council only has advisory powers.

The higher level of worker participation in enterprises in Yugoslavia was due to:

- the ability of workers to recall management;
- the fact that important decisions were decentralised to the level of the work unit – as opposed to the Taylorist methods of production predominant in the Mondragon co-operatives; and
- the fact that members of the workers' council still worked on the production floor.

Even so, Yugoslav workers felt higher levels of resentment than in, say, the USA, Italy and Austria. The implication is that participation in decision-making is less important than the structure of the work itself.

Critique

Enthusiasm for co-operatives should be tempered with a touch of realism. Only 2,5 per cent of Italy's non-agricultural labour force are employed in worker-owned firms, and this figure is the highest of any market economy. Spain, host of the successful Mondragon co-operatives, achieves a figure of 1 per cent. Comparable figures in France and the United Kingdom are 0,2 per cent and 0,03 per cent (Ben-Ner 1988). One's ideological predispositions notwithstanding, claims about the ability of co-operatives to redress unemployment significantly should be modest.

My view is not that co-operatives have no future, but that they have to target a more modest market niche. For example, it is unfair to look to the Yugoslav and Mondragon examples in the South African context. Worker ownership of large enterprises is unlikely in South Africa. Worker councils may well be represented on management boards, but they will have less influence. For a start, they will not have the powers of recall! Further, the sophisticated Mondragon co-operative groups, with their ability to engage in strategic and financial planning, research and development, and overseas marketing, seem unattainable in the foreseeable future.

Dickstein (1991) brings one back to earth. She notes that co-operatives are generally small (with a maximum of 500 employees), and are most often found in labour-intensive manufacturing, food processing and service industries. Co-operatives tend to avoid enterprises which require large amounts of capital, complex technologies, and international marketing, because both capital and entrepreneurship are in short supply and the ability to respond rapidly to differentiated markets requires a centralisation of authority. The performance of co-operatives is very uneven and generally declines as they age. Nevertheless, they have often been shown to outperform comparable capitalist industries.

Co-operatives also face structural obstacles to success. Access to finance is one example. The workers' membership contributions may only constitute a small proportion of the necessary investment. Lacking equity, the co-operative must approach a bank for a loan, but it appears seriously overgeared. The result is that co-operatives tend to be underfinanced. Another problem is that the managers of co-operatives can usually earn better wages in private firms. Unable to attract managerial skills, workers might know all about production and very little about, say, marketing. A further issue is that if the co-operative is successful and the value of the workers' share rises to high levels, the cost of membership might exceed the capacity of new workers to buy in and tempt existing workers to sell out.

From the point of view of assisting co-operatives, the appropriate lesson appears to come from the United Kingdom, the USA, and Canada. Here there have been policy interventions which address worker buyouts of plants that are closing or the creation of co-operatives in areas where there is high unemployment. This is in contrast to the 'informal' support systems that evolved among co-operatives in Spain, France, Israel and Italy to assist with the supply of services, marketing and the purchase of supplies.

Ideally we should look for a proactive strategy that creates conditions which facilitate the formation of co-operatives. These conditions include access to bank finance, an affirmative legal environment, assistance with training for the management of co-operatives, and the publication of material on how to structure co-operatives. In addition, government could create an agency that undertakes studies of potential co-operative ventures, including services, crafts, construction, printing, and select social services – all enterprises which require little capital, are labour-intensive, and serve local, easily identified markets.

SMALL ENTERPRISE

A healthy neighborhood economy has:
1. **Strong Purchasing Power**, with income high enough and costs low enough to keep the neighborhood affordable.

2. **Local Purchasing**, which keeps money changing hands within the neighborhood and creates local jobs.
3. **Local Ownership**, which gives residents financial security, a stake in the neighborhood, and more control over their economic futures.
4. **Local Jobs**, providing income for residents and drawing outsiders (potential customers) into the neighborhood each day.
5. **Local Reinvestment**, so that the community's savings help finance continued development.
6. **Local Sources for Local Needs**, which provide jobs for residents, reduce dollar drains out of the neighborhood, and improve the convenience and livability of the area.
7. **Opportunity and Diversity**, so that new people and new enterprises have a chance to get started, survive and prosper.
8. **Infrastructure That Makes Sense Locally**, so that the neighborhood's physical condition attracts and fosters activity instead of driving it away. (Center for Neighborhood Technology 1986: 13, emphasis in original.)

If these eight points represent the characteristics of a healthy neighbourhood economy, then apartheid has served the opposite end. African entrepreneurship has been severely restricted. Home ownership was prohibited. African wages were restrained through the prohibition, then harassment of the unions, and through inferior education. The banks take deposits but fail to serve the low-income housing market. Townships and informal settlements are distinguished by their lack of diversity. They often lack even the most rudimentary services. In other words, the townships lack the preconditions for economic success. Conditions are now changing, but only slowly.

The means to reversing the situation in the townships include:

- growth in the general economy, an increase in employment and an improvement in wages;
- enhanced municipal and social services; and
- the development of small business – which we address here.

Small enterprises include self-employed individuals and family labour in 'productive' small-scale production and 'marginal' activities, which range from peripheral low-productivity work such as shoe-shining and hawking to semi-legal and illegal activities. This definition embraces a great variety of activities, from informal enterprises (with no employees or only a couple, and a turnover which renders an income below wages in the formal sector) to small enterprises (which may render the owner relatively significant profits and which may have ten or more employees).

How to assist small enterprise

Page and Steel (1984) argue the issue of assistance to small enterprises in contrary directions. First, they hold that informal and small enterprises are not especially enticing. Such enterprises commonly provide little profit to their owners. The labourers, if any are employed, might work long hours, often under unsafe conditions, for low pay. But, after noting these drawbacks, Page and Steel argue that such enterprises are especially valuable since they provide employment at low cost.

The twist to their argument is that if this is the virtue of informal and small enterprise, then most efforts to assist them should be avoided since they have the perverse effect of adding to the cost of employment creation. That is, programmes that select a few entrepreneurs from the mass of small enterprises and provide subsidised credit, management training by highly paid professionals, subsidised rentals, and so on, only succeed in making cheap jobs expensive.

Elkan (1988) also supports the exclusion of training. He reports that while most training efforts in Africa are intended to improve management efficiency, as measured by keeping books, stock control and personnel management, there is no evidence that such courses result in improved performance. He also notes that most African enterprises are in fact managed with considerable business acumen, even though they do not necessarily distinguish between business and household expenditure and might well not require literacy. Elkan reinforces the earlier scepticism of Page and Steel that efforts to assist small enterprise primarily serve to make cheap jobs expensive.

In the light of the above arguments, assistance should take three forms: access to capital at market rates (which includes the transaction costs of supporting small enterprises), market enhancement and, it goes without saying, a favourable policy and regulatory environment.

Access to capital – comparative

Enterprises employ two types of capital: equity and debt. Equity is provided to a firm in exchange for a share of its future income. An individual's share of future income is proportional to his or her share of the equity. Small and informal businesses often use the savings of family and friends for equity purposes and, if they are relatively sophisticated, they can gain access to venture capital companies. The advantage of equity is that it is 'patient money', which means that the entrepreneur does not immediately have to devote a share of the business's income to paying interest.

Debt arises when the entrepreneur borrows money. Again, this is often obtained from family and friends, but all too often it comes from local money-lenders at exorbitant rates. Private banks are reluctant to lend to small businesses and, of course, especially to informal businesses. They prefer low-risk projects which have good collateral and an evident cash flow, and where the credit history and character of the borrower are favourable. If they are able to choose between a few large projects and many small projects, they prefer the former, due to the lower transaction costs. In addition, lending to an enterprise where there is (in the bank's view) a reasonable likelihood of having to foreclose on the loan raises potential public relations problems and hurts the bank's deposit-taking business in the neighbourhood. In effect, the lending practices of banks tend to exclude neighbourhood enterprises which are small, where the perceived risk/return ratio is inauspicious, and where the social distance between the bank official and the borrower means the official is less able to assess the credit worthiness of the borrower, and perhaps is even prejudiced.

It is clear that small and informal enterprises require start-up capital and that their future success depends on working capital. It is no wonder, then, that there are a variety of approaches to providing this service.

Community-driven

The goal of community financial institutions is to increase the flow of financial resources into their community, and to do so in a manner which enhances local control over the selection of projects which receive financial support. The specific contribution of local, financial CDCs is that they are geared to making small loans, knowing an area and the customer, and devising creative means of building collateral. The more common forms of financially oriented CDCs are described below.[20]

i. Packager/broker
    This CDC is typically a non-profit organisation that serves a specific area or constituency. It identifies sources of capital and maintains favourable relationships with them. For the borrower, the CDC pro-

vides access to capital, assistance in preparing loan applications, guidance in the management of a business, and, more generally, gives the borrower legitimacy in the eyes of the lender. For the lender, the CDC provides trustworthy information and a measure of the project's legitimacy. The lender knows that the CDC's reputation, and ultimately its survival, depend on successful projects; thus the CDC provides a rigorous filter for loan applications.

ii. Community loan funds
This refers to CDCs which try to capitalise and maintain their own funds to assist community development projects and to leverage external dollars. Most loan funds require fairly rigorous financial statements and personal loan guarantees, as they face strong pressures to lend to successful businesses and safeguard their money. Alternatively, community loan funds might use their funds to guarantee (a proportion of) loans made by private banks.

iii. Community development credit unions
Credit unions promote saving among, and provide loans to, their members. Credit unions may be united by occupation, association (for example, members of a religious or professional body), or residence. In the present context, they are useful as a means of keeping deposits within a specific geographic area and ensuring the availability of credit. An additional feature is that they facilitate democratic control, in that depositors may have voting rights which determine the union's policies.

However, financially oriented CDCs do not escape the usual constraints of having to safeguard loans through collateral or personal guarantees. Patty Grossman,[21] Executive Director of the Cascadia Revolving Fund in Seattle, says that if a CDC acts as a loan fund or credit union, it is essential that in addition to attracting commercial deposits it should receive foundation support, in order to have a financial reserve enabling it to undertake risky loans. This would allow the CDC to tolerate more than a 3 per cent loss rate. She holds that the heart of the issue is uncollaterised lending. Her experience is that the credit history of the borrower is a better guide to the security of the loan than apparent access to collateral. In her view, CDC financial institutions are best regarded as one channel to business credit, and as a source of assistance to prepare and carry out business plans.

Private non-profit

Perhaps the most popular example of how to deliver capital to informal and small enterprises is the Grameen Bank in Bangladesh. However, it is based in the rural areas of a low-income country and requires subsidy. This section therefore first refers to ACCION International, which operates in urban areas in a number of middle-income Latin American and Caribbean countries. ACCION provides an example of how to supply credit without subsidy and without requiring collateral.

i.   ACCION International
     ACCION's principal goals are to assist in the creation of job opportunities and improve the quality of life for low-income families. ACCION does not implement programmes directly, but rather forms an affiliation with local private development organisations and provides them with technical assistance relevant to programme implementation and institutional development. The services provided by ACCION and the local organisation are credit, training, and organising. The vehicle for these services is commonly a solidarity group, consisting of about five to eight people engaged in similar occupations. The group determines who should receive a loan, and its members assume mutual responsibility for paying back each other's loans. (This is a substitute for collateral and reduces the programme's administrative costs since only one loan is processed for all the group's members.) Once a self-selected group is formed, the members receive training to help constitute the group in a formal manner and to prepare them to operate as a group. At this stage the group members and the programme's field-worker develop a credit application based on a simple analysis of individual members' needs. The credit they receive is used for income-producing activities. It reflects the real cost of lending, is closely controlled for outstanding debts, and includes a monitoring system. The credit made available is short-term and is initially for small amounts like $50. The amount increases once a record of successful repayment is established.
     It is interesting to compare ACCION's lending to solidarity groups with its lending to larger clients, most of whom have a few employees and operate small manufacturing enterprises. Loans to the latter are guaranteed through collateral and co-signers. Loans to members of solidarity groups average $95 per member, whereas those to small entrepreneurs average $517. However, the cost of lending through

solidarity groups is $0,11 per dollar loaned, whereas that for the larger clients is $0,30. In addition, late payment among solidarity groups was 9,7 per cent, whereas that among larger clients was 16,1 per cent. Lending to solidarity groups clearly works.

There are three types of training. Firstly, each solidarity group receives three or four hours of 'orientation and information' before the first loan is approved. Secondly, periodic needs-derived training sessions occur throughout the life of a solidarity group and occur in larger groups of up to twenty-five persons. Thirdly, *ad hoc* individual technical assistance is offered on production issues. There is no formal business training, as ACCION has found this to be of little value at the level of the informal enterprise.

Organising originates from the solidarity groups. It takes the form of collective action to address problems the members face, but the social cohesion they have developed may also enable the solidarity group to address wider community issues. ACCION programmes are accessible to the functionally illiterate, to small businesses, and to women, who often own the smallest enterprises. Fifty-five per cent of ACCION's clients are women. ACCION's success is attributed to:

* loan application procedures which require minimal information and are quickly processed;
* subsequent loans following rapidly on the repayment of the previous loan;
* interest rates set at the commercial rate plus an additional fee for training and other expenses;
* the solidarity group using peer pressure to ensure timely repayment.

ii.   The Grameen Bank[22]

The Grameen Bank provides uncollaterised small loans (the average size is $60) to low-income rural households who lack access to formal credit. The Bank charges an interest rate close to the commercial norm, but one which is none the less subsidised. Lending is implemented through same-gender cells of five members. Six cells are organised into a centre and these in turn form part of a branch. By October 1989 the Bank had 632 branches, with 630 000 active members in 25 600 centres. Eighty-seven per cent of the borrowers are female.

.   The members determine loan utilisation, and before they sanction a loan an individual must convince her colleagues that the proposal is feasible and that there is a good chance of repayment. Initially only two members can receive a loan. No other members of a cell can get a loan if one member is in default. Loan payments start one week after disbursal and have to be repaid in full within a year. The members have an additional motivation to ensure the success of the operation – they control 75 per cent of the issued shares! (The government controls the balance.)

Unlike ACCION International, the members of a cell are not generally in the same occupation. Instead they are organised on the basis of proximity. This, no doubt, reflects their location in rural areas and the difficulties of travelling far.

The Bank has an extraordinarily high repayment rate of 98 per cent. However, its administrative costs are very high, and are met by concessionary financing.

The loans are credited with 'significant' increases in income among recipients. According to Hulme (1990) the Bank's success is related to its ability to constrain the costs incurred as a lending agency and to provide loans at attractive rates. The former is achieved by the high repayment rate and the avoidance of costs which arise from having to follow up on bad loans. The latter is achieved by keeping down the transaction costs that borrowers incur, by keeping the transactions close to the borrower's residence and ensuring there is no need for bribes.

Local authority

Municipal revolving loan funds (RLFs) are especially common in the USA.[23] These are development banks created by local governments in order to make loans for starting up or expanding businesses, as well as for business retention. Their purpose is to serve ventures which banks are reluctant to assist.

RLFs are unlike other forms of municipal development assistance which require ongoing, specific budgetary allocations, in that once the fund has been capitalised, its continued operation is assured through loan repayment. In addition, the RLF probably functions best at some distance from the local authority, since this prevents political criteria from influencing how the loan is steered. In this regard, the board of the RLF desirably combines the private sector, community organisations, and small business representatives. Private participation on the board augments the RLF's financial prudence and increases the likelihood that the RLF can be employed to leverage additional private funding. Interestingly, the RLF itself need not involve more than a technical director and clerical staff, since many of its functions such as loan monitoring, debt collection and legal support can be secured on contract.

Bank CDCs

Banks in the USA have been criticised for taking deposits in low-income communities and subsequently failing to make residential, small business, community development and consumer loans available in those communities. The Community Reinvestment Act of 1977 was passed to prevent the unfair treatment of prospective borrowers and ensure there was no geographic discrimination in lending patterns. The Act places an 'affirmative responsibility' on lending institutions to ascertain community needs and serve neighbourhood businesses, community members and organisations.

In a sense, the Act is comparable to the pressure on South Africa's large corporations to 'invest in the poor'. This pressure is reflected in the 'prescribed assets' debate – should banks and life assurance companies be coerced into devoting a certain proportion of their assets to, say, low-income housing? Recent press reports reveal that life assurance companies are indeed keen to avoid the prospect of prescribed assets, and wish to retain the freedom to choose where they will invest. It appears they are seeking alternative vehicles for social investment and the multi-bank CDC is being advanced in this light.

In the USA the terms of the Community Reinvestment Act are taken into account when, for example, a bank applies to open a deposit-taking facility in a low-income neighbourhood or when it attempts to acquire another bank which has such facilities. Unfortunately, the Act is not very specific about what compliance entails and its provisions are easily evaded. Some banks, though, have responded to the Act by establishing CDCs.[24] For example, while Chase Manhattan had long deliberated about establishing a CDC, it is surely more than coincidence that it set up a CDC soon after the Act was passed.

Bank CDCs are not equivalent to the CDCs depicted earlier, which have community boards and operate as non-profit institutions. Instead, bank CDCs can be founded by individual banks, bank holding companies, or groups of banks and other financial or corporate institutions; they can also take the form of public-private partnerships which link the bank with communities and other private or public investors. By the end of 1990, all but one of the bank CDCs in the USA were incorporated as for-profit institutions. There are about forty bank CDCs.

Sower and Milkman (1991) report that, in general, bank CDCs are established for individual projects, as public relations exercises or serious for-profit concerns. The advantage to banks of establishing CDCs is that they can engage in lending which is otherwise prohibited, either by federal regulation or by their own procedures and standards; and the bank can also invest in (take an equity position in) projects it supports. Especially when the bank CDC is operated as a for-profit enterprise, the regulatory flexibility enables the bank to reach sectors of the market which were previously barred to it.

Bank CDC support for economic development includes low-income housing, small business equity financing, commercial development and speculative industrial buildings, including business incubators. In practice, the bulk of CDC lending is directed towards residential transactions, usually in partnership with public housing agencies; their performance in small business lending is disappointing. Yet were the banks to successfully lend down-market, they would be a most promising institution, as they provide access to major sources of capital.

Access to capital – South Africa

There are many existing and proposed initiatives for small business lending in South Africa. This section examines just a few of the more prominent examples – Get Ahead, the Women's Bank, the Community Banking Project – and concludes with my proposal for a multi-bank CDC.[25]

Group lending, stokvels and Get Ahead

It is widely recognised that South Africa's stokvels make possible a form of group lending.

> A stokvel is a type of credit union in which a group of people enter into an agreement to contribute a fixed amount of money to a common pool weekly, fortnightly or monthly. Then, depending on the rules governing a particular stokvel, this money or a portion of it may be drawn by members either in rotation or in a time of need. This mutual financial assistance is the main purpose of stokvels, but they also have valuable social and entertainment functions ... (Lukhele 1990: 1)

There are various types of stokvels. Most common are savings clubs (41 per cent) and burial societies (21 per cent). Burial societies generally have about eighty members who contribute R39 per month. Savings clubs are more common among the urban, educated elite. They average sixteen members, with contributions in excess of R100 per member per month. The savings clubs have a variety of purposes. For example, members may subscribe funds to start up a business or undertake a shared investment. Alternatively, member subscriptions may be used to capitalise a money-lending institution in the township. Membership in stokvels is voluntary, but acceptance into a stokvel requires the trust of other members and results in peer pressure (and sometimes violence) if there is a failure to contribute. On the other hand, if this failure results from unemployment or hardship in the family, the stokvel is likely to be much more understanding than a formal financial institution.

Stokvels are courted by many of South Africa's financial institutions, in particular by NedPerm which has 80 000 stokvels as customers. One reason for this interest is simply that there are many stokvels and they save a great deal of money. For example, it has been estimated that there are 800 000 stokvels throughout the country, that 24 000 are located in the metropolitan areas, and that the urban stokvels generate an estimated R83 million a month (*Business Day* 11 August 1992).

Another reason for this willingness to deal with stokvels is the perception that lending to stokvels, with their built-in peer pressure to ensure repayment, parallels the successful group-lending practices of the Grameen Bank and ACCION International. However, Mark Peters[26] comments that while peer-group pressure within the traditional stokvel may be effective, it is less so when loans are made to stokvels by banks, since borrowers have a very short-term horizon and feel little obligation to repay loans.

It is in this light that one needs to embark on a sceptical review of Get Ahead. The Get Ahead Foundation's goals are to promote the communal and business interests of Africans. Get Ahead's business activities are primarily focused on micro (stokvel) loans which average R500, are limited to less than R1 000 and are made available without collateral. Get Ahead also offers larger business loans of between R1 000 and R20 000 and training in costing, bookkeeping and marketing.

Get Ahead's resources are limited. Between its inception in 1987 and November 1991, the total value of its micro loans was R4,88 million. Get Ahead is capitalised by individuals, corporate donors, and foreign aid agencies. Notably, Get Ahead's interest rate is 32 per cent, of which 10 per cent represents forced saving and is returned to the borrower once the loan is repaid. This interest rate is about double the prime rate available to large corporations, but is none the less below that of township money-lenders.

Get Ahead lends to what it terms 'stokvels', but this is a bit confusing as they are not stokvels in the sense described above. Instead, Get Ahead's groups consist of about five to nine persons, who need not be in the same business. The loans are used to help people start up and expand their businesses. More than 80 per cent of Get Ahead loan recipients are women. (Sixty per cent of stokvel members are women.) The loans are distributed as follows: hawking – 53 per cent; other retail – 19 per cent; manufacturing – 21 per cent; services – 6 per cent; and other – 1 per cent. On average there are 2,1 labourers in each business receiving a loan from Get Ahead.

Get Ahead claims a 96 per cent loan recovery rate and reports that much of the outstanding 4 per cent is put down to township unrest. This success is attributed to peer pressure and the fact that all the members of a group are 'jointly and severally' responsible for the whole loan. However, other sources hold that Get Ahead would be lucky to recover as much as 60 per cent. Time will tell whether this is an accurate assessment and whether the investment will be fully recovered.

One is a bit uneasy with these assertions since they cannot be substantiated. They do, however, suggest the need for caution in assessing both Get Ahead's performance and whether the model of group lending, implemented by ACCION International, is readily transportable. On the other hand, Get Ahead is important for trying to reach down-market with uncollaterised loans and will provide important lessons for small business lending.

The Women's Bank

The Women's Development Bank (WDB) is in the process of being formed. It will be a non-profit financial intermediary designed to provide women with access to credit and supportive services through a guarantee scheme operated in conjunction with commercial banks. The services to be made available by the WDB are credit facilities, mobilisation of savings, financial advice, and training on WDB delivery mechanisms and informal enterprise. The informal-sector orientation of the WDB is evident in its initial commitment to uncollaterised 'survival' loans of

R250 to R1 000, and micro-enterprise loans of R1 000 to R5 000. The WDB intends to move on later to more sizeable loans.

The role of the WDB is to identify women's groups and to advise for or against the provision of loan financing by the participating bank. Based on the WDB's recommendation, and subject to the bank being satisfied that the group understands its obligations, the bank is obliged to make the loan. The interest rate will be market-related.

The WDB's guarantee to commercial banks will itself be backed by a guarantee from the Development Bank of Southern Africa (DBSA). That is, the WDB is creating an indemnity trust fund, and the DBSA will provide a limited guarantee to a maximum of R250 000 as a back-up for the portion of the credit risk assumed by the trust. The purpose of the trust is to:

- act as principal guarantor to participating commercial banks;
- build up an equity base reducing the responsibility of donors and the DBSA;
- enable the WDB to finance bad debts; and
- render the WDB an income that will cover recurrent costs.

The income sources of the trust will be donations, interest received, and service levies on guarantees provided.

Community Banking Project[27]

The Community Banking Project (CBP) is presently being planned and various conceptions of it have been put forward. If implemented and successful, it will fundamentally improve community access to resources for home and business loans. I have described an early conception, which is closer to the ideals behind the project, and the most recent version, which reflects a more realistic approach.

With regard to the early version, the CBP is dedicated to the 'empowerment of people and communities by ... the establishment of institutional capacity which enables them to manage their own financial resources and access the financial and other resources of the formal sector in the development of their own communities'. This is taken to mean the recycling of funds within the community, community management of those funds, and access to the funds of the formal sector through community based-institutions.

The vehicle for these goals is a family of community banks, which will be 'community owned' in the sense that their profits will be retained in the bank. 'Community' may refer to a geographic area or to some common-interest group such as a labour union. The bank will be managed by elected community representatives, and each bank will have its own identity. This is to enhance community identification with the institution, and minimise the responsibility of other banks for losses. A 'National Community Bank' will provide infrastructure, managerial skills, access to bulk funds, systems and procedures, and training and development for member community banks.

The later version of the CBP envisages the acquisition of a large nationwide financial institution which has total assets of R3 billion, a transmission/savings account client base of 2 million persons, 200 outlets, and capital of R500 million. The intention is to transform the way business is done through a 'Core Bank' so that it becomes the lowest-cost provider of transmission facilities, an effective mobiliser of the savings of low-value clients, an efficient provider of low-cost housing finance, and an institution whose legitimacy enables it to recover costs and earn a satisfactory return on assets.

The vehicle for 'taking banking into the community ... [over] the long term' would be the 'Community Banking Foundation', which would work in partnership with the Core Bank. The Foundation would work with identified communities, establish a basis for the provision of banking services, and develop the capacity of each community to take control of the process. The products and services provided by the community outlets would focus initially on mobilising savings, providing partial collateral security, and establishing the necessary community cohesion. The goal is to have fifty community outlets functioning within six years.

Clearly the nature of the Project has changed substantially. From a family of community banks we now have a Core Bank and a circumscribed Foundation. The CBP would be very exciting, but we can't ignore the fact that if the Core Bank services loans other banks also find acceptable, it will be subject to powerful competition from institutions that offer a broader array of services. Alternatively, if the CBP services more dubious loans, then it will no doubt be welcomed by other financial institutions as a vehicle for relieving political pressure on themselves. In this case, however, the viability of the CBP would again be at stake.

The remarkable ambitiousness of the CBP may also be a flaw. First, the Mondragon co-operatives warn us that taking over existing businesses and transforming them is more difficult than starting from scratch. How easy would it be to transform the internal culture and practices of a large, newly acquired bank? Secondly, the sizeable amount of resources required will subject the CBP to conservative banking values and possibly, therefore, a relative loss of independence.

One hopes the CBP will succeed, but the bets are off.

Proposal for a multi-bank CDC

Why cannot South African banks engage in micro-lending through a multi-bank CDC? Certain observations which support the apparent feasibility of such an institution follow.

i.   The CDC could assume responsibility for the processing costs and could package loans for member banks. This will give the CDC the opportunity to learn the business while the bank takes care of the money.
ii. Processing costs for individuals will be reduced through lending at source and through the use of field-workers.
iii. Processing costs for the CDC will be restrained through shifting the cost of processing individual loans to the solidarity group, and through anticipated high repayment rates that will obviate the need to follow up on individual loans. The CDC's costs will be met by a premium on the loan.
iv. The risk to banks would be minimised through the CDC:
     • being capitalised by a number of banks;
     • starting small, and letting loans increase in size with proof of repayment; and
     • supporting a variety of projects/solidarity groups in many areas.
v.   The CDC Board would consist of representatives from participating banks, community organisations, and small and informal business. The Board should strive to avoid political representatives and a situation where lending is steered through patronage.

However, rather than launch immediately into a national bank CDC, it would be prudent to follow Robert Curvin and Wiseman Nkuhlu's advice.[28] They recommend that one starts with a limited project, selecting three to five sites where there is local mobilisation. The CDC should build local partnerships, and spend a few years gaining experience and coming to understand the elements of success and failure. Only at this stage should the project seriously envisage going national.

Market enhancement

Page and Steel (1984) concluded that *the* greatest stimulus to small enterprises is a growing economy and an increase in demand. Market enhancement programmes mimic the conditions of a growing economy and seek a means of increasing the demand for the products of informal enterprise.

The design of cities

In Chapter 10 David Dewar demonstrates how urban planning and shelter strategies can expand the market for small and informal enterprises. He shows that cities with higher densities, mixed land uses, and effective public transport systems[29] more often achieve the size and diversity of markets necessary for small and informal enterprises to prosper. Then too, urban design – for example, the design of bus termini – also influences whether the opportunities for local traders are enhanced. In my view his suggestions in Chapter 10 outweigh the proposals which follow.

Buy local, sell metropolitan

Low-income neighbourhoods generally have small markets and little economic activity. The result is that they have exceptionally small income and employment multipliers.[30] This means that because local residents spend most of their incomes on goods and services which are manufactured, distributed and sold outside the area, they contribute little to local income and employment generation.

The goal of 'buy local, sell metropolitan' campaigns is to increase the purchase of local goods and services by both local and area-wide businesses, government agencies and residents. At the same time, local manufacturers and retailers can be encouraged to engage in an import-substitution strategy and offer locally what hitherto was only available from external sources.

The types of actions retailers and manufacturers in a low-income neighbourhood can engage in are described below. It is assumed they will be assisted by civics and intermediate organisations.

i. Retailers should draw popular attention to the goods and services available locally, and publicise them.

ii. Retailers should explore ways of making the local shopping area more attractive. This could include both internal appearance and service; external issues such as street plans, parking, and crime; and sponsoring festivals on public holidays which boost allegiance to local retailers. (Note that this may constitute an export strategy, for example, when people from elsewhere in the city feel it safe to enter the neighbourhood and eat at its restaurants.)

iii. Intermediary organisations should guide local manufacturers by identifying those products which can be manufactured locally.

iv. An informal network of services, repairs and retailing probably exists already in the area. Child care, car repair, and the sale of second-hand clothes are examples. With assistance, could any of these enterprises expand and increase both jobs and incomes?

v.   With a view to replacing imports, local businesses, assisted by civics and intermediary organisations, might seek local franchises.

The above strategies should increase local sales somewhat and add to employment creation. However, it has often been demonstrated in America that residents of low-income neighbourhoods prefer to shop outside their neighbourhood, that is, in areas where they can obtain a wide choice, good service, and cheap prices. This is particularly true of consumer durables which involve comparison shopping, as opposed to consumption of daily staples that are often more conveniently purchased at 'mom 'n pop' stores (the American equivalent of South Africa's general dealers and spaza shops).[31] One has ultimately to recognise the constraints on development initiatives when they are targeted at specific neighbourhoods and based on local businesses and community organisations. In particular, the local economy will seldom be able to compete when it comes to manufacturing and marketing consumer durables.

Procurement set-asides[32]

In the USA, local and intermediary organisations pressure industries in the area and also government to engage in procurement set-asides. For example, in order to obtain a municipal contract a private contractor might be obliged to source, say, 20 per cent of the value of the contract from minority-owned business.

There are a few private initiatives in South Africa which have been launched without community pressure, but the country is remarkable for the limited number of such undertakings and the lack of government involvement.

There are two sides to government procurement strategies. On the one hand, given that American minority procurement programmes are closely related to the minority's political power within the constituency, it is to be expected that majority rule in South Africa will introduce government procurement programmes intended to benefit the majority. On the other hand, when the strategy calls for government to obtain goods and services from target groups, this is equivalent to saying that government will not itself undertake the supply of those goods and services – in other words, there will be privatisation. Many oppose such an outcome.

Private initiatives in South Africa involve gold-mining corporations which have attempted to foster small business. Although it goes unsaid, the initiatives are in fact directed at African enterprise. The approaches of the various corporations differ quite a bit. For example, the Anglo American Corporation requires that tenders from small business be competitive with those of other businesses. Anglovaal has a target of 10 per cent of all contracts going to small business, and Johannesburg Consolidated Investment (JCI) simply employs the fact that a tender comes from a small business as a favourable criterion when evaluating potential suppliers.

All three efforts are very small. Anglo's involves eight employees, JCI's a management trainee. The scale of effort probably reflects management's feeling that small business enhancement is the right thing to do, but is not a priority – and also the general sentiment that more extensive small business contracting is impossible due to the lack of entrepreneurs who can supply a product of a given quality on time and at cost. To a considerable degree, therefore, the respective small business units have to identify potential suppliers, provide them with assistance in respect of costing, establishing a financial system, and so on, and convince the buying officers of the companies comprising the corporation to experiment with small enterprises. Due to the limited staff (who, it is estimated, can serve no more than ten clients each), and reluctance on the part of many buying officers, the overall impact is limited.

Rupert McKerron of JCI is exploring the potential for franchising. Initially he focused on the franchisees, for whom JCI would supply some equity capital and the banks some loan capital. More recently he has begun to consider whether the issue might not be as much one of identifying appropriate products and establishing franchisers. This will certainly begin to address the limited reach of the current initiatives.

A further suggestion about how to reach a greater number of small entrepreneurs draws on the American experience, where large contractors develop relationships with minority enterprises and require quality, price competitiveness, and timeous delivery – and help enterprises to achieve these standards. Requiring large companies to subcontract 20 per cent of the value of a contract to African entrepreneurs might seem unreasonable when the company faces global competition; but when the context is one of local engineering companies, all facing the same tender conditions, then the potential inefficiency which might arise may be justifiable. In other words, mentoring relationships within the marketplace appear to be superior to direct contact with the small business units of large corporations.

The problem with these suggestions is that they fail to consider the fundamental conflict about who the target recipients should be. Should the programme have a redistributive focus and target particularly disadvantaged entrepreneurs, or should it promote the expansion of relatively established entrepreneurs who have managerial experience and above-average incomes?

With regard to the former, MacManus (1990) observes that most American minority enterprises are small, sole proprietorships, highly leveraged, and concentrated in retail and service trades. This rather limits the potential for subcontracting. It seems that when redistributive programmes are undertaken, then the beneficiary firms 'fail in droves'. The programmes fail.

On the other hand, if the focus is on the enhancement of African enterprise, then the question might be, why help those who have a proven ability to compete? The answer, it seems, is that in America such firms

- create jobs disproportionately among African-Americans;
- support investment in areas which white enterprises might avoid;
- create positive role models;
- need assistance since they are more highly leveraged (due to the lack of wealth in the African-American community) and consequently are more exposed to changes in the interest rate and economic cycles.

Bates (1985) argues that procurement set-aside programmes cannot forsake efficiency for redistribution, for then they create a permanent dependency on the programme. Indeed, he reflects on the fact that minority enterprises seldom achieve self-sufficiency and graduate into the marketplace. Instead, a few politically well-connected firms garner the bulk of government set-asides. These findings warn us not to assume that the mere fact of procurement set-asides will serve a redistributive function.

At the local level and with a view to taking this strategy further, civics should survey the skills and resources available within the community and see to what extent local entrepreneurs can match goods and services that are bought throughout the metropolitan area. Especially when the goods and services are purchased by government, the community can then pressure government to use local sources.

Should CDCs own enterprises?

The CDC record of owning and operating enterprises in America is dreary, with the single exception being the delivery of social services, the sector in which 86 per cent of CDC-owned and operated enterprises are located (National Congress for Community Economic Development 1989).[33] CDCs used to attempt to promote employment growth through starting their own enterprises, but most were unsuccessful. There has consequently been a shift towards a facilitator role, which entails the supply of equity capital, loans, industrial parks, incubator space and technical assistance. Even the South Shore Bank in Chicago, which has a distinguished record of investing in low-income communities, is reluctant to lend to CDC enterprises.[34] Should we be guided by the American experience?

Despite the fact that CDC staff in America had better training and more management expertise than civics in South Africa can anticipate having, their ventures failed. The main focus of CDC activity nowadays is the creation of stable, quality jobs. The primary vehicle for this is taken to be the expansion of local enterprise through, for example, enhancing access to capital or providing incubators.[35] CDC efforts to promote these enterprises are themselves often undertaken in partnership with government and the private sector in order to filter local businesses into the mainstream (rather than creating local dependencies on CDCs).

An affirmative regulatory and policy environment[36]

Most people now readily accept that 'it is the general economic environment and especially whether government policy is liberal or restrictive which determines whether people are prepared to venture into what is, by its very nature, a risky way of earning a livelihood' (Elkan 1988:181).

Indeed, this topic is nowadays overworked. The importance of small business and the absurdity of restricting it is widely accepted; the removal of restrictions, though, is not easily implemented.

Historical restrictions on African entrepreneurship have come from two sides. The first set of restrictions consisted of prohibitions on African urban entrepreneurs in order to impede employment creation in the urban areas and so restrain African urbanisation. These restrictions are now gone and this represents a major advance for African entrepreneurs.

The second set of restrictions arose from big business lobbying in order to prevent competition, and these restrictions are sustained by the weight of bureaucracy – the rationale for many jobs would dissipate if the regulatory environment were improved. Thus it is that for political reasons all three levels of government move very slowly when it comes to removing zoning, health, traffic, licensing and other regulations. The character of this officialdom is evident in the fact that they are not obliged to provide reasons for their rejection of applications for licences or zoning amendments.

The consequence of these difficulties is that people ignore the laws (and do not pay taxes). Businesses are established and operated. But, with a view to escaping notice, business expansion is constrained. When prosecutions do occur the effect is simply to create entrepreneurs with criminal records.

Rather than licensing inspectors, South Africa's local authorities need small business facilitators. Such an enabling environment appears to be a long way off.

CONCLUSION

Civics present a dilemma. We cannot always be sure that they are representative, many will probably not survive the political transition, and a large number of those that do survive will lack the capacity to implement development projects.

However, these apprehensions should not cause us to discard support for the civics. It seems that the future government will be founded on compromise with the NP and business, and will be indebted to *petit-bourgeois* groups and organised labour. In consequence the urban poor will be poorly served by urban policy and the allocation of resources. Civics and other institutions of civil society come closer to representing the interests of the poor than do any other force in South Africa.

What might the civics do? The preceding material deliberated on the merits of an advocacy role versus that of a development agency. My suggestion was that civics continue to organise in an advocacy mode and that adjacent civics combine to form development agencies. Such agencies will suffer from inadequate funding and be technically weak, but it seems that support from intermediary organisations will enable them to progressively strengthen their capacity.

Development agencies will confront many problems, the parameters of which are only now becoming apparent. For example, it was easy to unite people in opposition to apartheid. It is a great deal more difficult when the area comprises households with different incomes, male- and female-headed households, immigrants and illegal immigrants. Some will be able to pay for the anticipated benefits. Others will not. Illegal immigrants who fear being exposed by an upgrading scheme may oppose a development plan. The complexities are staggering.

The warning lights are also on for development agencies that seek to start co-operatives or own and operate enterprises. Comparative experience is inauspicious. From the point of view of promoting economic development, agencies would be more successful playing a facilitating role, for example:

- ensuring that local enterprises have access to capital;
- negotiating procurement agreements;
- protesting against regulations and other factors which inhibit small enterprise; and
- articulating a local development agenda.

The last function involves:

- canvassing the residents of a town in order to clarify what they view as the problems, opportunities and priorities;
- seeking agreement on the related economic development goals;
- surveying the resources within the community, potential external alliances, and sources of finance;[37]
- ascertaining which economic trends can be affected by community action and local businesspersons, and which are inexorable and not susceptible to local endeavour;
- formulating development strategies and presenting them to the community along with proposals for related projects as a starting-point for debate; and

- selecting a strategy as an advocacy organisation and/or a list of projects for implementation as a development agency.

The philosophy which underlies this approach reverses the civics' previous focus on development needs and appeals for external assistance, and instead tries 'to develop policies and activities based on the capacities, skill, and assets of low-income people and their neighborhoods' (McKnight and Kretzman 1989: 2). The approach is motivated by the belief that community development only takes place when there is local commitment, and the recognition that there are few external resources – whether public assistance or private investment and jobs – available for the community.

NOTES

1. The reference is to institutions that subscribe to the Freedom Charter.
2. The quote is taken from Sandi's response to questions from *Learn and Teach*.
3. For example, see the anonymous article in *Work in Progress* in December 1992.
4. Interview on 9 July 1992 at the Centre for Policy Studies.
5. The information pertaining to CDTs and section 21 companies was supplied by Erica Emdon of EFK Tucker.
6. The Partnership is described below.
7. Shiffman (1990) emphasises that it is important to differentiate between technical assistance groups and financial intermediaries. The former have independent boards and provide client-oriented services. The boards of the latter are accountable to both clients and donors and their function is both to assist clients and to judge whether or not their projects should be funded.
8. This description of LISC is taken directly from documents published by the organisation and also from an interview with Buzz Roberts in LISC's Washington office on 6 February 1992.
9. LIMAC is the Local Initiatives Managed Assets Corporation, a LISC affiliate.
10. Shiffman uses American terms. I have translated them.
11. Only?
12. Planact has still to receive domestic funding and is now dependent on foreign funding.
13. Zenzeleni 'is controlled by a board of trustees of union representatives elected from the union's national executive committee. The trustees appoint a board of directors and a general manager to run the factory. Six elected shop stewards represent workers to management, while two represent workers on the board of directors' (Jaffee 1992: 372).
14. My primary sources for this history are Sperry (1985) and Whyte (1988).
15. In 1986 the group managing the various co-operatives assumed the name of the product with the best-known trademark.
16. He is also known as Don Jose Maria and as Arizmendi.
17. The polytechnic was started first, and provided the technical skills necessary for the subsequent co-operatives.

18. For example, Arizmendi forged the signatures of leaders in the co-operative movement in order to present them with the creation of the bank as a *fait accompli.*
19. This section has largely been culled from Dickstein (1991) and Greenberg (1986).
20. The description is taken from Wiewel and Weintraub (1990).
21. Interview on 20 December 1991.
22. The description of the Grameen Bank is based on Hulme (1990) and Ashe and Cosslett (1989).
23. This section is based on Walker (1990).
24. See the *American Banker*, 28 March 1989, for a lengthy discussion of the issue.
25. See also the Sunnyside Group's useful summary, 'Access to finance for small business: A discussion document' (August 1991).
26. Interview on 18 August 1992.
27. The two descriptions of the Project are taken from 'Community Banking Project' (n.d.) and the later 'The Community Banking Project: Executive Summary' (completed in early 1992).
28. This paragraph is based on an interview with Robert Curvin at the Ford Foundation on 11 February 1992 and correspondence with Professor Nkuhlu.
29. Public transportation systems concentrate consumers at transportation nodes, points at which demand achieves a critical mass, as opposed to automobiles which leave consumers dispersed.
30. There are exceptions. For example, $1 000 of sales by Cuban enterprises in Miami generates another $630 of earnings within the community through subsequent rounds of expenditure. The equivalent figure for black communities in Miami is $140 as subsequent expenditure is largely located outside the community. This may be explained by cultural circumstances and also the fact that Cuban and Chinese entrepreneurs generally supply a greater diversity of goods and services (groceries, restaurants, *and* computer services) to their clients. (See Bendick and Egan 1991)
31. Spaza shops are very small local stores operating out of an individual's home or garage.
32. This section is based on interviews with Johan Kruger (Anglo American Small Business Initiative) on 3 August 1992; Hennie Bornman (Anglovaal Group Business Development Unit) and Rupert McKerron (Johannesburg Consolidated Investment Small Business Unit) on 10 September 1992; and MacManus (1990) and Bates (1985).
33. However, CDCs have proven effective in the rehabilitation and development of housing.
34. Interview with Michael Bennett, Vice-President of the South Shore Bank, on 21 January 1992.
35. An incubator, in the true sense of the word, provides space to fledgling enterprises; shared services such as secretarial staff, photocopying and fax machines; and an internal support network which includes assistance with gaining access to credit, preparing business plans, and other management consulting services. Incubators can be provided by communities or government, and have also been provided by the private sector. In the USA 40 per cent of all incubators are started by economic development agencies, 30 per cent by public-private partnerships, 17 per cent by universities with a view to creating facilities to exploit the products developed by faculty research, and 13 per cent by property developers (Steffens 1992).

    For example, Control Data Corporation used to franchise 'Business and Technology Centers' and 'City Ventures', but they proved unprofitable and the operation has been discontinued. The incubators were successful for the enterprises located in them, but proved a financial drain to Control Data since occupancy rates were low. The point is that a business incubator can only be profitable if the real estate is profitable. This means the building has to be small and have high occupancy. The real estate has to carry itself. But preleasing is not feasible – 'does one go from garage to garage searching for inventors with good ideas?' – with the result that there is a long lease-up period of four to five years. (My thanks to Jack Baloga of Control Data Corporation for these views.)

The general conception of public and community-run incubators is that they offer subsidised rentals, but here one returns to Page and Steel's (1984) warning that the effect is to make cheap jobs expensive. It can be argued that the enterprises located in incubators fail to create much employment. Instead, a few of the businesses that graduate from the incubators in search of larger premises can be a more significant source of employment. In effect, incubators are a long-term strategy whose primary purpose is to foster enterprise. In this light perhaps their major contribution is that whereas most new enterprises go out of business within a few years, it is the exception when this happens to enterprises located in incubators (Steffens 1992). Access to shared services and professional skills, and business camaraderie, clearly serve a purpose.

The South African experience has all too often been one of homeland bureaucrats expending their budgets on creating dreary, subsidised units in God-forsaken locations. Moreover, had the same expenditure been devoted to electrifying township housing, the contribution to the formation and productivity of enterprises would probably have been greater. Backyard enterprises do not need rental subsidies and ongoing administration.

36. This section has benefited from conversation with Gwynn Maine of the Sunnyside Group, 9 September 1992. For more detailed suggestions see the Sunnyside Group's 'Proposal for a small enterprise promotion act', 24 November 1987.

37. McKnight and Kretzman (1989) suggest that we map community capacity and identify:

    i.   Primary building blocks – assets and capacities located inside the neighbourhood and largely under community control. Examples include the skills, talents and experience of residents, individual businesses, personal income, business associations, and religious organisations.

    ii.   Secondary building blocks – assets located within the community but largely controlled by outsiders. Examples include schools, hospitals, libraries and parks.

    iii. Potential building blocks – resources originating outside the neighbourhood and controlled by outsiders. Examples include welfare expenditure, public capital improvement programmes and information.

Council, is that it is 'critically important for the city to be able to tap into the rich resources of the business community'.

Single projects

Public-private partnerships may be forged solely with a view to implementing a single project. The participants may include the local authority, or its quasi-public development agency, and either a company or a consortium.[3]

In the case of single projects, cities might provide the private sector partner with subsidies of some sort, allow crucial zoning variances, or help assemble parcels of land. As a *quid pro quo* they are able to bargain for things like private construction of low-income housing, contributions to the city's housing fund, or provision of public transportation facilities. For example, Park Tower Realty, which the city designated as the redeveloper for New York City's 42nd Street Redevelopment Project, was obliged to renovate the subway station beneath the project.

Bank CDCs

Bank CDCs have already been described. It is worth reiterating that they represent a private contribution to economic development that will be important in certain cities.

Consortia[4]

Consortia represent long-lived public-private attempts to promote urban economic development. Depending on where the consortium is active, its membership will include the local authority, private sector, unions and community organisations. Consortia are of special interest because they approximate the urban coalitions I am advocating in this book. In this section I examine three case studies: Pittsburgh, Baltimore and Detroit.

Pittsburgh is interesting because it contradicts Molotch's rather deterministic assumption that if large enterprises are unaffected by the condition of the local economy, they will do little to sustain it (Molotch 1976). For example, Richard King Mellon, probably Pittsburgh's foremost businessman during the 1940s, expressed a commitment 'to rebuild rather than abandon Pittsburgh'. To this end, in 1943 he formed the Allegheny Conference on Community Development.[5] (Pittsburgh is located in Allegheny County.) The point is that 'the attachment to locality is ideologically as well as economically constructed and, in the case of wealthy investors, does not result directly from dependency' (Fainstein and Fainstein 1991: 40).

Pittsburgh is also interesting because it shows that a city's primary income-earners may include the non-profit sector and demonstrates how a well-developed set of community organisations can be diverted from activism to an array of development projects.

Non-profit organisations represent an involuntary adaptation to a particularly harsh instance of economic restructuring. Table 7.1 makes the point. Between 1979 and 1988, Pittsburgh lost 100 000 manufacturing jobs. The decline was especially dramatic between 1979 and 1983, and accounted for 88 000 of those jobs. In a context of relatively stable total employment, the proportion located in the manufacturing sector declined from 35,4 per cent to 14,3 per cent between 1966 and 1988. Pittsburgh, hitherto a renowned industrial centre, had ceased to be an industrial city. The tragedy can be seen in the fate of Pittsburgh's steel-workers. They experienced a wrenching loss of jobs and face a future, as one of them put it, of 'flipping hamburgers' – low-paid jobs without medical insurance or pensions, and inconveniently located in other parts of the city.

Table 7.1 *Employment in the Pittsburgh metropolitan region (x 1 000)*

	1966	1972	1974	1976	1979	1987	1988
Manufacturing	299	256	266	218	225	124	125
Non-manufacturing	529	605	626	643	689	729	747
Total	828	861	892	861	914	853	872

Source: Sbragia 1990: 54.

Whereas manufacturing had been the city's largest employer, that position is now held by the universities and hospitals, in addition to government. The economic role of non-profits such as universities is evident in the $100 million Department of Defense research contract awarded to Carnegie-Mellon University. University research contracts, and the fact that the hospitals serve patients throughout the region, illustrate how some non-profits can be cast as export industries. The universities, hospitals and banks are now the foundation of Pittsburgh's economy, and development policy strives to exploit the advantages they offer.

An explanation of the role of the consortia requires that we return to the Allegheny Conference. The Conference was initially concerned with physical redevelopment. It hired professionals, developed the ideas, and prepared redevelopment plans. Richard King Mellon's counterpart in the public sector was David Lawrence, who led the state's Democratic Party, was Mayor of Pittsburgh, and later became Governor of Pennsylvania. Lawrence formed the Urban Redevelopment Authority, appointed the board and appointed himself chairman, thereby removing its decisions from public scrutiny. Lawrence was a powerful figure in his own right, and in Pittsburgh a collaborative public-private partnership was formed in which the local authority was an equal partner.[6]

The partnership undertook slum clearance and urban redevelopment and, in the process, dislocated former residents who, by and large, were African-Americans. In later years such programmes, in Pittsburgh and elsewhere, would arouse community opposition, but at the time it seems the city had no alternative ideas and, in any case, was not driven to seek such ideas by organised opposition. Community organisations only entered the picture during the 1970s when Mayor Flaherty made sure that such organisations became a part of the city's political and policy-making equation. Mayor Caliguiri, who followed Flaherty, thereafter ensured that neighbourhood revitalisation was emphasised along with downtown development, but revitalisation and development were still viewed as physical development.

It was only in the 1980s that economic development planning began to focus on development and employment creation through non-profits. The new orientation was epitomised by the Pittsburgh Technology Center which, as an advertising brochure put it, would be

> a hub of innovation, application and production, where emerging technologies are shepherded from creation to implementation. When complete, the Center will provide an attractively designed, high-quality environment to meet the needs of both established and new companies involved in the development or application of advanced technologies. As a means of speeding technology transfer, the University of Pittsburgh and Carnegie-Mellon University are joining forces with the business community. Each university is building an inter-disciplinary research center which will focus on developing and applying new technologies in the fields of biotechnology, bioengineering, artificial intelligence, robotics and computer applications.[7]

It is noteworthy that the Center is being built on the former site of the Jones & Laughlin Hot Strip Mill: the universities are taking over from the firm which was the largest non-governmental employer in Pittsburgh.

A further point regarding the emerging role of non-profits is that they represent new actors. The close relationship between the Allegheny Conference and the Urban Redevelopment Authority does not incorporate the universities and hospitals. Competition between these institutions, who often offer similar services, and the universities' protection of their own tax-exempt status, have created the need for the development of new institutional forms to accommodate these difficulties.

With regard to the community organisations, the fact that they were well organised and received support from Mayors Flaherty and Caliguiri enabled the neighbourhoods to exercise influence on government and facilitate consensual city policy-making. In particular, six CDCs dominate the neighbourhood agenda. Unfortunately, their focus is on the physical aspects of neighbourhood revitalisation rather than on economic development. They are not involved in the partnership and so miss the opportunity to express doubts about whether a strategy of economic transformation which creates high-technology jobs will benefit their constituents. The community organisations are on what they themselves describe as a 'gravy train' and their time has increasingly been devoted to development projects rather than activism.

It seems the CDCs have been diverted from assessing the implications of the city's overall strategy for their neighbourhoods, and are engaged in many small projects which are valuable, certainly, but of less consequence than the city's future development direction. However, one has to concede that their approach might make sense strategically. A strong public partner could not prevent the dramatic restructuring of the city's economy. As Ray Reaves, Director of Planning for Allegheny County, says, 'We're kidding ourselves if we think we can affect what happens, our deals aren't big enough.'[8] Local government directs services and projects to the neighbourhoods; beyond this, perhaps community economic development projects are all that one can hope for.

Pittsburgh is commonly viewed as a city that survived economic restructuring.[9] Before drawing conclusions on the potential lessons for a consortium, it would be best to describe two additional cities: Baltimore and Detroit.

Baltimore is often mentioned as a success story and it too was propelled into the future by a private consortium and a strong mayor. Baltimore is different to Pittsburgh in that only one *Fortune 500* corporation has its headquarters in the city. There was no interlocking group of corporate elites with an interest in sustaining the city. Instead, the Greater Baltimore Committee, comprising the chief executive officers of the city's 100 largest enterprises, was created in 1955. A major influence on the formation of this committee was the Citizens Planning and Housing Association, which supports neighbourhood and economic development and often provides technical advice to neighbourhood groups. Yet, despite a 'long tradition of civic organisations framing, evaluating, and sometimes implementing local economic development policy' (Hula 1990: 212), the premises underlying the Greater Baltimore Committee's first project – the Charles Center redevelopment plan – were that downtown commercial interests were the key to economic revitalisation, and that private enterprise should bear most (95,4 per cent) of the $180 million cost.

The second major project was the revitalisation of the Inner Harbor area. However, this project, intended for offices, commerce and tourism, was viewed as more speculative, and public subsidy was required for it to proceed. Both projects were successful, the latter spectacularly so. For example, instead of the anticipated construction of 150 000 square feet for retail and tourism space, one million square feet were supplied. Similarly, instead of supplying 200 to 300 hotel rooms, 3 500 were supplied. Over 18 million people visited the Inner Harbor during its first year.

The public counterpart to the Greater Baltimore Committee was Mayor Schaefer. Implementation of the Charles Center plan began prior to his election in 1971, but the Inner Harbor project stalled with little business support. His perseverance was necessary to 'get things done'. He was centrally responsible for Baltimore's successes, and the reputation he gained later saw to his election as Governor of Maryland.

Aside from the successes in terms of physical redevelopment, commerce and real estate, have the developments benefited Baltimore? Between 1970 and 1987 Baltimore lost over 50 000 manufacturing jobs and over 14 000 infrastructure jobs. However, the city also gained 36 000 service jobs, ending up with a net loss of 47 000 jobs. The question, then, is who benefited from this restructuring? The major growth in employment occurred in medical, financial, social and legal services. Surprisingly, tourism contributed only 2 000 additional jobs. Because of the character of medical and financial jobs, few benefits have been conveyed to the low-income residents of Baltimore; it is evident there is not an 'automatic link between downtown prosperity and neighbourhood well-being' (Hula 1990: 209). This problem raises two issues. First, the decisions were made by the private sector, and the mayor merely assisted its efforts. Secondly, had the community been more closely involved, could its demands have made a difference?

Some of the projects which one would have expected a community organisation to demand were undertaken by the city. For example, firms receiving financial assistance from the city were required to look to the city's Manpower Program for new employees and training. These firms were also required to pass work on to minority subcontractors. In addition, through the Baltimore Economic Development Corporation, the city attempted ancillary development schemes, including industrial land banking, the creation of business incubators and a free enterprise zone. These efforts notwithstanding, the most recent statistics show a continuing decline in manufacturing jobs. The Development Corporation now attempts to foster indigenous enterprise through the creation of a research centre and a waterfront business park. Again, it seems that few benefits will be conveyed to small enterprises and low-income groups.

The alternative to Pittsburgh and Baltimore is perhaps most graphically represented by **Detroit**. The city's urban fabric is falling apart and low-income neighbourhoods are 'disappearing' amid destruction and decay.

Two comparisons with Pittsburgh stand out. Pittsburgh used to be a one-industry town, dependent on steel. Detroit still is a one-industry town, dependent on an ever-declining number of automobile jobs. In addition, both cities have been home to transnational corporate elites; the difference is that in Pittsburgh they acted to safeguard the physical environment of the city, whereas in Detroit their engagement was sporadic and minor. For the most part they disinvested from the city.

A major contrast between Detroit and Pittsburgh lies in the nature of African-American politics in the two cities. African-Americans represent 25 per cent of Pittsburgh's population. They are dispersed among a number of neighbourhoods and riven by factional disputes. In Pittsburgh local politics takes the form of neighbourhood organisation rather than being structured along racial and class lines. Development assistance has largely gone to well-organised neighbourhoods and their CDCs.

In 1980, African-Americans constituted 65 per cent of Detroit's population. Between 1960 and 1980 the city experienced an extreme case of 'white flight' as its white population declined from 1 138 000 to 414 000 persons. Detroit is now among America's most segregated cities and local politics is specifically structured by racial issues. This is not to say that neighbourhood organisations have failed to organise, but their activism has been directed at unsuccessful attempts to block various office, university, medical and residential developments.[10]

Detroit has also lacked strong leadership for development purposes. Until the early 1970s Detroit suffered from an 'institutional hodgepodge', which meant that it lacked the ability to formulate a clear-sighted development strategy. In addition, since his election in 1974, Mayor Coleman Young has shown little concern for neighbourhoods and has targeted resources at industrial and riverfront development. The perceived need to concentrate investment for maximum effect is understandable given Detroit's loss of 98 000 manufacturing jobs between 1967 and 1982, and given also its advancing urban decay. However, the Baltimore example suggests that even if Detroit's Renaissance Center office development had proven successful, there would still have been few benefits for the city's low-income residents.

Further, the private sector had little motivation to contribute to Detroit's development. The spur to its activities was the 1967 riots rather than any enduring allegiance to the city itself. Indeed, of the Big Three car companies, only General Motors has its headquarters in the city – and it is not a 'city booster'. Thomas (1989: 148) hypothesises that the 'absence of a stronger redevelopment leadership by the economic elite' is also caused by the prominence of the Union of Automobile Workers in Detroit.

This tale of three cities argues against generalisation, but a few seem indisputable.

i.   Downtown redevelopment does not anchor the local economy.
ii. One should not side with Molotch (1976) and dismiss consortia as representing growth coalitions which articulate their self-interest solely in material terms. As Fainstein and Fainstein (1991) observe, Pittsburgh was more dependent on Mellon than Mellon was on Pittsburgh. Corporate leaders often develop attachments to cities which cannot be explained by corporate self-interest.
iii. Cities and their populations should be grateful if effective consortia arise. Yet, to be grateful is not to be blinded to the fact that consortia articulate a development agenda that reflects power relationships within the city.
iv. The initiatives taken by strong development mayors in Pittsburgh and Baltimore have been heartening, but one has to wonder about their capacity for independent action. Their strength lay in their

ability to assist the private sector with the formulation and implementation of development plans.

v.   The efforts of community organisations are easily side-tracked. For example, in Pittsburgh the mayor was able to spread resources to neighbourhoods, but liaison with the neighbourhoods and the formulation of development strategies were two distinct, parallel activities. Pittsburgh's CDCs were encouraged to do their thing while the consortia and the mayor plotted the city's future.

vi. Progressive groups should strive to articulate an alternative agenda which serves the economic potential and needs of low-income groups.

vii. All three examples demonstrate that if communities are to strive for more, then the issue is one of organisation and confrontation. The depoliticisation of local development strategies does not serve their interests. Their aim should be to participate in the formulation of development strategies, to ensure hard bargaining over the allocation of public resources, and to initiate development programmes which reach into the neighbourhoods.

Private development initiatives[11]

In addition to public-private partnerships, there are private initiatives that occur at arm's-length from local government. The source of these initiatives varies: they can be undertaken by individual companies, a consortium, business councils and, of course, institutions like the Chamber of Commerce. Of interest to us are the initiatives intended to affect a city or state's development policy and promote business development.

With regard to development policy initiatives, a further American example is apposite.

> The Business Council of Pennsylvania, Cleveland Tomorrow and the Bay Area Council, Inc. were formed by and remain dominated by top level business executives interested in influencing economic development policy. Generally, each was created in response to a prolonged period of economic decline and change. Their major activities are overall strategy development, advocacy and serving as forums for the discussion of important economic development issues. Operating at the regional or state level, each functions as a co-ordinating body on issues of local concern. Topics may include legislation, regulations or specific development projects. In addition, they have become

involved in some aspect of marketing their area and recruiting industry. ... Critical to the process and success of these organisations
is the fact that a group of CEOs of a similar mind can influence
public sector decisionmakers. (National Council for Urban Economic
Development 1984: 15)

Private sector development boards and corporations are organised as
non-profit corporations and have the same tax status as a chamber of
commerce. Their business development activities parallel the activities of
public and quasi-public development agencies. For example, they might
formulate and implement industrial attraction activities, target specific
industries for business retention, operate venture capital funds, and,
more generally, advocate measures to improve the business climate.

The private policy initiatives just mentioned use member contributions
and foundation grants and have never sought public assistance. In
general, business development corporations avoid using public funds as
part of their operating budget, but may seek public support for specific
projects or for projects directed at, say, minorities. It is in this sense that
they retain an arm's-length relationship with the public sector. Yet clearly
their agenda centres on public policy, regulations, and the allocation of
public resources.

The capacity of PSDOs to promote business development in addition
to their other activities depends on whether they are engaged in effective
public-private partnerships as well. For example, they can engage in
research and occasionally use public dollars to promote commercial
revitalisation, but if they are also to assist small enterprises with soft
loans and offer concessions as part of their business attraction programmes, then this presupposes some designated authority from, or
close co-ordination with, public authorities.

Chambers of commerce

Chambers of commerce occasionally act like PSDOs, but more usually are
member-driven organisations with more parochial interests. Like PSDOs,
they cannot offer soft loans to small businesses, invest in infrastructure or
provide worker training programmes. Thus, when a Chamber indicates
that it promotes small business, this means that it counsels its members.
PSDOs are often a reaction against the perception that Chambers are not
doing enough, and the result is tension between the two organisations – a
bit of a turf war.

SOUTH AFRICAN SURVEY

Attempts by business to promote local economic development can probably be divided into four categories:

- attempts to assist small business;
- indirect contributions via chambers of business, financial support for the Consultative Business Movement (CBM) and, for example, the funding of forum meetings (by providing premises and meals);
- participation in local initiatives; and
- adoption of a leading role in promoting local economic development.

Assistance to small business

There are many private schemes to assist small business. The Centre for Developing Business at the University of the Witwatersrand identified 89 institutions engaged in small business promotion. The activities and their distribution are: consulting (71); training centres (64); seminars (56); marketing support (51); research (49); lobbying (38); publications (37); legal advice (24); provision of premises (23); training of small-business consultants of other organisations (22); commercial loans (21); subsidised loans (less collateral and/or lower interest than banks) (20); venture capital (14); financial support to other development institutions (wholesaler) (7); and correspondence courses (5).

However, this list is flattering. Many of the surveyed institutions described activities that are included in their mandate rather than what they are actually doing. In the view of Mark Peters[12] of the Centre for Developing Business, not much is being done. Many institutions are concerned with small business issues, and many are prepared to contribute resources, but there is uncertainty regarding what might be attempted.

Conspicuously absent from the list are procurement strategies by local government and business. The areas of greatest activity are also worth noting: training, seminars, consulting, research, and marketing support. With the exception of marketing support,[13] these are precisely the types of activity that Page and Steel (1984) argue have the contrary effect of rendering expensive what was formerly a process of cheap employment creation.

Initiatives pertaining to access to capital, market enhancement and the regulatory environment were described in the preceding chapter. It suffices here to describe what is probably the most comprehensive private attempt to promote small business.

The Anglo American and De Beers Small Business Initiative (SBI) has three components – contracting, LITET[14] and the advisory centres.[15]

Contracting promotes the procurement of goods and services from small businesses. All contracts are governed by strict commercial considerations, requiring competitive pricing and high standards of quality and reliability. Unlike some other mining houses we do not specify that say 10% of contracts *must* go to small business as this will certainly negate the commercial principles we employ. However, the Unit does provide assistance such as implementing financial systems, assists with costing, advice in respect of quality control, simplified tender documents and even sometimes training. The Unit has assisted 106 small businesses of which approximately 65% are non-white. The value of these contracts at close of business on 31 December 1991 stood at R35 million. We hope to improve significantly on this figure in 1992. The success ratio of winning contracts for small business is approximately 20%.

LITET changed its focus from the creation of labour-intensive industries to taking minority equity stakes in emerging small businesses. LITET might also grant bridging finance to such small businesses in which they have invested. The loans bear reduced interest rates – i.e. below prime rate. ... LITET has greater potential than the contracting of small businesses into meaningful businesses which could participate in the mainstream economic activity of this country. The types of businesses LITET has invested in include companies in the fields of industrial cleaning, industrial catering, light engineering, retailing, pallet manufacture, import/export trading and a public telephone service.

In order to amplify the efforts of the SBI over a wider geographic area, **advisory centres** have been established in Welkom and Witbank. These centres ... play a key role in identifying opportunities for small businesses in their respective areas and in providing assistance with feasibility studies, costing and bookkeeping. In addition, the technical expertise of group employees is made available to small businesses interacting with the Group. (Fax from Johan Kruger dated 2 October 1992.)

Indirect contributions

A great deal of what the private sector does has very little immediate return. For example, I have attended numerous development conferences, workshops and forums where some corporation is credited with funding the venue and a meal. The corporation dispenses its social budget in this way but cannot be said to be directly engaging in development planning.

All too often, the participants in the conferences and workshops do nothing more than wallow in the muck. This was the title I bestowed upon a recent policy workshop where we yet again debated the role of civics, the negotiation process, and the development potential of the forums. The economy may be suffering but these workshops represent a growth industry, and hoteliers who have positioned their establishments in this market must be doing rather well.

Is such cynicism justified? Those attending these workshops are generally confused about their potential roles and responsibilities. They seem to think that development will result from the mere fact of talking to one another. This confusion regarding roles and responsibilities is widespread. Unions usually only participate at the regional level. This is true of the PWV Economic Development Forum, where competition among the centres suggests that the chances of reaching consensus on development programmes will be remote. (Metropolitan initiatives, such as the DFR Metropolitan Development Forum, face this obstacle to a far lesser degree.) Civics make do with listing their needs. Persons in local government often seek means of stimulating the local economy, but being uncertain of how to proceed make do with marketing efforts. Many in business are uncertain about collaborative relationships with the public sector and unions, and also about whether it is desirable to intervene proactively in the local economy.

In large part it is only a few individuals and service organisations who are beginning to articulate what the forums might contribute. But the service organisations, with their leftist inclinations, are often overly hopeful about the balance of power between communities and the private sector and also about what community organisations might hope to achieve.

This cynicism is unfair to select organisations such as the CBM. CBM is a voluntary organisation of senior business leaders and corporations who 'support the need for constructive transformation of South Africa's political economy'. CBM believes that management and ownership of the economy must be broadened to include labour and communities, and desires conditions and structures that support economic growth and a fair distribution of wealth. The service CBM provides is process consultation, which is 'a non-partisan method of consulting and communicating with political and community groups across the political spectrum in order to identify common goals and strategies'. CBM's role in facilitating the PWV Forum is an important service, as is its contribution to the NEF.[16]

In general, though, it is probably fair to conclude that the privately funded workshops should be perceived in different terms – as bringing opponents to the table and leading to mutual understanding. This is an important benefit. But it is unfortunate that so few of the forums are moving beyond a listing of needs and the search for resources to redress past wrongs. Economic development and the possibilities for development planning are seldom explored.

Chambers of business

I surveyed all the country's chambers of business, commerce or industry that are affiliated with the South African Chamber of Business and asked the following questions. Do you engage in activities intended to promote economic development within your area? For example, do you attempt to:

- attract industry?
- market the products of your members elsewhere in South Africa?
- market the products of your members elsewhere in Africa and overseas?
- provide assistance to small businesses?
- co-operate with the local authority in the formulation of local development strategies?
- co-operate with the local authorities in the formulation and implementation of privatisation strategies?
- co-operate with community organisations (church groups, civics, women's groups) to provide business services?
- co-operate with unions to chart a local development strategy or to resolve local labour issues?

If your answer to any of the above is 'yes', please elaborate.

To my surprise there were 'yes' (and 'no') answers to all the above questions. Positive answers tended to relate to attracting industry, co-operating with a local authority in the formulation of development strategies, providing assistance to small business and co-operating with community organisations and unions in the formulation of development strategies. The negative answers related to marketing the products of members and formulating privatisation strategies. This was particularly true of the smaller chambers.

The involvement in local development strategies takes place through local initiatives, and other efforts such as the urban development plans which are funded by the DBSA in many centres throughout the country. The chambers appear predisposed to contributing to local development. It seems they operate with a degree of sophistication that is surely induced by contacts with American and European counterparts. Thus, for example, the chambers:

- communicate with visiting business people, visiting chambers, and trade delegations;
- lead trade delegations overseas;
- publish trade digests for other chambers;
- use the South African Foreign Trade Organisation as a vehicle for marketing members' goods and services;
- attempt to formulate and/or support regulations and policies that favour informal and small businesses;
- initiate local development planning and participate in attempts by local authorities to market an area;
- consult directly with councils about how to increase the proportion of goods and services supplied by the private sector;
- co-operate with community organisations in respect of housing and other local initiatives; and
- participate with unions in forums which are mandated to prepare development strategies.

Participation in local initiatives

Business participation with government and civics in local initiatives has already been described in a number of places in this book. The chapters by Roland Hunter and by Jenny Robinson and Carlos Boldogh also consider the issue in detail. Little purpose is served in repeating the same material. It is much more interesting to speculate on the role of business when it *leads* development.

Business leading local development planning

Durban provides two obvious examples of what business has already done. One is Operation Jumpstart; the other is the Greater Durban

Marketing Authority (see Chapter 8). But the above material on consortia suggests a much more embracing model where business both seeks an economic development strategy that will chart new growth paths, and commits resources once investment opportunities have been identified. This generally translates into a strategic planning exercise and the preparation and implementation of a development programme.

A STRATEGIC PLANNING EXERCISE

Having examined a wide range of local authority, community and private efforts at development planning, we are at last in a position to describe the content of a strategic planning exercise.

The exercise should not take the form of a corporatist gathering of elites from the public and private sectors and from labour. The success of economic development strategies will depend on their political legitimacy. Rhode Island's experience with the Greenhouse Compact shows that planning has to build a constituency, both through who participates and through who pays or benefits. Thus I envisage that a coalition in Johannesburg would include local politicians, utility companies, large and small entrepreneurs, civics (who lack economic power but may be critical to legitimacy), and unions.

The key elements of a strategic plan 'are the establishment of long-term economic goals that may realistically be met, an audit and analysis of internal strengths and weaknesses, and an assessment of opportunities in the external world that may be exploited by the [area's] comparative advantages' (Eisinger 1988: 27).

The strategic plan should provide direction for a subsequent multi-faceted development programme which includes, for example, public and private investment programmes, changes in the regulatory environment, reorganisation of the institutional infrastructure to facilitate development and capacity-building training programmes.

The planning exercise can be disaggregated into the following components, which are intended to be illustrative, not exhaustive.

i.   Identify and prioritise development problems.
ii. Survey the public, private and community resources available to deal with the problems.
iii. Study national and international market trends with a view to determining potential niches which can be served by local entrepreneurs.
iv. Identify sources of competition, again national and international, for

domestic producers, and interpret their likely impact on the regional and local economy. Which industries have growth potential? Which industries have a comparative advantage?[17]

v. Determine:
   - which markets are accessible to local entrepreneurs;
   - which local industrial sectors employ a higher proportion of semi-skilled and unskilled labour; and
   - which local industrial sectors offer greater potential for expanding local linkage networks.

vi. Examine the capacity of the public sector to engage in the sourcing of supplies and services from small and community enterprises.

vii. Examine the capacity of community organisations to engage in the delivery of housing and other goods and services, to operate community enterprises and to facilitate the creation and expansion of small enterprises.

viii. Explore a tripartite development compact between government, management and the unions that:
   - enhances the competitiveness of local enterprise;
   - supports old and troubled industries;
   - attracts new industries; and
   - enables access to export markets.

Note that this will mean accepting the need for an improved business climate, investment in transportation and communications infrastructure, research in high-wage industries in which the city has a comparative advantage, a commitment by management to invest in target industries, and cut-backs on the workers' social wage.

ix. Prepare a development programme. This should detail the projects, budgetary implications and implementational responsibility necessary to create new growth paths for the local economy.

This presentation pre-empts discussion of whether a development strategy is desirable in the first place. While conservatives and neo-liberals debate the merits of industrial strategies, cities, states and countries around the world get on with implementing them. I have assumed that it is fatuous to debate this question in South Africa. This is because the ANC, COSATU and many business organisations accept that South Africa requires an *active* economic and industrial strategy which is directed at promoting both growth and redistribution. For us, the issue is not whether there should be such a strategy, but rather how successfully we are able to formulate and implement it at the local and metropolitan levels.

NOTES

1. It is notable that Africa's economic decline was not preceded by a fall in the amount of capital available for investment (measured as a proportion of the GDP). Instead, the blame lay in the allocation of resources to projects with a low rate of return, a slow rate of employment creation and a high capital output ratio. The same is true of public investment in South Africa.

2. Given that his retirement package from First Chicago pays him $780 000 per annum, Sullivan intends to donate his $118 000 New York City salary to charity!

3. This kind of consortium is devoted to a single project. In a separate section below we deal with consortia that play an ongoing role in development.

4. This section is based on Clark (1989), Fainstein and Fainstein (1991), Sbragia (1989), Sbragia (1990), and on interviews conducted in Pittsburgh between 25 and 29 September 1991.

5. His ability to form the Conference was enhanced by the fact that Pittsburgh has an extreme case of interlocking boards of directors. If development efforts are enhanced by personal contacts among corporate leaders, should we be encouraged by the fact that South Africa also has interlocking directorships?

6. One has to wonder whether the sense of equality would have been as pronounced if the local authority had had a different agenda. The impression one has is of a meeting of minds in an 'old boys' club'.

7. Bob Gleeson of Carnegie-Mellon University reports that the Pittsburgh Technology Center occupies a 49-acre site and has benefited from a $42 million public sector contribution. The site has been cleared and serviced but there has been no private take-up. The city has offered $17 million grants to the University of Pittsburgh and to Carnegie-Mellon to move ahead with their investment and to leverage private investment, and the facilities are under construction for both universities.

8. Discussion with Reaves was refreshingly realistic. He maintains that one has to beware of people involved in economic development. It is as if they have become so involved in marketing and the search for funds that they are unable to evaluate their own activities critically, or perhaps it is that they are unwilling to reveal their conclusions to outsiders.

9. The same is not true of some adjacent towns whose economies were solely dependent on the steel mills: they now look like ghost towns.

10. Interestingly, though, the protests caused the state to promulgate a law in 1972 which required that citizens' groups help direct redevelopment projects.

11. The next two sections are based on two reviews by the National Council for Urban Economic Development (1984, 1991) and a number of conversations with Kenneth Poole, Director of Technical Assistance and Research of the NCUED.

12. Interview on 18 August 1992.

13. This consists simply of marketing services provided by someone other than the entrepreneur producing the good or service. The marketing service may just involve producing and distributing brochures, or it may take the form of the Purchasing Centre, currently being established in Durban, where African entrepreneurs can shop for contracts to supply goods and services to large corporations. The entrepreneurs will also receive assistance in how to tender and receive loans, and the representation of the KwaZulu Finance Corporation and the Small Business Development Corporation at the Centre is intended to ensure access to capital.

14. LITET refers to the creation of labour-intensive industries.
15. This section is largely based on discussion and correspondence with Johan Kruger of the Small Business Initiative.
16. A similar service provided by the Institute for a Democratic Alternative for South Africa is described by Wyley and Talbot (1993).
17. See Carlson and Wiewel (1991) for a guide to industrial targeting.

Chapter 8

Operation Jumpstart
An Urban Growth Initiative in
the Durban Functional Region

Jennifer Robinson and Carlos Boldogh
for the Built Environment Support Group

During the 1990s there have been a number of locally based efforts to stimulate economic growth in South Africa's metropolitan areas. In the Durban Functional Region (DFR) much research and consultancy activity has been generated by a growing realisation on the part of business and local government that Durban faces a dire economic future unless urgent measures are taken to redress the local political and economic decline. There is no gainsaying the seriousness of the position: a national economic crisis is overlaid by a regional political situation characterised by endemic violence, as conflict between the ANC and regionally-based Inkatha has interacted with complex material and social forces operating at a micro level. Marketing the locality and attracting investment in such circumstances are difficult tasks.

Operation Jumpstart (OJ) – a broad coalition of public and private interest groups in the DFR – was born in late 1990 and arose at least partly in response to the crisis in the region. OJ declared that its aim was to stimulate, or 'kickstart', the local economy. As this chapter will suggest, its impact has been both limited and ambiguous in terms of a number of different criteria, but from the point of view of those interested in the wider problem of facilitating urban economic growth, OJ offers a most instructive case study.

We will demonstrate that the experience of OJ speaks to the following issues: the appropriate form for local growth coalitions, the value of different development projects, and the central limiting role of political and institutional factors in growth initiatives in the current transitional period. We will address, firstly, the origins and formation of OJ and then discuss in some detail two of the development initiatives in which it was crucially involved. Finally, we will assess OJ in terms of its value as a model for future efforts at local urban development.

THE ORIGINS OF OPERATION JUMPSTART

OJ was launched in October 1990 at an Economic Development Conference held in the Durban City Hall. The event was hosted by the white Durban City Council and facilitated by a prominent firm of management consultants, Deloitte Pim Goldby. After a number of addresses by people ranging from Simon Brand of the Development Bank to Don Mkhwanazi of the ANC and Bobby Godsell from Anglo American, the conference divided into predefined 'action groups' to discuss a variety of different topics which the organisers had identified as crucial to the future of economic growth in the DFR. At the end of the conference, a Steering Committee was appointed with representatives from each of the action groups, as well as from major players in the region (the city councils, ANC, Inkatha, the provincial administration and the Joint Services Board). Before we describe these action groups or discuss the activities of Jumpstart, however, it will be useful to explore the prehistory of the Economic Development Conference and of Jumpstart itself, for it was in this early phase that the foundations for Jumpstart's later activities were laid.

The various participants in OJ have somewhat disparate views on 'how OJ started'. The different accounts, which are clearly based upon the participants' various experiences and ideological preferences, range from the view that OJ's 'source can be found in Arthur Anderson's work on San Francisco, and the SWOT (strengths, weaknesses, opportunities and threats) technique that was used in Pietermaritzburg 2000' and adopted by Deloitte Pim Goldby in their research into Durban's economy (Procter 1992); to the argument that OJ was a straightforward derivative of the Victoria & Alfred Waterfront development in Cape Town. The ideas behind this development filtered up to Durban through consultants such as Roland Starkey, who became a key player in OJ. Starkey has argued that 'when I came to Durban, I gave the papers I had been using to a colleague of mine, who went and saw Jan Venter (then Mayor of Durban). To his credit, he picked up the opportunity' (Starkey 1992). Simultaneously, a more technical initiative was taking place in the City's planning bureaucracy and a series of technical reports were drawn up concerned with the 'workings' of the region. Furthermore, 'pressure from various private sector directions and community sectors' came to fruition during the short period between 1988 and 1990, when the Tongaat-Hulett[1] Planning Forum was established, with Umgeni Water, the Natal Provincial Administration (NPA), and the Durban City Council (DCC) working more or less in parallel on a 'City-Region' initiative that intended to identify and tackle the DFR's various developmental crises.

The most direct instigator of OJ, however, was the DCC. Early in 1990 the DCC decided to set up, by itself, a Project Steering Committee (PSC) which would co-ordinate economic development in the DFR. This committee consisted of representatives of the DCC, the Durban Chamber of Commerce, the Natal Chamber of Industries, the KwaZulu/Natal Chamber of Commerce, Spoornet, Portnet, and the Small Business Development Corporation. The PSC believed that 'with the aid of Pim Goldby Consultants acting as facilitators, this group [would] set about developing a set of outline strategies and action plans for the region' (Van Kralingen 1990a: 2). After much research and debate, the following strategies for promoting local economic growth were recommended:

- promoting and marketing the DFR to local and overseas investors;
- identifying and assisting in the development of major projects, for example, the harbour and Point areas;
- reducing the difficulties in obtaining permission for development;
- cutting out unnecessary bureaucratic controls;
- developing the DFR's infrastructure in respect of water, serviced stands, industrial land, electricity and transport networks;
- developing innovative funding avenues to provide capital for development;
- encouraging the development of small business;
- promoting technical training, and upgrading education and health services; and
- promoting job creation where this is economically justified.

To begin with, the council proposed a major International Investors' Conference for the region. This was aimed at promoting Durban as a place for future investment by foreign capital which, they hoped, would be streaming back to South Africa once the post-apartheid order had been established. The 'post-apartheid' era, then, signalled the ending of restraints on international contacts, and the opportunity for capital to take centre stage in future plans for economic growth. But the council's consultants cautioned against an international conference: Durban's negative image was not very attractive for business, they argued, and unless the council actually lied about the conditions, investors were more likely to be frightened away by such an event. Instead, the council and their consultants decided on a locally based, more participatory conference which would attempt to overcome the obstacles to investment in the area, and thereby create the conditions for future international investment. The conference was scheduled for November 1990.

The participation process involved taking a brief and somewhat unoriginal analysis of Durban's strengths, weaknesses, opportunities and threats to a variety of identified interest groups in the area. While certain political organisations were invited to presentations, the consultants concentrated on approaches to the business community. Their lack of experience of extra-parliamentary groups probably resulted in an incomplete inventory of interest groups, and community representatives certainly express the feeling that they were not properly included in the participation process.

Rather naively, however, the PSC under the guidance of Pim Goldby's Mike van Kralingen did not count on the World Bank, who had been invited to the Investors' Conference, contacting the ANC for advice. The ANC's response was blunt. They argued that while they supported development initiatives in the DFR and were themselves involved in one such initiative (together with the Urban Foundation, the Joint Services Board and Tongaat-Hulett), they felt nevertheless that 'the time is not ripe for such a conference simply because (i) major actors were not consulted ... and (ii) the key white political actors organising this conference have just recently been involved in political machinations which ensure the character of the city council remains very conservative' (Mji 1990).

The Council and Pim Goldby retreated rather rapidly and within three days negotiations were set up between the ANC and Jan Venter on behalf of the City (Sutcliffe 1992). The City immediately offered to publish a joint press statement with the ANC to the effect that 'Councillor Venter, as Mayor of the City of Durban ... confirms the City of Durban's commitment to the move towards negotiated democratic national and local government' (*Daily News* 30 September 1990). Pim Goldby decided to go ahead with preparations for the November conference, albeit with informal liaison with the ANC, since

> an apolitical framework would be put in place within which the entire DFR community could participate on a consultative and mutual self-interest basis ... with the ANC [playing a key role] in the

parent Economic Development Committee (EDC) as well as in each of the sub-committees concerned with:

- core development projects
- big business development
- small business development
- health, housing and infrastructure
- education and training, and
- land use and regulation. (Van Kralingen 1990b)

SOME INITIAL ASSESSMENTS

'Behind-the-scenes politics' comprise a large part of the activities of states everywhere, and are frequently very important in local economic development initiatives (Grant 1990), but the phrase is perhaps even more appropriate in relation to those actors who are never seen as political agents at all, those who are permanently off the public stage. In the case of urban development initiatives in South Africa at the moment, it is the management consultant who is shaping the politics of the future from this off-stage position. The implications for political accountability are of course serious, but in addition, the 'formula' approach to urban development (Harvey 1989) is mediated through these agents, who emerge as important makers of urban environments of the future in the place of states, or once influential professionals such as health officers. With the professional ideas of planners, engineers, finance officers and others relocated from the public sector to the private sector and infused with the private enterprise spirit reflected in the high fees charged by consultants, we certainly see a new force emerging to shape our cities, one closely tied up with the restructuring of the service sector internationally.

In Durban one particular consulting firm has redesigned the management structure of the city, seeking to reorient all transactions and services – even those within the city bureaucracy – to the 'market'. This firm has also acted as the prime co-ordinator of Operation Jumpstart. In addition, people from consultancy backgrounds are very heavily involved in the various committees of OJ. Three of the seven elected/appointed members of the steering committee are present or former employees of management consulting firms and these actors, who have a common background and approach, can potentially exert a great deal of influence. The consultants on the whole promote a pro-capitalist, pro-growth position, and suggest that wider social development ('upliftment') projects are relatively valueless in the problematic area of urban development: if anything, these projects represent constraints on the possibilities for development. Such ideas coincide well with those presented by the various business interests involved.

Because of the ANC's rather belated involvement in the proceedings, many aspects of the November development conference had already been decided upon, including the allocation of chairpersons to the various sub-committees which were to be formed at the conference. However, from this point onwards, crucial contributions from regional ANC members shaped the broad agenda of the conference, and certainly influenced the strong populist tone of the address delivered there by the conservative Mayor. In a signed press statement the ANC declared that they saw 'the need for an economic development initiative for the benefit of the region as a whole, [and expressed] their resolve to participate fully and positively as a key player in the Economic Development Committee to be set up at the conference in November'.

Clearly both of the major alliances here – the state and business on the one hand, and the ANC and community organisations on the other – have made something of a compromise: the former has incorporated left-wing forces in the city into the coalition, and the latter has become involved in a process which more conservative state and business interests have already shaped, at least partially, and definitely dominate. The outcomes of this compromise will become evident in the discussion which follows on the activities of OJ.

An important point to emerge from this prehistory of OJ is the new power of the ANC and popular movements to shape the agendas of the ruling classes with threats of mass action and international influence. This signals a new phase of political activity on the Left. After many years of boycotting state structures and exerting mass pressure from the outside, the widely accepted ability of the ANC to mobilise popular support around local issues is now a weapon in the hands of a leadership who are engaging the state in an effort to shape concrete outcomes. New political dynamics and new forms of political organisation have become apparent and important. The nature of the relationship between the leadership and the 'masses', for example, has become an important issue for community-based and left-wing political organisations, and the possibility of divergent agendas on the part of different groupings on the Left becomes ever more real. In addition the political tactics of states everywhere – secrecy and behind-the-scenes negotiations – become increasingly useful to all parties.

Both of the alliances engaged in OJ have some idea of how to interpret the compromise which their involvement in the initiative necessitates. A formal model of the coalition itself (see Fig. 8.1) reveals the perspective of the pro-market consultants on the compromise. The central pivots of the coalition's structure are the Big and Small Business Action Groups, where the 'real' problem of promoting economic growth will be addressed. In addition, the Major Developments Action Group (later called the Special Projects Action Group) is seen to be the forum for immediate and effective action, and the people involved in it are used to ensuring that such action occurs; they are property speculators and independents who are not encumbered by the committee and report-back structures which big businesses impose upon their employees. Included in OJ's structure are also three action groups dealing with 'obstacles' to economic growth including health, housing and infrastructure; land use and regulation; and education. These groups, according to the main consultants to the

Figure 8.1 *The organisational structure of Operation Jumpstart*

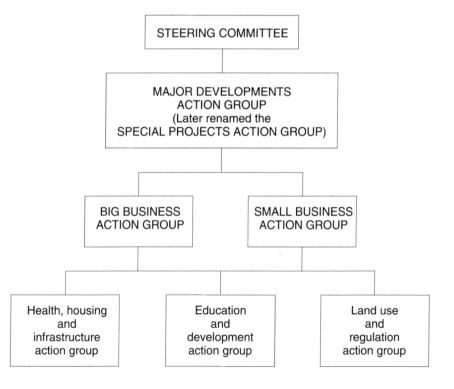

initiative, are not worth 'a can of beans', and it is in the business groups that the real action will take place. They are most pleased, therefore, for community activists and progressive political organisations to be crowded into the three groups concerned with social problems leaving business to move into the groups in which they have a direct interest. This view of the compromise favours the realisation of the interests of local capital and of economic growth with little concern for broader development issues.

However, the popular forces also feel that they have done rather well out of the compromise: achieving consensus around left-wing policies in the field of social services and housing has been identified as one of the primary short-term ambitions of the coalition as a whole. This means that at least some popular demands are likely to be acceded to in one form or another. Business interests have been predominantly (although not completely) relegated to longer-term strategies which might possibly never even take off. The key role played by some of the few left-wing political activists on the steering committee and on the committee planning the development of Cato Manor is seen as a safeguard against capital's plans. However, the Left's position is made at least a little problematic by the need to deliver community participation and support, which is by no means ensured in the present state of organisational chaos, and incipient ethnic and political divisions in the region.

But, as was apparent in the incident concerning the World Bank and the Investors' Conference, the left-wing grouping in OJ has a power which does not rest only upon delivering popular support. A measure of discursive legitimacy surrounds the positions they adopt and, more broadly, the policies they advocate. At least two competing discourses have been shaping growth initiatives in the DFR. The first promotes the free-market system and capitalist economic growth as the value nexus likely to generate efficient development and without which all other social and political ambitions will not be realised. The other is a radical discourse centred around the restructuring of the apartheid city, in terms of both political representation and urban form. The path which this latter discourse has followed, from being a marginalised position amongst left-wing academics and community organisations to playing a key role in shaping urban policies both nationally and locally, is most interesting (see Tomlinson 1992). The need for information and for creative solutions to very serious economic and political problems has resulted in the previously discounted radical discourse of urban and political transformation being translated into concrete and widely acceptable policy recommendations. Alongside the free-market rhetoric, a radical redistributive, transformative discourse inhabits the domain of Durban's latest growth initiative.

The strength of the new urban-planning discourse evolving among radical or formerly radical intellectuals provides one reason why OJ might have been steered towards the interests of the popular classes. Through the involvement of such intellectuals in a number of planning/lobbying arenas, a coherent set of policy proposals based on a left-wing analysis of the apartheid city has emerged and includes the strong claim that available central land should be used for housing for the poor. This is especially relevant in Durban where several fairly large tracts of well-located land are still available for development, having been cleared under the Group Areas Act. Cato Manor, one such piece of land, became central to OJ's development interventions. Morally based demands for retribution in respect of apartheid injustices have been broadly accepted by most parties involved. The vision of the compact city, with vacant land and buffer strips filled in by low-income housing and mixed uses, and the idea that employment creation close to living places is essential to eradicate some of the contradictions of the apartheid city, have been taken up successfully by OJ as well as by other local planning exercises, such as that promoted by Tongaat-Hulett. The idea of participation, too, is well entrenched within the structures of the coalition, and is being pursued at least formally by various committees.

Because of the different interests, and the different discourses, which have come together in OJ there is a potential for not inconsiderable disagreement or contradiction. We will explore this potential – which can also be interpreted as a conflict between the popular forces and capital – by following some of the debates and activities which have come out of two of the committees set up as part of OJ: one concerned with Special Projects, and the other concerned with health, housing and infrastructure. The potential for the speculative and entrepreneurial interests in OJ to dominate the initiatives of more populist forces will be considered.

THE ACTIVITIES OF OPERATION JUMPSTART: URBAN ENTREPRENEURIALISM OR COMMUNITY-BASED DEVELOPMENT?

OJ's short history can be crudely divided into three periods: first, the period of 'optimism' from December 1990 till mid-1991; secondly, the period that saw a recognition of developmental 'reality' and the obstacles which confronted development proposals in contentious areas such as the Point/Victoria Embankment[2] and Block AK;[3] and finally, the present, a period in which some assessments of the exercise have been offered.

OJ began with a tremendous sense of optimism. Plans to achieve an 8 per cent growth rate in the DFR economy and to create at least 300 000 jobs were publicised, and the group aimed to initiate some high-profile projects within six months in order to convince the public that OJ was going to be a success. The Steering Committee's first informal meeting was held on 3 December 1990, immediately after the Development Conference. Here it was decided that the organisation's objectives would be directly derived from the DCC's 'Durban Business Initiative: Position Statement' (adopted on 20 November 1987). In a significant amendment it was decided that the term 'business plan' would be replaced by 'economic, infrastructural and social plan' and that 'caring for the people' would be made an important principle. A later meeting suggested that OJ's aim should be to 'create a positive environment for wealth creation through job opportunities'. It was also emphasised that any policies that were made should use 'countries like Hong Kong and Singapore as a model of achievement' (Minutes 5 December 1990: 8).

In structuring various initiatives some effort was put into ensuring that the chairpersons of committees had the appropriate entrepreneurial acumen and influence. Hence, Bruce Forssman, a representative of the property giant RMS Syfrets, was allocated the task of lobbying international investors by the External Business Environment Group. Natal's Regional Development Advisory Committee chairperson, Chris Procter, was asked to look into financing some of the business initiatives, and at a later stage to examine the possibility of lobbying the government to support an Export Processing Zone for Durban. Tongaat-Hulett's Gordan Hibbert was given the task of addressing the Chambers of Industries and Commerce, the Sakekamer, and Business Forum, to win support for OJ. In the 'Land-Use' initiative, Helgaard Botha (also of Tongaat-Hulett) was asked to address the need for getting rid of 'red tape' surrounding projects like Cato Manor and to bring in property interests such as the South African Property Owners' Association (SAPOA). Finally Roland Starkey, because of his previous experience in Cape Town's Waterfront development, agreed to direct the 'Special Projects' committee, where it was argued that the development of waterfront areas such as the Point/Victoria Embankment should be linked to wider issues affecting the tourist industry such as the dropping of legislation against gambling.

By April of 1991 things were getting off the ground and the various action groups were ready to report on their progress. Terry Rosenberg, the chairperson of OJ, reaffirmed the coalition's commitment to maintaining a broad membership, and was pleased to announce that a number of international companies had already expressed interest in investing in the region, although they were highly concerned about the current violence and instability. Gordan Hibbert also made a point of reaffirming the 'importance of the partnership approach between the various major players if the goals of 8% growth and 300 000 formal sector jobs were to be achieved by the end of the decade' (Minutes 15 April 1991: 1). From the point of view of the Business Sector Committee he identified the need for an international conference centre in Durban, for the upgrading of the Louis Botha Airport and, generally, for measures which would 'attract the A-Grade income tourist back to Durban'. The committee's proposal was to establish a Greater Durban Marketing Authority which would concentrate on tourism, exports and developing the manufacturing industry (Minutes 15 April 1991). Roland Starkey of the Special Projects Action Group stressed the urgency of implementing the ideas which OJ had generated. He felt 'that to retain credibility it would be necessary to have projects running within a twelve to twenty month time-frame … [and] … was concerned with the facilitation of the Point Area' (Minutes 15 April 1991). Finally, with regard to the Cato Manor initiative, Mike Sutcliffe pointed out that negotiations for the development of the area were well underway and that a moratorium on current building was being negotiated with the government so that a structure plan could be prepared and discussion around the creation of a development company could proceed.

Soon after this, however, participants in OJ began to be concerned about the lack of visible action, and a number of obstacles arose to disrupt the enthusiasm and capacity of the organisation. The contradictions within the coalition were also exposed in the process. We will explore these interruptions by examining in some detail two key sub-committees, namely the Special Projects Action Group and the Greater Cato Manor Action Group. We will examine not only the obstacles which confront development initiatives in South Africa's metropolitan areas in the present phase of political negotiations, but also the implications of the specific compromises which had been effected amongst the partners in this local coalition.

Urban entrepreneurialism: The Waterfront developments and the property/tourist lobby

The shape of cities across the world has been much influenced by the activities of growth coalitions, and in the recent period this has taken the form of large, architecturally adventurous consumption spectacles designed to replace the industry lost by ailing Western cities. Such developments have already begun to emerge in South Africa's cities, and the business lobby in OJ was much influenced by this kind of vision.

During the November conference, the consultants' presentation to the Special Projects Action Group (variously named Core Projects, or Major Developments) stressed the importance of market principles in development, and opposed state-directed development. Despite the frequent failure of the market to promote development in particular localities, it was argued that capital was the key to promoting growth in the region. But, given the problem of market failure, this would need to take place within the context of public-private partnerships. Exceptionally high investment risks, compounded by uncertain and slow returns, had made capital most unwilling to invest both generally in South Africa and more specifically in the Durban area. The role of the public sector was therefore to supply funds to reduce the risk for capital, to assist with land and resource provision in order to ensure that development occurred rapidly and to speed up the realisation of returns by investors.

The focus of this group in terms of concrete projects was on the generation of highly visible, very short-term developments which would convince the public that the Jumpstart initiative could succeed and thereby gain popular support for the coalition. The types of developments mooted included central developments around the harbour, the promotion of tourist facilities and industrial parks, possibly an international convention centre, and even the possibility of making a bid for the 1996 Olympic Games. In addition to these, key focal points for the committee were the extensive areas of land which had been lying vacant for decades, emptied of their inhabitants by removals under the Group Areas Act. The Warwick Avenue Triangle, Block AK, Cato Manor and the under-utilised Durban Drive-In became the pivots for these proposed high-profile developments (see Fig. 8.2). Clearly the danger was that these well-situated lands, lost to the poor and disenfranchised, would be colonised by speculative capital eager to realise an enormous potential surplus. This is exactly what happened to many other areas of the

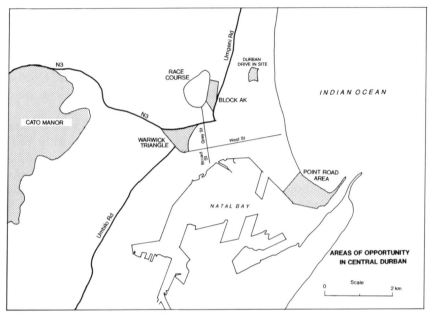

Figure 8.2 *Areas of opportunity in central Durban*

country cleared under earlier rounds of urban rejuvenation/removal. South End in Port Elizabeth, for example, was colonised by yuppie townhouses, and District Six in Cape Town by an educational institution and some housing before popular protest put an end to further development. But the compromise achieved within OJ regarding the future use of these lands in Durban is, on the whole, remarkable. That lands of which people have been dispossessed by apartheid should be used predominantly for lower-income housing has generally been accepted by this committee. The search for appropriate sites for high-profile major developments has had to turn elsewhere.

The other key projects envisaged by this group involve another important shaper of the form of South Africa's cities, namely the harbour authorities. Portnet has been commercialised along with three other increasingly independent and self-financing entities, formerly divisions of the South African Transport Services network. With no cross-subsidisation of passenger transport envisaged within a year or two and vast expanses of property in and around South Africa's major ports (all in the centre of large towns), Portnet has already begun to research and implement ways of benefitting from these assets. In Durban a marina on

the western end of the harbour and undisclosed tourist, retail and residential developments on the beachfront side of the harbour are in the
pipeline. But the autonomy of the harbour authorities from the city, and
the emergence of conflicts between the business and community lobbies
within OJ, have made negotiations over the future developments slow
and these high-profile projects have yet to be realised.

On 25 June 1991 Steering Committee members were told that the Point
& Victoria Embankment Redevelopment Committee had already produced a structure plan for public perusal and that a workshop would be
set for July or August. Furthermore, the Council had allocated the funds
to investigate the proposal and appoint a consultant to 'manage the
process through Portnet and the intention was to hand over the area to a
development agency and/or set up a utility company' (Minutes 25 June
1991). However, when the Point Waterfront Workshop was convened on
1 August, it was clear that the community-based constituency had been
completely neglected by the organisers. The only 'community' grouping
invited was the ANC whose single delegate, Mike Sutcliffe, was ranged
against a host of some 120 delegates representing the Government, the
Council, the discredited Local Affairs Committees, big business, developers, property interests, and those with a major stake in the recreation
field. A key theme in stressing the urgency of the development was
encapsulated in the comment made by city councillor and vice-chair-
person of the Point Redevelopment Committee, Peter Mansfield: 'I would
like to give Cape Town the reassurance that we do not plan to imitate
their scheme. I would also like to warn them, in the spirit of friendly
competition ... that the reason we do not plan to imitate V & A[4] is that
we plan to better it' (*Daily News* 2 August 1991).

From the point of view of business interests in OJ, projects were
progressing well. A proposed convention centre, for example, joined the
Point development as a priority in the minds of OJ Business Sector
participants. The OJ Steering Committee decided that the time was ripe
to spend some of the City's money to hire a well-known marketing consultant (who had previous links to entrepreneurial Council projects)
to produce promotional media that would 'sell the vision of Durban
becoming the Conference and Sports Centre of Southern Africa' (Minutes
2 August 1991: 72). Other projects such as the promotion of the Export
Processing Zone concept, a lottery, and the launch of the Greater Durban
Marketing Authority (a more powerful and 'jazzed-up' version of the
discredited Durban Publicity Association) were already in the pipeline.

By the end of 1991 and the beginning of 1992 OJ was becoming increasingly concerned about 'completing its mission'. But as meetings got smaller, despite the fact that they only took place once a month, and various business sectors (large developers and housing interests) saw that apart from tourism OJ had little to offer, interest waned. The fragility of the coalition between business and the popular forces was also highlighted when OJ's Internal Business Environment group decided to chastise COSATU for its proposed two-day stayaway-for-peace in Natal, scheduled for November 1991. The group complained that the stayaway was ill-considered because 'small businesses were going out of business; while big businesses were retrenching people' and the economy was 'sick as a dog' (Minutes 17 October 1991: 90).

Simultaneously, the notion that 'things were nicely in the pipeline' began to take hold of the various committees involved in the Business Sector initiatives. And to an extent they were: USAID and the World Bank were showing an interest in funding housing projects; R200 million was offered by the Council to fund the conference centre; Export Processing Zone legislation was being considered nationally; preparations for the lottery were in place; plans were being made to attract the Olympics; it was expected that 'a development company would be established by the board of Transnet during February 1992 [which] would consider the Victoria Embankment' as a development that should be linked to the whole future of the Point (Minutes 23 January 1992). Finally, OJ had been integral to facilitating the creation of the Greater Durban Marketing Authority which would, it was believed, take over some of OJ's projects. Members of the Steering Committee began arguing in March 1992 that 'OJ should be phased into the [Marketing Authority] which could be properly constituted and represented by both the private and public sectors, would have status, finance and an entry into organisations *who would and could implement projects*' (Minutes 31 March 1992: 116, own emphasis).

The net result of such confidence was a backlash from both the Left and interestingly the private sector over the release of a joint Council-Transnet plan for the Point development. This plan had arisen out of a Council-Transnet steering committee – a strategy reminiscent of the Council's old style of operating without consulting community groups. The controversy revolved around the fact that, firstly, the City Council and Transnet had commissioned their own private development and structure plan for the area and unilaterally intended implementing it. Secondly private developers salivating on the sidelines with 'billions in foreign investment', were furious at being left out and hopping mad that the Council-Transnet plan would be phased over a fifteen-year period. And finally the ANC, represented by Mike Sutcliffe of the OJ Steering Committee, were equally unimpressed by the fact that they had not been consulted about a scheme that involved the privatisation of thousands of rands worth of public land in the heart of the city.

As was to be expected, pressure on the ANC grew from all sides. Peter Mansfield (now chairperson of the Management Committee – MANCO) argued that planners such as Dr Sutcliffe had been involved in the consultation process (*Natal Mercury* 10 April 1992) while the Chamber of Commerce's Mike Norris claimed to be disgusted by the 'interminable wrangling' between Transnet, the Durban Corporation, and the ANC (*Daily News* 22 June 1992). Furthermore, dissension within the ranks of the OJ Steering Committee grew. Members began to argue that 'various projects like the Point and Victoria Embankment developments were suffering through political interference ... which was retarding development and the legitimacy of the representatives of the people to question the economic justification and feasibility of these projects was queried' (Minutes 12 June 1992). However, as a civic organisation leader has sarcastically pointed out, 'all the business sector has to do is phone the MANCO chair ... and that amounts to pressure, and the Council then promptly responds to this pressure' (Gordhan 1992). True to the nature of OJ, members now began to argue that 'pressure be placed on Transnet and the City Council ... and the City Council (through Peter Mansfield) be requested to remove all obstacles and apply initiative planning to these areas as soon as possible' (Minutes 12 June 1992: 123). Compromise, however, was waiting in the wings, and a local newspaper editorial suggested that:

> The city council, flawed as it is an all-white relic of apartheid, is still the legally constituted local authority. It must certainly consult widely before embarking on a development project, but then it must act decisively. The general welfare of the city is too important to wait for the politicians to stop posturing – for that day may never come. (*Natal Mercury* 26 June 1992)

Indeed by August the 'pro-Point' lobby in OJ was sounding a little less belligerent and voices were heard to argue that 'community participation was necessary and it was stated that the people could not be pushed ... that the people themselves did not have the basic necessities of life and they needed to be convinced that for every ten tourists one job would be created' (Minutes 27 August 1992: 130). Finally, because financial institutions were now wary of the project's 'profile', 'the interests of the community' would be safeguarded by the creation of a Trust which would deal with issues 'such as cross-subsidisation, [and] the sharing of profits' (Minutes 27 August 1992: 130).

Despite the fact that the community-based grouping had left the field of high-profile developments wide open for business interests, strategic intervention in various proposals had opened up a space for some influence in terms of the direction and pace of development. However, the powerful City Council still holds the reins of central city developments, and holds the purse-strings too. The Council has pledged large sums of money to meet the development needs of informal settlements on the outskirts of the city, and has attempted to support the civic structures in terms of their capacity to make an intervention into economic decision-making. In addition Council officials have devised plans for financing the spectacular downtown developments (the conference centre and the Victoria Embankment) which do not involve any loss to the ratepayers or others with claims on the city budget. They plan to cash in some investments made in terms of the substantial Capital Development Fund (which is the foundation of Durban's unusual debt-free status), and to use only the profit from this for funding the proposed developments, reinvesting the capital amount. However, this still amounts to an expenditure foregone on other items.

More importantly, however, while the Left has made a substantial conceptual intervention in terms of the Cato Manor development (see the following section), its contribution in terms of economic development has been purely reactive. It would seem that a more sustained and proactive contribution on future economic strategy should be seen as a crucial goal of more radical forces: or else the business coalition will continue to dominate policy formulation and growth coalitions in the region – albeit with a caveat suggesting that consultation or participation is necessary. For this participation to be meaningful, community groups and left-wing political groupings need substantially increased research capacity and staff. Even attending meetings is often beyond the capabilities of local groups: how much more difficult, then, to formulate policy at a local level on the wide range of issues raised by a growth coalition such as OJ.

However, as the following section demonstrates, even when community groupings put a lot of resources into a project such as the development of Cato Manor – and, indeed, take the leading role in the initiative – other obstacles become apparent. In particular, the fragmentation of state structures at the local level and the persistence of conservative elements within these structures have hampered this local development initiative and others around the country.

The development of Cato Manor: Housing for all in a phase of transition?

In contrast to the stalled initiatives in the Point and other downtown areas, OJ's involvement in Cato Manor has been described by all parties as something of a success. Having set up a consultation process involving all the major players in the Cato Manor development, OJ was able to disband its Greater Cato Manor Action Committee in January 1992. By this time the OJ Committee had been able to play a crucial role in shaping the negotiations process as regards the planning and development of the area.

The fate of the Cato Manor area is extremely controversial. Cleared of settlements under the Group Areas Act, Cato Manor has lain vacant for the greater part of thirty years, although there have been piecemeal developments in some areas recently. Land-ownership is fragmented amongst local councils, the House of Delegates and the University of Natal, and the final responsibility for land-use planning rests with the Province. The variety of authorities with jurisdiction over pieces of this land is confusing to all but the most informed and securing consensus on the development of the area has been extremely arduous.

Within the context of OJ, the Cato Manor Committee was the preserve of the left-wing political grouping, although some construction interests were also represented. But from the point of view of the community-based forces, the Cato Manor Committee was the primary focus of their activities. Here well-developed, local, radical ideas concerning the restructuring of the apartheid city and the need to provide housing for millions of informal-settlement residents, as well as to redress the wrongs of apartheid removals, could be mobilised. Agreement was reached within the Committee regarding the type of development (low-income, with some commercial and industrial development to assist with employment and financing the scheme); and regarding the development process (to form a section 21 company to implement the project, outside the jurisdiction of any of the local authorities competing for control over the area).

But initial efforts to persuade the central government to support the proposals by consolidating all land-holdings in the implementation body and freezing all developments until a coherent plan for the whole area could be agreed upon were fruitless. Instead the state mounted its own counter-initiative against what it saw as a radical hijacking of the local development initiative. The Province, local councils (except for the DCC), the House of Delegates and the House of Representatives were drawn together into an alliance to try and reassert their control over local developments. However, the DCC and OJ refused to be drawn into this alliance and managed to broker a meeting between the Provincial representatives and the extra-parliamentary groupings involved in the Cato Manor discussions. A negotiated structure was agreed upon but after consulting with the Cabinet, the minister who had been conducting the local negotiations returned with a series of recommendations which caused the community groupings to walk out of the meeting. The disagreement revolved around whether the resulting committee was to be an advisory or an autonomous body, whether the chairperson was to be appointed or elected, whether the body would have powers of implementation, and how representation was to be effected. After much negotiation (brokered to a large extent by OJ and DCC members) agreement was reached amongst the major participants. This even included the House of Delegates who had been undermining attempts to consolidate the land in a last bid to deliver to their particular constituency before the apartheid structures on which they depended were dismantled.

While it seems as if an agreement acceptable to the community-based groupings has been arrived at, the present arrangements give central state actors such as the Province and the House of Delegates, who have a strong interest in preserving their institutional and political power bases into a post-apartheid era, a lot of control in directing a development which will have a major influence on the physical shape of the city as well as on the balance of political forces in the city. But while 'negotiating in bad faith' (Planact 1992a) may be the state's strategy in the current phase, alliance-building is crucial to the politics of the Left. In this respect, Cato Manor signals the problems associated with development initiatives in a phase of such fluid politics: apartheid forces are using their institutional bases to further their own political ends, which makes negotiating a particularly hazardous undertaking for opposition forces; and community-based and ANC-aligned forces are seeking support from many different quarters in their efforts to oppose and undermine the present state's strength and to demonstrate that they are able to deliver to their constituency. Whether the interests of the very poor and homeless survive the vagaries of such politics remains to be seen. A crucial disabling factor here is the relative weakness of ANC-aligned groupings in terms of resources and skills. In general more support for the infra-structural capacities of these groupings will be necessary if negotiations over developments at local level are to be meaningful in the present transitional phase.

CONCLUSION

All of the projects have been a part of the 'behind-the-scenes' push-ing of officials. (Starkey 1992)

The relationship between the City and OJ is a very privileged one, and one that is highly undemocratic. It continues as a long-standing political culture in this city, where the business sector always has the ear of the City. (Gordhan 1992)

OJ is very derivative, so that they simply follow Cape Town's V & A without coming up with really bold ideas; instead they are more cautious and conservative. (Maughan-Brown 1992)

OJ was so 'wishy-washy' from the beginning. They were all business people and it was clear to me from the beginning that it was an attempt to co-opt the Movement into a framework that would allow them to advance the economic and business interests of Durban. (Forster 1992)

... the lack of [civic] involvement was partly a capacity problem, [but] we took a conscious decision with COSATU to play a gate-keeping role, while they said they felt more comfortable acting in the usual bilateral role with business. (Sutcliffe 1992)

Assessing an exercise like OJ is quite difficult, as the varied perspectives of different participants in the process cited above suggest. Clearly the coalition did have a number of impacts on the development process in the DFR: a lottery to raise funds for development needs has been success-fully launched; decisions concerning Cato Manor, conference centres and waterfront developments have been helped along; and a basis for future negotiations regarding local development has been laid. But there remain many different grounds for offering a critique of the organisation, includ-ing the rather heady ambitions of the founding committee. Our perspective here will be that of those parties concerned with future growth initiatives in South Africa's metropolitan areas: what could we do better in the future, and what positive lessons can we learn from the Jumpstart initiative?

The first and often the most crucial ground for criticising growth coalitions of this sort is the process which led to their formation and which informed their method of operation. Here OJ has received a great deal of criticism, especially concerning the absence of representation from civic and trade union organisations. The predominance of business interests was only offset by the strength of the radical planning discourse within the local context, and by the legitimacy accorded to the positions adopted by community-based organisations and the ANC in the current political conjuncture. Experiences elsewhere support the idea that it is very important to the success of growth coalitions that a reasonably representative spectrum of interests be included on an equal basis. Thus a more democratic form of representation could have been secured in the initial stages of OJ, and initiators of future efforts should learn from this.

The second problem concerns the methods adopted by the coalition. As the public moments of disagreement suggest, consultation with all interested parties was not always well effected, and a number of OJ's initiatives have been taken into the implementation phase by the white City Council. While this is certainly a pragmatic move in the present transitional period, it also exposes the developments to methods, practices and ideas which have existed within the City Council and its bureaucracy for decades. Thus the planning of initiatives in steering committees or standing committees sets agendas and strategies in an undemocratic fashion, and consultation is frequently too late and insufficient – especially given the lack of capacity of the civic groups and left-wing political parties. While the Council has made efforts to resolve this problem (for example, funding consultants for civics to make an input on various issues, such as the proposed convention centre), both Jumpstart and progressively-inclined state bodies could do a lot more to facilitate democratic economic and urban planning in the transitional phase.

In considering the importance of democracy, left-wing forces could also assess their own democratic practices. While it may not be tactically advisable on many occasions (as when trying to present a united front on the Cato Manor issue), it is quite important for actors in development strategies to acknowledge that a diversity of opinions and interests often goes into constituting 'the Left' or 'the community'. If the interests of the most powerless are not to be sacrificed to those whose access to decision-making structures is more secure, and whose political interests may well diverge, then it is important that observers and advisers/consultants to community groupings should be sensitive to these differences as well as to those amongst the ruling groups involved. The time for closer and more public analysis of left-wing politics has arrived if development ambitions are to be realised in a manner appropriate to the interests and needs of the poor.

An interesting observation about the processes and politics of the OJ initiative concerns its reliance on key personalities, both on the Left and in business circles. Experience elsewhere suggests that it is frequently the case that key individuals, who have charisma and who appeal to a wide cross-section of the community, are crucial to the success of growth coalitions such as OJ. As we have noted, a number of key business people with a great deal of legitimacy in the business community were chosen to participate in Jumpstart in an attempt to ensure the support of this constituency. The desire to safeguard such support certainly shaped and constrained Jumpstart's interventions from time to time. However, in order to counter the 'spoiling' role of the ANC and civics, key individuals from this constituency with an interest in this sphere of politics also became involved and were able to deliver 'community support' for different initiatives on occasion. Stitching together a coalition which is both democratic and functional will probably always depend on the presence of key individuals, as well as on the objective conditions which gave rise to the perception that economic growth in the locality is urgently needed.

However, future growth coalitions could certainly expand their horizons beyond the rather limited and derivative strategies for growth identified by OJ: a waterfront development (like Cape Town and Boston and Baltimore); a convention centre (like Johannesburg and Birmingham); an export processing zone (like Hong Kong and Mauritius and China); the Olympic Games and tourist developments. The point is that there was not a great deal of specificity in the developments proposed, and very little in the way of grassroots development initiatives, except those associated with housing plans, which grew out of a need to meet the reproductive needs of people rather than a desire to stimulate development. Much more thought could be put into an appropriate industrialisation strategy for the DFR given its present and past economic standing, and into ways of promoting sustainable and long-term development that does not rely on attracting speculative capital investments or abandoning regulations for industries locating in a special industrial area. These may well be useful strategies, and left-wing activists have proved relatively pragmatic in assessing ventures such as the international convention centre or the Point developments. But it could be argued that OJ's long-term impact on the city may have been greater if it had focused more on the local potential of the economy rather than on spectacular, large-scale projects requiring great investment of funds with an uncertain return. Simple manoeuvres were required, like sourcing all local-authority requirements locally, or adopting an investment strategy which supported local entrepreneurial or industrial ventures rather than real estate speculation in other towns – although clearly this is the source of a great deal of the surplus funds with which future development initiatives could be supported. It is at this level of planning for economic development that future consultations and negotiations need to take place, and not only at the stage of implementation.

Operation Jumpstart, therefore, which continues the tradition of high-profile growth initiatives in many other parts of the world, is not necessarily the most appropriate model for a development vehicle in the present situation. If, in addition, we take into account the fundamentally disabling role which the current institutional fragmentation plays in the process of development, we might conclude with three recommendations on local-level economic development in South Africa in the short to medium term.

First, a strongly democratic process would secure consensus and enable conflicts of opinion to be resolved within the context of negotiations; it would also signpost a form of development appropriate to a post-apartheid, democratic urban future. Secondly, institutional reform in terms of local government and development agencies is an essential prerequisite, not only to facilitating development practically, but also to 'levelling the playing field' amongst the major participants. For conservative forces wield a great deal of power in their control of institutions and, as the Cato Manor episode indicated, they are not hesitant to use it. Urgently needed developments are unnecessarily delayed by parties in order to secure sectarian interests. This point raises questions about the wisdom of the Left's insistence that local-level political reform should follow after a national-level political settlement (even though local-level negotiations on a variety of development issues have been pursued). And thirdly, some creative and innovative research concerning appropriate development strategies for the DFR is crucial to the launching of a successful growth initiative. The derivative strategies of Operation Jumpstart need to be replaced by locally developed, locally specific and sustainable, if perhaps more modest, exercises.

NOTES

1. Tongaat-Hulett is a major industrial company in the region.
2. This area has the potential to become a major commercial and residential development alongside the harbour.
3. This is one of the first inner-city squatter areas.
4. The Victoria and Alfred development is a large and successful commercial development in Cape Town's harbour.

Chapter 9

Local Economic Development Strategies in the PWV

Roland Hunter for Planact

By the beginning of 1993, the importance of local and regional economic and development initiatives had become obvious. The last three years have seen, along with a great deal else, a flowering of such initiatives all over South Africa. From regional initiatives in the Orange Free State, the Eastern Transvaal, and (finally) the PWV; through metropolitan programmes such as 'Growing the Cape' and Operation Jumpstart; to local initiatives such as those in Klerksdorp and Atlantis, a series of sub-national economic development initiatives has begun to take shape. Politically these initiatives are very much a phenomenon of the transition: they are negotiation-based and have a participatory flavour.

An additional origin of the initiatives is that local authorities are also paying increasing attention to the health of their local economies. For example, the Pretoria City Council recently appointed a Marketing Manager whose strategy for local development includes developing a marketing plan and competing to attract potential investors. The Johannesburg City Council has a Director of Commerce and Industry with similar responsibilities, despite the difference in title. In addition, in the duel between Cape Town, Durban and Johannesburg over which South African city should host the Olympic Games early in the next century, the central concern was the anticipated positive impact on the local economy.

Finally, initiatives whose focus is on housing, hostel upgrading or other aspects of development are also laying increased emphasis on the economic dimension: this is largely based on the recognition that local housing projects have little long-term prospect of success unless the people who live in the houses are able to find work. Variants on this argument have been the key issues in examples as diverse as the struggle in the Metropolitan Chamber[1] over the TPA's plans in Rietfontein[2] and the hostel-upgrading project in Mohlakeng.

Of course, none of this is to say that until now South Africans have had no awareness of local economies or that development projects have not long included an economic dimension. The DBSA's well-developed Urban Development Plans focused on promoting economic development and, as long ago as the 1970s, Pietersburg had the good fortune to have a Town Clerk with the vision, drive and contacts to make a distinct impact on the local economy. Nevertheless, it is clear that recent years have seen an increased emphasis on the local and the regional as sites of economic strategy-making and action.

Notwithstanding this interest in development planning, the lack of professionals with knowledge and experience in the field, and indeed the lack of university courses in the subject, are a further indication of how recent the emphasis on local economic strategies is.

Yet, local or regional economic strategies are by no means uncomplicated or unequivocally 'the right thing to do'. On the contrary, they pose a number of serious challenges and issues, the careful consideration of which is a prerequisite for success. Furthermore, international successes in local economic strategies are not particularly frequent, and conditions in South Africa are less than ideal. It may be that the recent energy and enthusiasm in this field are based more on hope and on the severity of the depression than on a realistic appreciation of what can be achieved.

WHY TRY LOCAL ECONOMIC DEVELOPMENT STRATEGIES?

For the purposes of this chapter, a local economic strategy will be defined as a set of deliberately connected policy initiatives and projects which seeks to improve the condition and functioning of the economy of a particular locality, and which originates and draws its momentum primarily from within that locality.[3]

The endogeneity in the definition refers to the source of the momentum and the primary object of concern. It does not necessarily imply anything about the nature of the local strategy or the origin of resources to finance policy initiatives.

There are a number of reasons why attempts to promote a local economic strategy may appear an attractive option. Perhaps the most compelling of these is related to the depth of the current depression and the extent of unemployment. With formal sector employment now reaching only about half the national workforce, and with little prospect of any substantial economic revival, there is little sense in relying on national economic policy alone to transform the situation. Indeed, this does not apply only to South Africa: national economic policies in other countries have generally had just as little success. Furthermore, national strategies may operate to the detriment of particular local economies. Under the circumstances, it can be argued that local strategies may succeed where the national have failed, or at the very least, that the extent of the depression requires that South Africa develop as many sites of potential initiative as possible. Economic strategies for particular localities would appear to have significant potential for those localities and also for the economy as a whole.

National and local strategies may also be seen as having different functions in overall economic strategy formulation and implementation. For example, although 'national policy sets the parameters within which growth occurs, local governments and people can play an important role in taking advantage of available opportunities' (Ferguson 1990b). Something along these lines appears to guide COSATU's participation in subnational development initiatives: while the NEF is considered to be the place where an enabling economic-policy environment should be negotiated, the subnational initiatives are seen as the arenas which can achieve concrete delivery.

Taking this point further, it is clear that there are things which local initiatives, local governments and other local actors can do which their national counterparts cannot, or can do only with very great difficulty. National initiatives and governments can intervene in the overall price system; they can have some effect on distribution, and they can mediate with the world market. National initiatives may be able to deal more easily with circulation than with production. Local initiatives and governments, however, are closer to the particular and the detailed, and can therefore perform specific planning, animating and financing functions more effectively. They are also in a better position to have an effect on industrial restructuring (Murray 1989: 2).

In general, when local areas have obvious local needs and obvious unused local skills and resources, it seems self-evident that the two should be combined in a strategy. The common-sense thrust of this argument makes it hard to argue against local economic strategies (Beauregard 1992).

Finally, local economic strategies may be favoured because they are potentially a means of exposing economic development to democratic pressures (Murray 1989: 3). This is obviously worthwhile in its own right, but it may also be a means of ensuring the sustainability of a development initiative both because there is the prospect of drawing on local ideas and knowledge and because local ownership of an initiative may generate commitment and enthusiasm which national strategies have little hope of achieving.

Nevertheless, it is easy to be over-optimistic about the potential impact of a local economic strategy. A typical cautionary remark is that, given the nature of the current global economy, attempting a local economic strategy is like trying to empty the sea with a teaspoon (Planact 1992c: 8). Even major practitioners and proponents concede that, if the goal is economic regeneration, local economic strategies are likely to have only minor effects (Cochrane 1988: 164).[4]

Furthermore, South Africa in the 1990s, like Britain in the 1980s, is a less than ideal environment in which to launch local economic strategies, particularly left-oriented strategies. While the flurry of such initiatives, especially the negotiations-based initiatives, would seem to contradict this assertion, it nevertheless remains a reasonable one. As will be discussed later, local economic strategies raise a series of social contract issues that are currently far from resolved. Furthermore, the initiatives have yet to mobilise substantial resources. The experience in local-level negotiations around service delivery issues is that they have achieved gains for local communities only where resources have been available from outside the local area. So far, such negotiations have not managed to unlock local resources for development of service provision (Planact 1992d: 41).

ONE STRATEGY, TWO INITIATIVES: THE CENTRAL WITWATERSRAND AND THE PWV

South Africa now has two major economic and development initiatives in its economic heartland. The purpose of this section is to provide some background to the emergence of these two forums: the Economic Development Working Group of the Central Witwatersrand Metropolitan Chamber,[5] and the PWV Economic and Development Forum. It will then be possible to discuss some of the special issues that arise when attempting to develop a local economic strategy in areas which generate a substantial proportion of the national product.

The Central Witwatersrand Metropolitan Chamber

The Central Witwatersrand Metropolitan Chamber is the primary forum in which the future system of local government for the central Rand area is being negotiated. This forum, the most developed in the country, was established as a result of the signing of the Greater Soweto Accord in September 1990. Although the Accord dealt with short-term issues including writing off of arrears and ending of the rent boycott, a key element of the agreement was the establishment of a Metropolitan Chamber to oversee the dismantling of the apartheid urban system in the central Witwatersrand. It was the Soweto People's Delegation[6] who insisted that a body would be required to formulate policy on longer-term issues[7] during the interim period.

It was agreed that the Chamber would comprise representatives from local authorities and civic associations[8] in the metropolitan region as a whole. Policy work would be co-ordinated by a Joint Technical Committee, and would be undertaken in six Working Groups, each dealing with a major subject area: Constitutional Development, Institutional Development, Physical Development, Financial Development, Social Development, and Economic Development.

While the immediate priority of the Chamber was to design a non-racial and democratic system of local government, it was also required to develop new policies with regard to land use, housing, transport, social and recreational facilities, economic development, and other key aspects of an urban policy for the metropolitan region. In short, the Chamber is a mechanism to supervise the urban transition. The most significant paragraphs in the Accord which expressed this are worth quoting in full:

> Generally, the Chamber shall also serve as a forum within which political participation, dialogue, and interaction may take place during the period of constitutional transition in South Africa.
>
> The Chamber shall be committed to exploring and formulating short, medium and long-term practical democratic and non-racial solutions to the problems of local government and finance ...
>
> The Chamber shall be considered to have fulfilled its mandate as soon as an appropriate system of local government and administration has been established for the region.

In summary, the constitution of the Chamber envisages a three-fold role, namely:

- a negotiating forum;
- must formulate policy alternatives premised on the principles of non-racialism, democracy and redistribution; and

- must ensure the implementation of a new system of local and metropolitan government.

The Economic Development Working Group (ED:WG in Chamber short-hand) is the last of the Working Groups to be established: in fact, at the time of writing it had yet to be formally launched. This has much to do with the way in which the Chamber was established and its composition: although civic associations and local authorities are full members of the Chamber, business interests and trade unions are not. Early Chamber meetings which sought to establish the Working Group soon ran up against the fact that there was not much point in starting an economic development initiative for the Central Witwatersrand without the participation of both those interests. It was decided to invite organised labour and business to participate in the activities of the Working Group, and although business groups (including the Johannesburg Chamber of Commerce and Industry and the Afrikaanse Handelsinstituut) did take part, major labour groups, particularly COSATU, declined to do so on the grounds that they would prefer to take part in economic development initiatives on a regional level.[9]

The PWV Economic and Development Forum

At this stage it was felt within the Metropolitan Chamber that it might be advisable to establish a PWV-scale economic development forum. After a number of discussions among various parties about the issue, a preliminary informal meeting to discuss the possibility took place in May 1992, and was attended by a range of organisations from business, the trade unions, civic associations, and regional authorities.[10] It was decided to ask CBM[11] to convene a first plenary session, and to invite five delegations: one each for organised business, organised labour, political parties, civic associations, and regional government. It was also decided that if technical advisers and organisations attended the plenary, they would do so as part of the delegations of principals, and not in their own right. Finally, it was decided to ask each participating organisation to deliver an input on their conception of a PWV economic and development forum. These would be complemented by presentations on the economic and development characteristics of the PWV, and on the other regional and national economic and development forums.

The plenary, which took place in June, was the first of three to be held in 1992. It was convened and chaired by the CBM, paid for by

Siemens, and took place against a background of political impasse at national and at metropolitan level.[12] Attendance reflected the diversity of the invitation list and the intention to be inclusive. The strongest delegations were those of the civic associations and regional government, followed by organised labour and organised business. There were also a number of observers, mostly technical support personnel from various camps, but also including a representative of the Metropolitan Chamber.

The presentation on the economic and development characteristics of the region highlighted a recurring theme in local and regional development work in South Africa: the paucity of information which is relevant to the task at hand and which has been collected on an appropriate scale. Although considerably more such information is available for the PWV region than for the Central Witwatersrand, it has a number of deficiencies, including the fact that it does not quantify needs and that it reflects the lack of resources available to the representatives of those excluded from formal power.

The presentations from the participating organisations focused on the need for a regional economic development forum, what issues the forum should concentrate on, who should participate, the boundaries of the area 'covered' by the forum, committee structure, and the relationship with other forums and negotiation processes taking place at national, regional or local level. Most debate occurred around the issues of participation, although there was also some debate on the geographical focus and objectives of the forum. An interim steering committee consisting of three representatives from each delegation was established to finalise these points and to draw up a constitution.

The second plenary session, which took place in September 1992, was held to consolidate the vision, objectives and structure of the Forum, and to find a way forward. To this end, the meeting considered a report of the Interim Steering Committee on the structures of the Forum, a statement of intent and objectives, criteria for determining boundaries, criteria for participation, procedural and constitutional issues, and a programme of work. On this occasion, the most vigorous debate centred around the meaning of consensus and mandates as they were to apply to participants in the Forum. The TPA was concerned to emphasise that, as the statutory authority, it carried ultimate responsibility for development decisions in the region. As the TPA is a participant in the Forum, any consensus reached would exert moral pressure, but no more than this, on the TPA to comply with the consensus: the TPA representatives would in all cases be subject to the decisions of the Executive Committee of the TPA. The civic and labour delegations objected to this point: they rejected the notion that the TPA would simply take advice from the Forum, and felt that the consensus principle would be used to brush important issues aside. After a break for caucusing and informal conflict-resolution processes, the meeting continued with the TPA recommitting itself to the process and to consensus, and stressing the force of the moral obligation it would be under to implement any decisions reached to which it had been party. This assurance was accepted by the other participants. However, the point highlighted the still unresolved issue of what force would accrue to decisions and proposals of negotiations-based economic and development forums.

The meeting also went through details of its emerging constitution. CBM was appointed as the permanent secretariat of the Forum, and the Steering Committee was mandated to develop a programme of work and a budget for presentation at the next plenary.

The main item of business at the third plenary session, which was held in November 1992, was discussion of a proposed work programme for the Forum. Despite a specific request for delegations to get involved in drawing up the proposal, in fact only technical resource people took part in its development.[13]

The proposal presented to the plenary sought to resolve one major tension: between the need to deliver concrete proposals and actions rapidly and in a visible and effective manner, and the need to develop a comprehensive and well-considered economic and development strategy for the region. Implementable policy proposals need to be developed and implemented soon, but they must also fit into an overall policy framework which will be several years in the making. The proposal was therefore to run two exercises over a six-month period.

Firstly, there was a 'specific projects' programme, to produce actionable project or policy proposals. The projects were to be proposed by delegations on their own initiative: this was basically a mechanism for parties to the Forum to propose specific projects and policy actions, develop these into complete, well-considered and if necessary financed proposals, and put them up for consideration.

Secondly, there was a 'rapid review' programme: a quick-sketch and overall analysis of the economic and development status of the PWV. The emphasis would fall on trends and their implications, and could cover issues such as the decline in gold mining, general industrial change, the varying comparative advantage of sub-regions in the PWV, the impact of public investment in transport infrastructure, and so on. The purpose of the review would be to identify the key development issues in the region, provide information support to the 'specific projects' programme, and provide an initial framework within which policy debate could occur. The exercise would be carried out by a team appointed by the Steering Committee.

The intention was that these concurrent processes would be able to interact in a constructive manner, so that by the end of the six months, an outline perspective of the 'economy of development' in the PWV would be available together with a number of implementable policy proposals. At this point, decisions could be made on which of the projects to implement, and whether to embark on a more comprehensive policy research exercise.

The proposed work programme was adopted with some minor alterations.

The PWV Economic and Development Forum was formally launched in January 1993. Documents distributed at the launch set out the salient features of the Forum, including the organisations involved, the *modus operandi*, and the work programme. Membership of the Forum at this stage included:

Organised labour:	COSATU, National African Congress of Trade Unions, FEDSAL, and Federation of Independent Trade Unions.
Organised business:	South African Chamber of Business, National African Federated Chamber of Commerce, Foundation for African Business and Consumer Services, Afrikaanse Handelsinstituut, and Congress of Business and Economics.
Civics:	Civic Associations of the Southern Transvaal.
Public authorities:	Transvaal Provincial Administration, Regional Services Council, Transvaal Local Government Association, Department of Regional and Land Affairs, and the KwaNdebele and Bophuthatswana governments.
Political organisations:	ANC, Democratic Party, National Party, Pan African Congress, and the South African Communist Party.[14]

These organisations were launching a Forum with the following statement of intent and objectives:

1. The primary objective of the PWV E & DF is to promote and encourage the growth and development of the region in the interests of the people of the region and the nation.
2. The PWV E & DF is founded on the principle of development as a process conducted by the people of the region for the people of the region. On this basis the Forum aims, through its representative structure, to encourage the widest possible participation in the development and implementation of strategies related to the growth and development of the region and the welfare of its communities.
3. The PWV E & DF shall, within its means, consider and where appropriate, initiate action respecting the full spectrum of socio-economic and physical development issues, and related to the political context within which the region functions.
4. Priorities shall be determined by the Forum from time to time in the light of changing circumstances.
5. The PWV E & DF shall strive to reach consensus on issues pertinent to growth and development in the region on the basis of research, discussion, and open debate. The Forum shall endeavour to give effect to this consensus in consultation with interested parties, including local, regional and central government, technical agencies, and other stakeholders.

The *modus operandi* document set out the basic structure of the Forum. The principal participants are organised into five delegations, each having an equal vote: Business (12 individuals), Labour (12), Public authorities (16), Political parties (14) and Civics (12). Delegations may be accompanied by advisers and consultants, provided these are limited in number. Observers are permitted, and the Metropolitan Chamber is one of these. The Steering Committee consists of three people from each of the groups *excluding* political parties, plus a chairperson and secretary (both from CBM). Working Groups were to be set up as and when required, and would probably reflect the structure of the work programme.

Back to the Economic Development Working Group

Despite the launch of the PWV Forum, there remained a feeling in the Metropolitan Chamber that its still-unlaunched Economic Development Working Group should make some progress. Late in 1992, therefore, a workshop was held with the intention of developing a set of principles in line with the Chamber's overall policy development approach. The workshop began with a presentation of such salient features of the economy of the central Witwatersrand as it had been possible to assemble at short notice. However, the issue that had bedevilled the Working Group a year earlier arose again: there was not much point in developing an economic strategy for the metropolitan region without union participation. It was decided not to formally adopt a set of principles, and instead to commission a small research effort to further investigate some of the policy issues highlighted during the presentation. It was hoped that the research report could be used as the basis for another metropolitan-scale initiative, possibly taking the form of a conference, which could evolve into a more realistic and inclusive strategy development process.

In early 1993, therefore, both the Metropolitan Chamber and the PWV Forum were engaged primarily in information-gathering exercises. It remained unclear whether either would prove capable of developing the momentum necessary to have any significant impact on the regional economic environment.

Some political and process issues

What are the issues which lie behind the formal processes of establishing negotiations-based economic development initiatives on a metropolitan or regional scale? The purpose of the following two sections is to outline some of these issues as they have emerged in the Economic Development Working Group of the Metropolitan Chamber and the PWV Economic and Development Forum. No claim is made that the list is comprehensive, nor will each issue be exhaustively treated.

The first point to be made is that *two* initiatives on large but different scales are in the process of being established. This reflects a number of factors: the difficulty of defining an appropriate scale for economic development activities, even in the abstract; the regional organisation of participants (COSATU's regional structure more closely corresponds to the PWV than the central Witwatersrand); the different political forces operating at the different scales (civic associations at metropolitan level are closely involved with the Metropolitan Chamber, whereas there is considerable hostility to the Chamber at regional level); the organisation of information available (there is information on several different definitions of the PWV/Region H, and less information on different definitions of the central Witwatersrand, etc.); capacity issues; and so on. Despite the involvement of the Metropolitan Chamber in establishing the PWV

Forum, and despite its observer status in the Forum, the possibility exists that a certain amount of rivalry could develop between the two initiatives. The Metropolitan Chamber is a well-established forum with considerable momentum, and, because of the involvement of the local authorities and the RSC, considerable capacity to deliver. The PWV Forum could be seen by some regional participants as a rival vehicle for delivering to constituents.

However, it is perhaps unlikely that the two initiatives will produce economic development strategies which are sharply in conflict, if only because of the overlap of technical and policy-research personnel involved at each level. This highlights a second fundamental issue: the capacity of the mass-based organisations to participate effectively in such initiatives. Effective participation requires sufficient involvement in all the activities of the forum to be able to influence its direction significantly. Following a pattern which is all too characteristic of the strategic shift 'from resistance to reconstruction', on this point the cards are stacked against the civics, unions and political movements. This is evident, for example, in the lack of involvement thus far of members of mass-based organisations in developing the work programme of the PWV Forum; and the same organisations will probably require assistance to develop complete project or policy proposals. The public authorities, by contrast, are able to devote very substantial resources to producing comprehensive policy proposals.

The power and implementation capacity which was the subject of such heated debate at the second plenary of the PWV Forum (see above) is a third key issue. It is very important, especially to the mass-based organisations, that the initiatives deliver, and that they be seen to deliver. But despite moral pressure, the public authorities and the business delegations here also hold most of the cards. Projects will need to be financed, and policies will need to be implemented; until there is a new government, there is not too much that the mass-based organisations can do when the authorities drag their feet. This point should not be made too starkly: the mass-based organisations do bring considerable power to development forums; but it is a form of power which is difficult to wield in a negotiations-based development initiative.[15]

A fourth issue involves the risk that the economic development forum merely becomes a vehicle for high-profile delivery to constituencies, and that little attention is paid to the fundamental, long-term and difficult task of developing a comprehensive strategy. The risk might become more acute as the first non-racial elections approach. Against this concern, however, it is possible to set the following observations: the Metropolitan Chamber has a policy development approach which is focused on the long term and which all working groups must follow; and in its 'rapid review' and 'specific projects' programmes, the PWV Forum has developed a device to finesse the issue. Furthermore, the two initiatives provide vehicles for mobilising investment resources which could become very important in the face of private investor hesitancy, or even capital strike. Finally, the political organisations who will stand for election are not central to either the Economic Development Working Group or the PWV Forum.

A related fifth issue concerns the question of whether fundamental political realignments are taking place in forums such as the two being discussed here, or whether the forums are papering over divisions which they have little prospect of overcoming at this stage. One way of looking at the numerous forums which have emerged in recent years is that they are attempts to forge social compacts at each level and in each locality. If this is the case, they would be an appropriate vehicle for local economic strategies, which, if they involve labour and community groups at all, usually involve a social compact deal of some kind. If, however, the forums are for delivery to constituencies, and divisions are being papered over, then they are unlikely to be suitable for developing and implementing local or regional economic strategies.

Finally, and again on a related point, there is the issue of what economic approach will be adopted by the initiatives. Currently there is no clarity about economic policy directions in the PWV Forum or the ED:WG. The 'specific projects' programme of the former may throw up proposals which are so divergent in conception and direction that it will not be possible to implement them all. This will force participants to engage in the economic policy debate which has been notably absent from the proceedings thus far. Unfortunately, there is little clarity on a regional or metropolitan economic direction in progressive circles either. Support for a radical statism in the economy has lost ground, to be replaced by a focus on measures such as anti-monopoly legislation, fiscal redistribution, and so on. But this provides little direction for regional or metropolitan economic strategies.

Some economic and development policy issues

The first issue under this heading is also obvious: both the PWV Forum and the ED:WG are concerned with developing regional/metropolitan strategies for areas which are South Africa's 'economic heart'. There are two aspects to this. Firstly, the link between the national, regional and metropolitan economic strategies becomes especially important, since a large part of the national strategy will relate directly to the economies of the central Witwatersrand in particular and the PWV in general. Alternatively, the metropolitan or regional strategy may come close to also being the national strategy. The political and other issues which arise in these cases are particularly intractable: from the perspective of the subnational process, it is essential to examine the features of the metropolitan economy, and link them to those of the economies of the PWV, South Africa and the international world. If the concept of a local economy is in doubt anywhere, it is in the central Witwatersrand.

The second aspect of this issue involves whether the central Witwatersrand and the PWV are net recipients of resources from the rest of the country, or whether they are net donors. This point, so difficult to show empirically as it would involve tracking inter-personal, intra- and inter-corporate, and state financial flows, is of great political and developmental significance. Considering its relative wealth, numerous corporate head offices and so on, the viewpoint most often expressed elsewhere in the country is that the centre is a net recipient. The implication is obvious: mechanisms must be found to transfer more resources from the centre to the less favoured areas. On the other hand, if the centre is a net donor, such a policy could stifle the economic heart and retard the development of the whole country.

A second issue which faces economic and development policy in the PWV more than in other areas is the question of illegal immigrants. Because the PWV in general and the Witwatersrand in particular offer so many of the available work opportunities, these areas have attracted a great many immigrants, especially from Mozambique and Zimbabwe, but increasingly from further afield as well. This is of great importance to the regional and metropolitan economies, and raises some very difficult policy issues which will ultimately have to be decided at national level. One dimension of this is that immigrants have only a tenuous grip in the urban areas: they are subject to deportation and so must survive in informal residential and work situations. In some parts of the Witwatersrand, small enterprises make a point of employing illegals at one-third of the wages in formal and unionised factories. In some cases, they may even accommodate the workers on site, to lessen the chance that they will be discovered by the police. A second dimension is that because illegals must live in informal situations (shanty settlements and hostels provide their most obvious toe-holds in the urban areas), they are threatened by development projects which involve upgrading and formalising services and accommodation. When the illegals are also involved in arms smuggling, or have access to arms, then they are in a position to put a stop to any development project which threatens to expose them. The policy issues here are very difficult to resolve: either a concerted effort will have to be made to expel all the illegals (this hardly seems very likely), or their position will have to be made more secure (but this would amount to an invitation to more immigrants, with dangerous effects on unemployment and wages of South Africans). The third alternative involves attempting to make some form of (covert) provision for illegals in any development or upgrading project where they are present: but this, too, seems unlikely to succeed.

The question of the illegals was discussed at the first plenary session of the PWV Forum. It points to the need to examine the PWV economy in relation to all the other economies of Southern Africa as well.

NOTES

1. The Metropolitan Chamber is discussed below.
2. Rietfontein is a 'green field' site which is being developed for low-income housing despite its distance from potential employment.
3. Coffey and Polese (1984) use a similar definition.
4. For example, John Benington, a leading British practitioner whose experience includes economic development work for the Sheffield City Council and with the Motor Industry Local Authorities Network (MILAN) acknowledges that the direct impact of local economic strategies is likely to be negligible (cited in Cochrane 1988: 167).
5. Henceforth, 'the Chamber'.
6. The negotiating arm of the Soweto Civic Association during the time that the latter was banned.
7. Including: transferring houses to the people, upgrading of service standards, affordable service charges, and a common fiscal base.
8. The founding signatories were civic associations and government bodies. The civic associations were the: Soweto People's Delegation; Soweto Civic Association; Western Rent Action Committee; Kliptown, Eldorado Park, Klipspruit West Interim Democratic Civic Association; Riverlea Civic Association; Ennerdale Civic Association.
    The government bodies were the: Transvaal Provincial Administration; City Council of Soweto; City Council of Diepmeadow; City Council of Dobsonville; City Council of Johannesburg; City Council of Randburg; City Council of Sandton; City Council of Alexandra; City Council of Roodepoort; Davidsonville/Fleurhof Management Committee; Lenasia South Management Committee.
9. COSATU was concerned not to stretch its capacity too far, and felt that while effective participation at regional level would be possible, participation at metropolitan and local level would not.

10. Organisations represented at the preliminary meeting included the Civic Associations of the Southern Transvaal, Civic Associations of Johannesburg, Soweto Civic Association, COSATU, Foundation for African Business and Consumer Services, Federation of South African Labour Unions (FEDSAL), Federation of Independent Trade Unions, Johannesburg Chamber of Commerce and Industry, National African Federated Chamber of Commerce, South African Chamber of Business, Transvaal Provincial Administration, and the Central Witwatersrand Metropolitan Chamber.

11. The CBM was concerned not to be seen as driving the process, and stressed that it would act as a facilitator and not as a player in its own right. This concern has been expressed by CBM staff-members throughout the process to date: participants, however, seemed unconcerned, and have repeatedly endorsed the CBM's role.

12. National negotiations had ceased with the failure of CODESA II, and the Metropolitan Chamber had just been suspended when the plenary took place.

13. This highlighted the issue of the relationship between delegations representing constituencies and 'development experts'.

14. The Azanian People's Organisation requested membership soon after the launch.

15. For example, local-level negotiations over the last two years have generally been able to make substantial progress only when it has been possible to find an external source of development finance (Planact 1992b).

Chapter 10

Urban Planning, Shelter Strategies and Economic Development

David Dewar

Although South Africa has had a low-income housing policy for some decades, urban housing remains one of the biggest problems facing the country. The backlog in formal housing is currently estimated at over one million units. Moreover, largely because of the legacy of apartheid, there is a strong racial bias in the pattern of shortfall: the shortfall for whites is minimal; the backlog in the coloured and Indian communities is estimated at 100 000 units, while that for blacks is estimated to be at least 850 000 units and possibly as high as one million units (De Vos 1987). Over seven million people (mostly black) live in informal housing circumstances (in free-standing or backyard shacks, outbuildings, garages and so on). About 70 per cent of urban blacks do not have direct access to running water or electricity (Urban Foundation 1990a).

Although reliable statistics do not exist, it is apparent that rates of urban growth, too, are high. Durban, for example, has reputedly grown 100 per cent over the last ten years, which would make it one of the fastest-growing cities in the world. The overall population of the major metropolitan areas is expected to increase almost threefold during the period 1980-2000 (Urban Foundation 1990a). Accordingly, the absolute magnitude of urban housing needs is escalating daily. It is estimated that an additional 130 000 dwelling units will have to be built each year in order to provide adequate housing for the urban black population (excluding the homelands, for which statistics are not readily available) by the year 2010. Recently, annual supply has been less than a quarter of this (Urban Foundation 1990b). Clearly, whatever the form of non-racial government which emerges from current negotiating processes, it will have to address the housing question vigorously and as a matter of urgency.

Equally clearly, the question of *how* the housing issue should be tackled cannot be examined in isolation from dominant contextual realities, particularly those of urban structure and form (of which housing is the major and most rapidly growing component) and the need to combat poverty and unemployment. Of particular importance in the South African context, where the formal economy is failing to generate jobs at a rate anywhere near sufficient to match demand, is the need to create opportunities for small-scale, self-generated employment. The reality is that, for the foreseeable future, large numbers of people will have no option but to seek survival through self-generated employment.

These issues seem self-evident, and yet there is little understanding of how such concerns – housing, urban management, and unemployment and poverty – impinge upon each other. This chapter seeks to address this problem. Specifically, it identifies some urban management and housing actions which need to be taken to maximise opportunities for employment generation and to assist in combating poverty.

COMPACT THE CITY AND IMPLODE GROWTH

Three spatial patterns, more than any others, characterise South African cities. The first is explosive low-density sprawl, the direction of which is largely uncontrolled. The second is fragmentation: the grain of the urban fabric is very coarse and there is limited continuity of urban fabric. Development tends to occur in relatively discrete 'blobs', more or less adjacent to each other. The third is separation: races, income groups and land uses are separated to the greatest degree possible. These patterns are strongly underpinned by entrenched practices in housing provision: in particular, the fact that the end-product of the housing process is seen as nothing but a free-standing house on a large plot, and everything is geared to producing this; the fact that housing schemes are undertaken primarily as large programmes requiring large parcels of vacant land – parcels which can only be found beyond the existing urban fringe; and the use of space as a buffer between race groups, until recently, and now between income groups.

In combination, these characteristics have a savage impact on the lives of the majority – the urban poor (Dewar *et al.* 1990a, 1990b). The sprawling, fragmented urban system generates an enormous amount of movement, but fails to create the preconditions for the emergence of viable, efficient and widely accessible public transportation systems. The costs of this movement to urban-dwellers, in terms of time and money, are becoming increasingly intolerable: the structural system is significantly aggravating the major development problems of poverty, unemployment and inequality. It is economically inefficient, inflationary, and militates against economic growth. The large distances and low densities ensure that distributional costs form an inordinately high proportion of total costs in the cost structures of most businesses.

Further, the system differentially affects very small businesses. The market concentration necessary to generate vibrant local economies does not exist and the limited number of points of high accessibility, in combination with the spatially extensive market catchments, ensures that only large economic units can really flourish: the physical structure thus promotes economic centralisation and monopolisation. It fails to generate high levels of social and commercial services; indeed, the costs of providing the sprawling system even with adequate utility services are becoming prohibitive. It wastes society's scarce resources such as land, energy and finance. It is resulting in extensive environmental destruction and pollution.

These dormitory housing areas make desperately poor living environments. They are highly inconvenient, particularly for those huge numbers of people without motor cars. Because of their fragmented, introverted nature, individual housing areas, in effect, need to be self-sufficient in terms of social and economic infrastructure: there is little reinforcement or interaction between areas. In reality, because of low thresholds, service levels are extremely low. Indeed, for many the average day is dominated by survival activities such as the search for fuel and water and desperate attempts to generate a meagre income.

Being poor in these areas is an expensive business. Transport costs, although heavily subsidised in the case of public transportation, bite deeply and commodity prices are generally higher than in the wealthier areas.

In the face of this, there is an overwhelming case for using housing policy to insert or implode new housing within the boundaries of the existing cities. Instead of continually pushing the urban edge further outward, densities should be increased. New growth should be seen as a resource to restructure the cities and to improve the performance of existing areas. There is considerable residual land within South African cities to implement policies of this kind.

There are a number of sound economic arguments for pursuing such a course. It will, over time, increase the efficiency of all businesses by reducing distributional costs. It will reduce the cost of urban development by making maximal use of historical investments in utility and social infrastructure. It will result in indirect transfers to the poorer members of society (via savings in transport, cheaper serviced land and other costs), thereby increasing local markets. In a real sense, it will change the nature of urban economics. It will improve labour productivity by reducing travelling time. Finally, and perhaps most importantly, it will maximise the generative capacity of urban systems. The more compact the local market, the greater the range of potential economic opportunities and the wider the range of viable locations to manufacture and trade which present themselves to all inhabitants: accessibility in this case is not defined primarily by the configuration and intersection of transport routes – points that can be dominated by larger enterprises. Compaction, therefore, is the key to encouraging specialisation and diversification. This is particularly important in the case of small economic enterprises.

Four types of implosion policies suggest themselves. One is structural implosion: increasing unit densities around strategically significant parts of the cities, in order to maximise their potential (for example, the inner-city areas, around stations, along public transportation channels and so on). A second is economic implosion: facilitating an internal tightening by encouraging people, within certain performance constraints, to subdivide land parcels they own – benefiting themselves in the process. A third form is social implosion: encouraging existing communities to identify residual land in their areas which can be used to reduce the chronic overcrowding within housing units, while maintaining community ties. A fourth form is surgical implosion: strategically inserting higher-density units into the fabric in order to give a sense of scale and enclosure to currently ill-formed, unscaled and dangerous public spaces (Dewar and Uytenbogaardt 1991).

MAINTAIN A FIXED, PERMANENT EDGE BETWEEN URBAN AND RURAL AREAS

Small-scale agriculture must be seen as a vitally important land use in and around South African cities. The primary agricultural sector in South Africa can and will have to play an increasing role in supporting people. Because of a lack of alternative forms of income generation, many people will have no option but to seek sustenance from the soil, either in a primary or a supplementary way. Evidence indicates that urban and peri-urban agriculture can play a vital role in supplementing income. The degree to which small-scale production can occur, however, is strongly influenced by how urban growth is managed.

The smaller the scale of agricultural production, the more significant the unit cost of transporting produce to market becomes. And the further away small farmers are from marketing points, the more they are forced to rely on the services of 'intermediates' serving a number of producers. These operators, because they are in a monopolistic position, are able to engage in considerable price exploitation to the detriment of both producer and consumer in the longer term.

The greatest opportunities for small-scale agriculture, therefore, lie close to dense urban markets. Conversely, a sprawling, shifting, low-density urban edge ensures that larger and larger producers supply the urban population, via centralised distribution points.

The implication of this for urban growth management is that if agriculture is seen to be an important urban land use, as indeed it should be, then a stable relationship – a fixed edge – between dense urban areas and agricultural land is essential. Such a relationship also allows for urban waste, such as water run-off and partially treated sewerage, to be returned easily to the land and put to productive use.

If we are to deal with the urban management problem in a constructive way, our starting-point must not be where urban development should go, but where it should *not* go. This is an important distinction. The current approach to urban land is to identify land parcels where urban development should go and then develop these to the exclusion of almost all others. Their very uniqueness places great pressure on them and results in major problems. The approach outlined here recognises that the dynamics of urban growth play themselves out in many places simultaneously, through a variety of decisions and processes. A range of options is clearly necessary, but it is important to ensure that the range is not unlimited and that these embryonic dynamics are channelled into a system which grows together over time into a cohesive, continuous, integrated urban system with an enduring relationship to the countryside.

Finally, while the emphasis here has been on small-scale agriculture, other forms of primary production are equally important. It is now widely accepted that aqua-farming is suitable for small-scale production and has significant economic potential. Woodlots (the planting of trees as a fuel source) also offer economic potential to small-scale operators, and can be particularly valuable when they double as shelter belts to modify micro-climatic impacts.

ENCOURAGE DECENTRALISED WHOLESALING SYSTEMS

A third economically stimulatory action, made possible by the first two outlined above, is to encourage decentralised wholesaling systems.

A vital factor affecting both the extent and profitability of small-scale vending is the spatial relationship between vendors and their primary sources of supply (Dewar and Watson 1990). Given this, wholesaling outlets can be used as 'triggers' to stimulate small-scale economic activity. This has potential in many cases (for example, building materials, firewood, and so on) but a particularly important one is the urban fresh-produce wholesaling system, as basic foodstuffs are the primary products sold by small-scale vendors, especially in low-income areas.

When small traders have easy and close access to a wholesale outlet, the cost of produce to the vendor is relatively lower and the cost of transporting supplies back to the point of sale is reduced. Further, additional supplies can easily be obtained in the case of unexpected demand and the trader can more closely match supplies with sales. Conversely, when easy access does not exist, flexibility is reduced, supply costs increase, profits decrease, and costs to the consumer rise. An important structural change also occurs: larger, more successful vendors, who often have their own transport, are able to gain an advantage over smaller traders. Hence, minimum capital requirements for vending are increased, larger operators dominate the market and small traders suffer.

This underlines the need to decentralise wholesaling outlets, and to integrate the location of these with the public transportation system, to provide for the majority of vendors who do not have their own transport. In Bombay, India, for example, this need is recognised in part: the last coach of every train is reserved for vendors and their wares.

Significantly, the more dispersed the form of the city, the more necessary it becomes to centralise wholesaling.

In South African cities, the fresh-produce wholesaling system is entirely centralised. It is poorly serviced by the public transport system and is generally inaccessible to the vast majority of small-scale traders. As a result, a second, and far more decentralised level of wholesaling has emerged: many small traders buy their supplies from larger informal traders or from wholesale supermarkets. The effect of this, however, is to raise costs, reduce profits, and limit the extent to which small informal traders can engage in food distribution.

Increasing dislocation between urban and rural areas, therefore, has two main effects: it promotes the emergence of larger food producers at the expense of smaller ones; and it demands a high level of centralisation of distribution sources within the urban areas. Conversely, the closer the integration, the greater the opportunities for small producers, for a decentralised wholesaling system and for small-scale distribution.

PROMOTE A GREATER MIX OF LAND USES

For a number of decades, urban planning and housing policy have been dominated by a belief in the need for the spatial separation of urban land uses. Housing programmes are implemented via mono-functional housing schemes: residential areas are viewed as needing protection from commercial and manufacturing activities and from heavier traffic movement. This attitude negatively impinges on the generation of economic activity, particularly small-scale activity. The exclusion of small operators from residential areas (under zoning, traffic and health-related regulations) increases their operating costs significantly: operators must pay for separate and often specialised locations and services, and endure increased travelling costs to and from points where they can operate legally.

The separation of small operators from residential areas also constrains their productive time severely and hence reduces turnovers and profits. Small sellers and producers frequently rely on extended working hours to compete with large businesses and this requires that they operate from home. Home-based activity should therefore be encouraged and the extent of such activity will certainly increase as the cities compact.

Historically the authorities have opposed home-based activities because of a concern that they will constitute a nuisance and thus impinge on the rights of surrounding residents. Obviously, some activities are nuisance-generating and in these cases the rights of residents should be protected. However, a number of points must be made about the issue. Firstly, many productive activities which can be conducted from home do not cause a nuisance at all. Secondly, in many cases, it is only one part of the process which is nuisance-generating and that part can be separated and accommodated elsewhere. Thirdly, many activities have no nuisance effect until they reach a certain scale; blanket regulations tend to throw the baby out with the bath-water. Fourthly, research shows that even home-based activity does not occur at the same intensity everywhere (Dewar and Watson 1981). Greatest opportunities lie around lines and points of greatest movement intensity, which tend to be places that are noisier and less private in any event: to an extent, therefore, the land market resolves the issue of conflict naturally. When considerations of nuisance are as complex as this, the issue clearly cannot be controlled through a set of rigid, standardised rules or regulations. What is required is a performance-based licensing system where the onus is upon the operator to show the local authority, to whom residents may appeal in the case of transgressions, that performance requirements in terms of noise, smell, light and air are being met.

Related to the issue of home-based economic activity is that of electrification. Bearing in mind that electricity is the cheapest and cleanest form of energy in South Africa today, there is no doubt that large-scale electrification would significantly increase economic opportunities, and thus levels of employment, in the poorest areas. Electrification, wherever viable, should be an important aspect of housing policy.

USE TRANSPORT ROUTES TO INTEGRATE URBAN AREAS AND TO CREATE ACTIVITY SPINES

South African cities have been fragmented by apartheid, by housing programmes undertaken on discrete parcels of land, and by the simplistic belief that social 'communities' can best be created in new residential areas if they are designed as physically discrete, self-centred suburbs. The fragmented form of the cities hampers the generation and diffusion of income-generating opportunities.

Urban energy is expressed largely in terms of flows – of people, goods and investment. And this energy determines the distribution of the most intensive activities, those activities such as economic enterprises, commercial facilities, social and cultural events and so on which are dependent on high levels of public support for their existence. Significantly, the potential expressed in this energy is not realised through the process of flow: it can only be realised when the flow is broken – when stopping and gathering occur. Obviously, too, for the potential to be realised, more intensive activities must be able to respond to the energy.

A corollary of the current sprawling, fragmented urban form is that the movement hierarchy tends to be highly simplified. The main continuous routes tend to be limited-access freeways, which, from an urban structural perspective, have little positive impact, since there is little or no stopping and more intensive activities are prevented from locating along them. This movement is channelled to a limited number of points (for example, egress points or the intersection of two freeways) and more intensive activities are restricted to those points. In effect, the accessibility surface of the city takes the form of a limited number of peaks connected by movement routes. At a lower level, most other routes are purely local routes internal to housing areas; individually, they do not carry sufficient volumes of movement to make them really viable locations for activities dependent upon public support.

There are several disadvantages which result from this: the range of opportunities available to the more intensive users is limited; those opportunities that do exist tend to be monopolised by larger activities; the system is dominated by car-owners; over-specialisation occurs at particular points or centres, such as the CBDs, thereby increasing their vulnerability; the connectors do not serve to integrate the city but to divide; and the system generates enormous amounts of movement.

The resolution of these problems lies in breaking the pattern of fragmentation. The key to this, in turn, lies in promoting a hierarchy of interconnecting continuous routes or, preferably, systems of movement modes, to carry both public and private transportation; in orienting development to these interconnecting systems and using housing policy to reinforce them through higher-density housing; and in allowing more intensive activities to respond to the flows along them, resulting in linear corridors of activities or 'activity spines'.

There are several advantages which result from this structural form. Firstly, it maximises the generative capacities inherent in urban agglomeration. When the movement system is structurally clear, when connector- or through-routes are easily identifiable and dominant, through-traffic naturally gravitates towards them. Because flows are channelled along defined routes, enterprises and activities of different sizes, with different generative capacities in their own right, can find viable places along them. Larger enterprises tend to dominate the most accessible, and therefore most desirable points along the line (for example, at the intersection or confluence of different movement modes). However, in this structural configuration smaller, more fragile enterprises can benefit from the flows of energy generated by these larger concerns, by taking up interceptor locations between or adjacent to the major generators. Similarly, activities with different space, rent-paying and accessibility requirements can find a place in the system. Effectively, therefore, the system allows a wide range of different types and sizes of enterprises and activities to coexist with a high degree of complementarity, and this maximises economic efficiency.

All activities benefit to some degree from the generative capacity of others; all gain from and serve both passing traffic and the local areas which they abut. Consequently no activity is entirely dependent for its support on its immediate local community.

Secondly, the system promotes equity, in the sense that it has the potential to reach a greater number of people than exclusively node-based forms of development. In the former system, activities are taken to the people; in the latter, people have to come to the activities. The former seeks to maximise accessibility; the latter, ease of movement. Further, the more integrative system allows the poor to benefit from the purchasing power of the wealthy, and the variety of activities supported within the local areas is much greater and of a higher order than could be supported by the local population of any one area alone.

Once the linear system advocated here is viewed not as a single activity spine with a diverse pattern of accessibility along it, but as a system of interlocking spines of different intensity, it becomes apparent that the pattern of urban accessibility and therefore the pattern of economic opportunity becomes far more complex, differentiated and spread than in the point-related system.

CREATE LOW-OVERHEAD OPPORTUNITIES FOR SMALL ENTREPRENEURS TO MANUFACTURE AND TRADE IN THE MOST VIABLE LOCATIONS WITHIN THE CITY

In the ongoing processes of building and rebuilding which are shaping South African cities, two interrelated tendencies in the places of greatest economic potential – the main commercial centres – are observable. The first is ever-increasing specialisation. The centres are increasingly dominated by office and service functions; over time, through the operation of the urban land market, housing and commercial components have been systematically displaced. The second tendency is displacement of small businesses by larger ones.

Ironically, both of these tendencies threaten the future of the centres themselves. There is therefore a strong case for using housing policy to implement sustained, intensive housing programmes in order to create large amounts of affordable housing for lower-income people close to these centres. This would make it possible to rebuild these centres from the bottom up, and to stimulate diversity by creating opportunities for small-scale retailers, manufacturers and providers of services. This could take many forms. A particularly important one is the conscious stimulation of periodic and permanent markets in public spaces and selected streets. Markets – physical agglomerations of small traders and producers – are potentially powerful instruments for stimulating informal-sector activity (Dewar and Watson 1990). Because of their collective size, and the range of choices which this offers to consumers, markets enable small enterprises to compete with larger formal ones, which otherwise tend to monopolise trade. The stimulation of diversification can take many other forms: the use of low-cost, clip-on infrastructure (kiosks) to enliven institutional buildings and other 'dead' facades; the use of hives for small industry on the edges of centres; alternative forms of service provision, such as metered water and electricity standards, for periodic use; and so on.

The principle of using public space to organise and structure economic activity and public facilities does not only apply to commercial centres: it should be entrenched in housing policy and should apply in all settlements, including informal ones. The public spaces, which should be integrated with the major movement routes, should be supported by a network of bulk services, including water, electricity and sewerage. This means that economic activities and intensively used public facilities such as schools and clinics can make use of necessary services even though surrounding residents may choose not to do so. The proximity of the bulk service network also means that when people's circumstances do allow them to take up particular services, the link-up costs are low.

USE THE PROCESS OF HOUSING DELIVERY TO STIMULATE EMPLOYMENT GENERATION AND WIDE INCOME CIRCULATION

There is intensive debate in South Africa over whether or not a vigorous housing policy has a major role to play in promoting economic growth via 'inward industrialisation'. Regardless of the macro-economic potentials, it is clearly sensible, in the face of very high rates of unemployment and poverty, to use housing policy to stimulate employment. The potential is considerable, particularly since the construction sector is relatively labour-intensive. The role of the state should be to inject substantial and sustained amounts of capital into the housing process, broadly defined. It also has a major role to play in stimulating the organisational and institutional changes necessary for capital to circulate as widely as possible, for example, large-scale training programmes to develop extensive networks of small builders; the promotion of labour-intensive public works programmes to provide and maintain infrastructure; the use of subcontracting to promote small business, not only in housing but in related fields such as making institutional furniture and uniforms; the establishment of wholesale building caches; and so on.

CONCLUSION

It is apparent that the problems of housing, urban development and economic development are closely interrelated. Indeed, for housing policy to have any real meaning it must be consciously used to tackle urban and economic problems and, over time, to change the nature of urban form and urban economics. This is not happening now. For housing policy to contribute to a better urban future, it needs to encourage urban compaction; at the moment it is a major force entrenching the characteristic sprawling, fragmented form of the South African city. For it to contribute significantly to economic development, it needs to promote vigorous processes of housing consolidation and to stimulate a restructuring of the construction sector, in order to encourage a wide spread of income and labour-intensive practices. Currently, the policy emphasis is on the provision of serviced sites, while major obstacles to vigorous consolidation remain; the housing sector remains relatively capital-intensive; and finance invested in housing has a relatively narrow circulation.

Chapter 11
CONCLUSION

Development planning is usually born in crisis, when economic misfortune and unrest among the poor prompt a city's leaders to promote growth. However, initial enthusiasm for development planning soon confronts the competitive pressures inherent in global capitalism. It is easy to oversell development planning. Thus, Markusen and Carlson (1989: 49) comment that

> The following policy tools, and strategic elements were prominent: smokestack chasing, job retention, industrial targeting, location incentives, small business incentives, research parks, venture capital funds, export promotion, and human capital strategies. Some have proved to be better than others, but as a group they have not been successful against the tide of restructuring forces ...

This is a fair comment, but there are exceptions to the rule. Judd and Parkinson (1990) cite the relative successes of what they term 'intentional cities': those cities in Western Europe and North America where urban coalitions sometimes brought about a reversal in the decline of manufacturing employment, more often reduced the rate of manufacturing decline relative to the region and comparable cities, and initiated new and more diversified growth paths.

These cities did not make do with limited and ill-co-ordinated programmes initiated by the local public and private sectors. Instead, agreement was sought among major local economic and political actors about a long-term strategic direction that encompassed a co-ordinated investment and marketing programme.

This is an encouraging conclusion, and one which is supported by two additional arguments for development planning. The first argument is simply that development planning is getting better. We should think back to Chapter 5 and the so-called 'Third Wave' in economic development strategies: while the focus is still on indigenous development, increasingly development programmes are organised in concert with the private sector, are demand-driven, and are targeted to specific sectors and industries within those sectors.

The second argument is that the process of development planning generates a better understanding of development problems and the resources available to deal with them. In South Africa development planning has the potential to bring the major players together and create a common perception of development problems and opportunities, and of the resources available to deal with them and how they should be approached. This could build trust and help repair the damage caused by apartheid.

LIKELY PARTICIPANTS

The following characterisation of the motives of the various participants in the urban coalition represents a 'South Africanisation' of the question asked in Chapter 4: 'Why engage?' I first list the participants and then discuss their motives. The list is not exhaustive but rather intended to highlight the major players.

The players will have a crucial decision-making role. This is because the planning process will not consist of a technical expert in government or a consultant being given a task and asked to return with a recommended 'solution'. Rather, planning will be a process in which a steering committee formed by the coalition interacts with the technical expert in order to explore strategic options and make informed decisions.

i.   The core members of an urban coalition, the decision-makers who steer the development planning process, will probably include local politicians, chambers of commerce and industry, prominent businesspersons, small business representatives, unions, and metropolitan civic structures. While the public and private sectors and the unions are obvious participants in any exercise intended to chart a city's economic future, the legitimacy of the exercise and commitment to it will be enhanced if planning is not undertaken in a corporatist fashion. Community groups must be included. Economic power and political capital are not easily separable.

ii. A coalition's membership will mushroom through the creation of sub-committees, task teams or working groups. These will be necessary to address the numerous issues for which policy research and recommendations are required. The outcome, ideally, is that commitment will ripple outwards as more groups are drawn into the process.[1]

iii. Aid agencies and utility companies will contribute to the main steering committee and the task teams. They will not and should not have voting powers, but their power will none the less be implicit. For it is they who influence how a development problem is articulated, make decisions on whether or not to fund a project, and determine the conditions under which to offer funding. Many sins are concealed by conditionality and technical expertise, and the development agenda of the steering committee may be distorted by these means.

Inevitably, there will be tensions between the various participants and between different types of participants.[2] Again, initial enthusiasm will have to confront certain realities. The Central Witwatersrand Metropolitan Chamber is lucky to have Frederik van Zyl Slabbert in the chair, just as Operation Jumpstart and the Metropolitan Development Forum in the DFR are lucky to have Terry Rosenberg. When development issues are so intertwined with the legacy of apartheid and the politics of the transition, are figures of such stature a precondition to success?

From the local authority's point of view,[3] participation will depend on:

• its expectation that development will entail more benefits than costs;
• whether the proposed development benefits important constituencies; and
• the degree to which it has powers which will influence the outcome.

Although the constitutional uncertainty in South Africa makes it difficult to gauge the enthusiasm with which most local authorities will embrace development planning, the large number of local initiatives that already exist suggests that the approach is popular. In general, this enthusiasm will reflect:

• the distribution of responsibility for development planning between levels of government;
• where the local authority's finances come from;
• whether local politicians are linked to and depend on the support of

a national party or, if the party system is weak, whether their careers depend on contributions from the private sector in order to fight elections;

- whether the prevailing ideological structure emphasises entrepreneurship and growth;
- whether local initiatives will be supported or opposed by central government; and
- the priority given to economic development by the local initiatives.

For the private sector, including major business and financial institutions, companies and individuals, participation will be influenced by:

- the state of the local economy;
- the sense that a public-private partnership can influence the state of the economy;
- anticipation that the costs of development efforts will to a large degree be borne by the public; and
- the degree to which public powers have a bearing on the success of individual projects.

For small and informal enterprises, participation in the development process will seem necessary in order to obtain a more favourable regulatory environment, and will also be encouraged by the many opportunities for government largesse which result from majority control of city government. An obvious example is government contracts which are awarded subject to, say, 20 per cent of the contract going to small enterprises.

For their part, community organisations will have an interest in:

- the way development problems are defined;
- how expenditure priorities are determined; and
- their own role either in receiving funding and supplying services, or in influencing who receives funding.

As far as the unions are concerned, it is evident that their interests are at stake if there is a declining local economy and there are attempts to restructure that economy. The fact that COSATU is presently reluctant to participate in the local initiatives rather contradicts this assertion. However, my feeling is that when the initiatives become more sophisticated and proceed to attempts to restructure metropolitan economies, COSATU will see greater value in participating in development planning forums.

In this regard, Dirk Hartford's article in *Business Day* (25 February 1993) is encouraging in that he points out how COSATU's attitudes are changing from 'resistance to reconstruction'. Reconstruction includes programmes to create jobs and alleviate poverty, and the linkage with development planning is immediately apparent.

Finally, it is in the nature of aid agencies and utility companies to seek both projects and cost recovery. The former is the standard by which they are measured, the latter is a precondition to their survival. Given that they presently struggle to disburse resources due to violence, local disputes, and the illegitimacy and limited implementational capacity of many borrowers, development planning forums which offer projects and legitimacy are likely to be highly prized.

PROBABLE INTERVENTIONS

The following actions have all been discussed in the body of the text. Here I bring them together as a check-list which South African practitioners might consider.

I assume that the development planning process will be guided by an urban coalition and that the day-to-day decision-making within the coalition will be undertaken by a steering committee. Their actions can be summarised as follows.

Strategic plan

The participants should prepare a strategic plan. This plan should provide guidance to the committee in respect of:

- the targeting of specific industries and services with a view to formulating a co-ordinated investment strategy which serves the domestic and international markets;
- efforts to attract related investment when synergistic outcomes seem possible;[4]
- the formation of vertical networks between large, medium and small firms, and horizontal networks between medium and small firms – both to create development opportunities for the latter firms, and so that they can achieve economies of scale;
- how to foster an entrepreneurial culture;
- affirmative policies, especially with a view to promoting African enterprise;

- a regulatory environment which nurtures economic development; and
- reviewing and revising the factors that contribute to an inefficient and inequitable city, and limit opportunities for economic development.

Medium and small enterprise

The structure of the South African economy is notorious for its 'missing middle'; the economy is dominated by large corporations. It is instructive that small and medium firms account for 75 per cent of Japan's manufacturing output, whereas in the USA the figure is 35 per cent. It was earlier shown that integrated manufacturing networks between large and small manufacturing firms in Japan benefit all and facilitate flexible specialisation. For medium and small firms, also, horizontal networks bring the advantages described in respect of FMNs in Chapter 5. Efforts should be made to enhance the potential for vertical and horizontal networks.

Entrepreneurial culture

The notion of an entrepreneurial culture is nebulous and probably in disrepute due to the failure of enterprise zones. Yet there can be little doubt that creating links between, say, business and universities which enable universities to offer high salaries and superior research facilities to engineering professors, may be a better marketing and economic development strategy than expensive attempts to lure foreign industries. Similarly, the public and private sectors could provide the seed capital for a venture capital programme; the civics could be trained to serve as a conduit for business loans to the informal sector; or assistance could be made available in respect of the identification of markets. All these initiatives could enhance entrepreneurship within the area.

African enterprise

When local industries face competition from elsewhere, it is difficult to argue that affirmative policies which increase inefficiency in the production and cost of their products are justified. However, when it is possible to impose the same conditions on all potential suppliers, then procurement clauses, for example, which state that companies bidding for a municipal contract must subcontract a minimum proportion of the value of the contract, are worth considering. This will create partnerships between large and small firms, provide instruction in business methods, improve quality control, and lead to the establishment of additional enterprises.

Regulatory environment

The regulatory environment affects every facet of conducting business: ownership, governance, finance, operating procedures, interaction among firms, the social wage, environmental conditions and so on. This either hinders or enhances economic development. The combination of restrictions based on apartheid and others derived from a First World British tradition has not served South Africa well. While a less cluttered regulatory environment is desirable, it would be a mistake to articulate the issue in these political terms. Rather, the goal is to ensure that the private sector is able to respond to a changing economy and the associated forms of organisation and activity (Fossler 1992).

The apartheid city

Given my urban-planning background, I cannot conclude this list of probable actions without again bemoaning the inefficiency and inequity of the apartheid city, whose form is inimical to economic development. David Dewar's chapter provides a succinct assessment of what needs to be done.

POSSIBLE INSTITUTIONAL ARRANGEMENTS

Planning for economic development is intended to bring about a lasting and continuing change in the local economy ... Economic development is an institution-building process. As a result, it requires the emergence of *planning systems and institutions* that can manage the development process over extended periods of time. ... An institution with specific responsibility to co-ordinate each step of the local economic development process is essential. The development strategy plan, as well as the process itself, requires fiscal resources, technical expertise, leadership, and imagination. Some type of fully staffed, locally based institution must be available ... (Blakely 1989: 252, emphasis in original)

Irrespective of the form of the development organisation, it should have both the authority and the resources to undertake research, strategic planning, and the co-ordination of the activities of related institutions. The last point is the key. It is unlikely that the development planning institution will be given the power necessary to implement the actions described above. Instead it will co-ordinate the actions of a university, which undertakes research; a chamber of commerce, which is responsible for marketing; city government, which will review regulations that are obstacles to the informal sector; and so on. In other words, the power of the development institution is of a different sort: it consists in winning the commitment of the main players, the ability to co-ordinate an investment programme, access to information, and the legitimacy which arises from political credibility and superior technical expertise.

This conception of the development institution leads directly to the third of Blakely's (1989) three models. The models are:

- a government agency, which benefits from access to political decision-makers, but suffers from bureaucratic inertia, limited credibility in the private sector, and poor access for community groups;[5]
- a PSDO, which is circumscribed by vested interests and seldom pays more than lip-service to the agenda of community organisations and unions; and
- 'joint power' organisations which comprise business, government, community and union interests.

The joint-power organisation is instantly recognisable as an urban coalition, supported by a professional staff. The mandate and functions of the coalition will obviously have to be negotiated between the coalition members. In my view the coalition should not be under the control of any one of the member groups, for then it will be in a better position to broker agreements between its members and to foster relationships of trust. The location outside government may be contentious, but offices of this sort all too easily become a vehicle for politicians. In addition, if weighed down with a bureaucratic style, the office will be insensitive to market trends and lack the ability to formulate creative responses.[6]

The following structure is illustrative. The coalition will build the broad economic and political consensus required. The steering committee will see to the everyday operation of the coalition and will be assisted by a professional secretariat or consultant. If a secretariat is preferred, then rather than develop into a bureaucracy it should employ consultants to facilitate information-gathering and informed decision-making. The task teams will themselves be served by consultants.

Urban coalition

|

Steering Committee

|

Professional secretariat
or consultant

|

Task teams:
Strategic planning
Networking
Marketing
Opportunities (entrepreneurial, African)
Regulatory

The institutional complexity within which the coalition will have to operate is apparent when one looks at investment promotion. Wells and Wint (1990) describe three generic institutional forms of investment promotion, all of which are undertaken at the national level. The forms are consultant to government; a quasi-governmental body; or government itself. The form chosen depends on the nature of the task. The necessary activities include:

* negotiating with foreign investors;
* minimising bureaucratic hurdles;
* targeting industries and sectors; and
* marketing.

Consultants might be good at marketing, but then lack clout when it comes to minimising hurdles. Having a single ministry responsible for promotion will provoke jealousy and subterfuge from other ministries. The most common institutional form identified by Wells and Wint therefore included representatives from different government ministries, was undertaken within a quasi-governmental agency, and relied on consultants for assistance.

By way of illustration: it is desirable to separate the job of marketing a country from that of targeting specific sectors and industries for investment within an area. The former task can adequately be undertaken by the quasi-governmental agency. The latter task, when it concerns a large urban area, can be led by an urban coalition.

NOTES

1. Of course, to be less gung-ho for a moment, we could also experience fracturing, schism and a loss of coherence and momentum.
2. For example, Gilroth and Mier (1989) cite three examples from Chicago where local coalitions were jeopardised by tensions arising from:
    i.   the closure of an industrial facility which had benefited from public assistance but failed to reach promised employment levels, and was now consolidating industrial plants at another location, again with public assistance. Here, community and labour networks led the struggle against the firm, which culminated in it being sued by the city.
    ii. the displacement of small industrial businesses as a result of the redevelopment of neighbourhoods adjacent to the city centre for service and residential functions. Here a community organisation fought developers, with the city being left as the judge.
    iii. a city initiative to create industrial task forces in the steel and apparel industries which would make recommendations on how to reverse the decline of these industries and ameliorate the situation of dislocated workers. This initiative left the private sector unconvinced and needed support from the coalition.
3. The criteria in respect of local government were assembled from Harding (1991), Judd and Parkinson (1990) and Molotch and Vicari (1988).
4. The random targeting of possible investments – the 'Shoot anything that flies' syndrome – and the failure to understand in which industries a city (and region) have a comparative advantage, will lead to a waste of resources as government, chambers of commerce, and other institutions squander their efforts in an undirected fashion. Effective planning requires insight into a city's opportunities and threats, as determined by the market, and ideally the urban coalition will agree on an investment and marketing strategy which exploits the opportunities available to the area.
5. For those who believe that development planning is primarily the responsibility of the public sector, the lesson from America is that development problems and initiatives no longer call forth new programmes administered by monopolistic government agencies. Contracting, privatisation, partnerships, or simply support and encouragement to private and community groups are typical of the 'Third Wave' of development planning.
6. This is a bit of a stereotype. Glasgow's remarkable turn-around illustrates successful public sector planning, financing and implementation of an urban development strategy. But even here, with a Labour Party-controlled local authority and with the funds of the Scottish Development Agency, the benefits are spatially selective and some wards within the city still experience unemployment in excess of 45 per cent (Boyle 1990).

References

Abu-Lughod, J.L. 1980. *Rabat: Urban Apartheid in Morocco*. Princeton: Princeton University Press.

Alonso, W. 1991. The coming global metropolis: Cities of the next century. *Journal of the American Planning Association* 57, 1:3-6.

Alonso, W. 1989. Deindustrialization and regional policy. In L. Rodwin and H. Sazanami (eds), *Deindustrialization and Regional Economic Transformation: The Experience of the United States*. Boston: Unwin Hyman, pp. 221-37.

Archer, S.H. and S.M. Maser. 1989. State export promotion for economic development. *Economic Development Quarterly* 3, 3:235-42.

Ashe, J. and C.E. Cosslett. 1989. *Credit for the Poor: Past Activities and Future Directions for the United Nations Development Programme*. New York: UNDP Policy Discussion Paper.

Balkin, S. 1989. *Self-Employment for Low-Income People*. New York: Praeger.

Bates, T. 1985. Impact of preferential procurement policies on minority-owned businesses. *Review of Black Political Economy* Summer: 51-65.

Beauregard, R. 1992. Industrial diversification as economic policy. In D. Fasenfast (ed), *Community Economic Development*. Macmillan, pp. 109-12.

Bell, R.T. 1983. The growth and structure of manufacturing employment in Natal. Occasional Paper No. 7, Institute for Social and Economic Research, University of Durban-Westville.

Bendavid-Val, A. 1991. *Regional and Local Economic Analysis for Practitioners* (4th ed). New York: Praeger.

Bendick Jr, M. and M.L. Egan. 1991. *Business Development in the Inner-City: Enterprise with Community Links*. Community Development Research Center, Graduate School of Management and Urban Policy, New School for Social Research, New York, NY.

Ben-Ner, A. 1988. Comparative empirical observations on worker-owned and capitalist firms. *International Journal of Industrial Organization* 6, 1:7-31.

Bennett, L., G.D. Squires, K. McCourt and P. Nyden. 1987. Challenging Chicago's growth machine: A preliminary report on the Washington Administration. *International Journal of Urban and Regional Research* 11, 3:351-62.

Bingham, R.D., E.W. Hill and S.B. White (eds). 1990. *Financing Economic Development: An Institutional Response*. Newbury Park: Sage Publications.

Birch, D. 1987. *Job Creation in America: How Our Smallest Companies Put Most People to Work*. New York: The Free Press.

Birch, D. 1979. *The Job Generation Process*. Cambridge MA: MIT Program on Neighborhood and Regional Change.

Blakely, E.J. 1989. *Planning Local Economic Development: Theory and Practice*. Newbury Park: Sage Publications.

Bluestone, B. and B. Harrison. 1982. *The Deindustrialization of America*. New York: Basic Books.

Bond, P. 1992. Re-using the spaces of confinement: From urban apartheid to post-apartheid without post-modernism. *Urban Forum* 3, 1:39-55.

Bond, P. 1991. *Commanding Heights and Community Control: New Economics for a New South Africa*. Johannesburg: Ravan Press.

Bovaird, T. 1992. Local economic development and the city. *Urban Studies* 29, 3/4:343-68.

Bridgman, D.H., I. Palmer and W. Thomas. 1992. *South Africa's Leading Edge? A Guide to the Western Cape Economy*. Cape Town: WESGRO.

Budlender, D. 1992. Women in economic development. In G. Moss and I. Obery (eds), *South African Review 6: From 'Red Friday' to CODESA*. Johannesburg: Ravan Press, pp. 352-63.

Burnier, D. 1992. Becoming competitive: How policymakers view incentive-based development policy. *Economic Development Quarterly* 6, 1:14-24.

Buss, T.F. 1991. After communism, Hungarian city pursues development. *Economic Development Abroad* 5, 6:3-5.

Carlson, V. and W. Wiewel. 1991. *Strategic Planning in Chicago: How to Select Target Industries*. School of Urban Planning and Policy, Center for Urban Economic Development, University of Illinois at Chicago.

Castells, M. 1983. *The City and the Grassroots*. Berkeley: University of California Press.

Center for Neighborhood Technology. 1986. *Working Neighborhoods:*

Taking Charge of Your Local Economy. Chicago: Center for Neighborhood Technology.

Center for Urban Economic Development. 1987. *Community Economic Development Strategies: A Manual for Local Action*. Chicago: Center for Urban Economic Development, University of Illinois.

Chant, S. 1991. *Women and Survival in Mexican Cities: Perspectives on Gender, Labour Markets and Low-Income Households*. Manchester: Manchester University Press.

Cheshire, P. 1991. Problems of regional transformation and deindustrialization in the European Community. In L. Rodwin and H. Sazanami (eds), *Industrial Change and Regional Economic Transformation: The Experience of Western Europe*. London: Harper Collins, pp. 237-67.

Clark, G. 1989. Pittsburgh in transition: Consolidation of prosperity in an era of economic restructuring. In R.A. Beauregard (ed), *Economic Restructuring and Political Response*. Newbury Park: Sage Publications, pp. 41-68.

Clark, G.L. 1989. US Regional Transformations in the Context of International Economic Competition. In L. Rodwin and H. Sazanami (eds), *Deindustrialization and Regional Economic Transformation: The Experience of the United States*. Boston: Unwin Hyman, pp. 199-220, 296-302.

Clarke, G. 1991. Urban management in developing countries: A critical role. *Cities* 8, 2:93-107.

Clavel, P. 1986. *The Progressive City: Planning and Participation, 1969-1984*. New Brunswick, NJ: Rutgers University Press.

Clavel, P. and W. Wiewel (eds). 1991. *Harold Washington and the Neighborhoods: Progressive City Government in Chicago, 1983-1987*. New Brunswick, NJ: Rutgers University Press.

Cochrane, A. 1988. In and against the market? The development of socialist economic strategies in Britain, 1981-1986. *Policy and Politics* 16, 3:159-68.

Coffey, W. and M. Polese. 1984. The concept of local development: A stages model of endogenous regional growth. *Papers of the Regional Science Association* 55:1-12.

Collinge, J. 1991. Civics: Local government from below. *Work in Progress* 74:8-12.

Croeser, G. 1991. Autonomy in local authority finance. In M. Swilling, R. Humphries and K. Shubane (eds). *Apartheid City in Transition*. Cape Town: Oxford University Press, pp. 139-50.

Cross, C., S. Bekker, C. Clark and C. Wilson. 1992. *Searching for Stability:*

Residential Migration and Community Control in Mariannhill. Durban: Rural Urban Studies Unit, Working Paper No. 23.

Dabney, D.Y. 1991. Do enterprise zones affect business location decisions? *Economic Development Quarterly* 5, 4:325-34.

De Guademar, J. and R. Prudhomme. 1991. Spatial impacts of deindustrialization in France. In L. Rodwin and H. Sazanami (eds), *Industrial Change and Regional Economic Transformation: The Experience of Western Europe*. London: Harper Collins, pp. 105-32.

Development Research Group. 1992. Towards a framework for national development. Mimeo.

De Vos, T.J. 1987. The complexity of housing in South Africa. Paper delivered at the 2nd Techno-Economics Symposium, CSIR, Pretoria, 28 January 1987.

Dewar, D. and R.S. Uytenbogaardt. 1991. *South African Cities: A Manifesto for Change*. Urban Problems Research Unit, University of Cape Town.

Dewar, D. and V. Watson. 1990. *Urban Markets: Developing Informal Retailing*. London: Routledge.

Dewar, D. and V. Watson. 1981. *Unemployment and the 'Informal Sector': Some Proposals for its Stimulation*. Urban Problems Research Unit, Citadel Press.

Dewar, D., V. Watson and A. Bassios. 1990a. An overview of development problems in the Cape Town metropolitan area. Urban Problems Research Unit, Working Paper No. 40, University of Cape Town.

Dewar, D., V. Watson and A. Bassios. 1990b. The structure and form of metropolitan Cape Town: Its origins, influence and performance. Urban Problems Research Unit, Working Paper No. 42, University of Cape Town.

Dickstein, C. 1991. The promise and problems of worker cooperatives. *Journal of Planning Literature* 6, 1:16-33.

Eisenschitz, A. and D. North. 1986. The London industrial strategy: Socialist strategy or modernizing capitalism. *International Journal of Urban and Regional Research* 10, 3:419-40.

Eisinger, P.K. 1988. *The Rise of the Entrepreneurial State: State and Local Economic Development Policy in the United States*. Madison, WI: University of Wisconsin Press.

Elkan, W. 1988. Entrepreneurs and entrepreneurship in Africa. *Research Observer* 3, 2:171-88.

Fainstein, S. 1990a. The changing world economy and urban restructuring. In D.R. Judd and M. Parkinson (eds), *Leadership and Urban Regeneration*. Newbury Park: Sage Publications, pp. 31-47.

Fainstein, S. 1990b. Economics, politics and development policy: The convergence of New York and London. *International Journal of Urban and Regional Research* 14, 4:553-75.

Fainstein, S. 1987. Local mobilization and economic discontent. In M.P. Smith and J.R. Feagin (eds), *The Capitalist City: Global Restructuring and Community Politics*. Oxford: Basil Blackwell, pp. 323-42.

Fainstein, S. and N. Fainstein. 1991. Public-private partnerships for urban (re)development in the United States. Mimeo.

Fainstein, S. and N. Fainstein. 1989. Technology, the new international division of labour, and location: Continuities and disjunctures. In R.A. Beauregard (ed), *Economic Restructuring and Political Response*. Newbury Park: Sage Publications, pp. 17-40.

Fallon, P.R. 1992. An analysis of employment and wage behaviour in South Africa (draft). Southern Africa Department, World Bank.

Ferguson, B.W. 1990a. Paths to local progress: Development, political reform, and cultural change in Brazilian municipalities. Doctoral Thesis in Urban Planning, University of California at Los Angeles.

Ferguson, B.W. 1990b. Local growth strategies in developing countries: The case of Brazil, Parana, Brazil. Mimeo.

Fisher, R. 1984. *Let the People Decide: Neighborhood Organizing in America*. Boston: Twayne.

Foley, P. 1992. Local economic policy and job creation: A review of evaluation studies. *Urban Studies* 29, 3/4:557-98.

Forrant, B. 1990. From training consortia to technology networks. In *Proceedings of a Dialogue on Flexible Manufacturing Networks*. Conference organised by the Consortium for Manufacturing Competitiveness, Ramada Beach Resort, Fort Walton Beach, Florida, 16 January 1990.

Forster, C. 1992. Interview with J. Robinson and C. Boldogh, 18 November 1992.

Fossler, R.S. 1992. State economic policy: The emerging paradigm. *Economic Development Quarterly* 6, 1:3-13.

Freund, W. 1986. Some unasked questions in politics: South African slogans and debates. *Transformation* 1:118-37.

Friedman, J. and R. Bloch. 1990. American exceptionalism in regional planning, 1933-2000. *International Journal for Urban and Regional Research* 14, 4:576-601.

Friedman, S. 1991a. Soweto: Managing the transition? *Politikon* 18, 1:97-111.

Friedman, S. 1991b. An unlikely utopia: State and civil society in South Africa. *Politikon* December: 5-19.

Gans, H.J. 1990. Deconstructing the underclass: The term's dangers as a planning concept. *Journal of the American Planning Association* 56, 3:271-77.

Goldsmith, M. and K. Newton. 1988. Centralisation and decentralisation: Changing patterns of intergovernmental relations in advanced western societies – an introduction by the editors. *European Journal of Political Research* 16:359-63. Gordhan, P. 1992. Interview with J. Robinson and C. Boldogh, 13 November 1992.

Gore, T. 1991. Public/private partnership schemes in UK urban regeneration. *Cities* 8, 3:209-16.

Gouws, R. 1991. Economic policy changes for a new South Africa. In R. Lee and L. Schlemmer (eds), *Transition to Democracy: Policy Perspectives 1991*. Cape Town: Oxford University Press, pp. 41-66.

Grant, J.A. 1990. Making policy choices: Local government and economic development. *Urban Affairs Quarterly* 26, 2:148-69.

Greenberg, E.S. 1986. *Workplace Democracy: The Political Effects of Participation*. Ithaca: Cornell University Press.

Hall, P. 1982. Enterprise zones: A justification. *International Journal of Urban and Regional Research* 6, 3:416-21.

Harding, A. 1991. The rise of urban growth coalitions, UK-style? *Environment and Planning C: Government and Policy* 9, 3:295-317.

Harvey, D. 1989. From managerialism to entrepreneurialism: The transformation in urban governance in late capitalism. *Geografiska Annaler* 71B, 1:3-17.

Haygarth, G. 1992. Interview with J. Robinson and C. Boldogh, 17 November 1992.

Heymans, C. 1991. Privatization and municipal reform. In M. Swilling, R. Humphries and K. Shubane (eds), *Apartheid City in Transition*. Cape Town: Oxford University Press, pp. 151-73. Hibbert, G. 1992. Interview with J. Robinson and C. Boldogh, 20 November 1992.

Hill, R.C. 1989. Comparing transnational production systems: The automobile industry in the USA and Japan. *International Journal for Urban and Regional Research* 13, 3:462-80.

Hindson, D. 1987. *Pass Controls and the Urban African Proletariat*. Johannesburg: Ravan Press.

Hirst, P. and J. Zeitlin. 1989. Introduction. In P. Hirst and J. Zeitlin (eds), *Reversing Industrial Decline: Industrial Structure and Policy in Britain and her Competitors*. Oxford: BERG Publishers, pp. 1-16.

Hofmeyr, J.F. 1990. The rise of black wages in South Africa. Paper delivered at the biennial conference of the Development Society of

Southern Africa, University of the Witwatersrand, 5-7 September 1990.

Hollander, E. 1991. The Department of Planning under Harold Washington. In P. Clavel and W. Wiewel (eds), *Harold Washington and the Neighborhoods: Progressive City Government in Chicago, 1983-1987*. New Brunswick, NJ: Rutgers University Press, pp. 121-45.

Hula, R.C. 1990. The two Baltimores. In D. Judd and M. Parkinson (eds), *Leadership and Urban Regeneration: Cities in North America and Europe*. Newbury Park: Sage Publications, pp. 191-215.

Hulme, D. 1990. Can the Grameen Bank be replicated? Recent experiences in Malaysia, Malawi and Sri Lanka. *Development Policy Review* 8:287-300.

Innes, D. 1991. Empowerment in the workplace. *The Innes Labour Brief* 2, 4:6-7.

Jaffee, G. 1992. Co-operative development in South Africa. In G. Moss and I. Obery (eds), *South African Review 6: From 'Red Friday' to CODESA*. Johannesburg: Ravan Press, pp. 364-77.

Joffe, A. and D. Lewis. 1992. A strategy for South African manufacturing. *South African Labour Bulletin* 16, 4:24-31.

Judd, D. and M. Parkinson. 1990. Urban leadership and regeneration. In D. Judd and M. Parkinson (eds), *Leadership and Urban Regeneration: Cities in North America and Europe*. Newbury Park: Sage Publications, pp. 13-30.

Kagiso Trust. n.d. *Kagiso Trust: A Dossier*. Johannesburg.

Kahnert, F. 1987. Improving urban employment and labor productivity. Discussion Paper No. 10 Washington DC: World Bank.

Kane, M. and P. Sand. 1988. *Economic Development: What Works at the Local Level*. Washington DC: National League of Cities.

Keeble, D.E. 1989. High-technology industry and regional development in Britain: The case of the Cambridge phenomenon. *Environment and Planning C: Government and Policy*, 7:153-72.

Kieschnick, M. 1983. Taxes and growth: Business incentives and economic development. In M. Barker (ed), *State Taxation Policy*. Durham NC: Duke University Press, pp. 155-280.

Knox, P.L. 1988. Public-private cooperation: A review of experience in the US. *Cities* 5, 4:340-46.

Krauss, E.S. and J. Pierre. 1991. Targeting resources for industrial change. In K. Weaver and B. Rockman (eds), *Do Institutions Matter? Government Capabilities in the United States and Abroad*. Washington DC: The Brookings Institution.

Kudrle, R.T. and C.M. Kite. 1989. The evaluation of state programs for international business development. *Economic Development Quarterly* 3, 4:288-300.

Lassar, T.J. (ed). 1990. *City Deal Making*. Washington DC: The Urban Land Institute.

Lawless, P. 1988. Urban development corporations and their alternatives. *Cities* 5, 3:277-89.

Le Gales, P. 1990. Economic regeneration in Rennes: Local social dynamics and state support. In D. Judd and M. Parkinson (eds), *Leadership and Urban Regeneration: Cities in North America and Europe*. Newbury Park: Sage Publications, pp. 69-85.

Lemon, A. 1992. *Homes Apart: South Africa's Segregated Cities*, Cape Town: David Philip.

Levine, M.V. 1989. The politics of partnership: Unequal development since 1945. In G.D. Squires (ed), *Unequal Partnerships: The Political Economy of Urban Redevelopment in Postwar America*. New Brunswick: Rutgers University Press, pp. 12-34.

Levy, B. 1992. How can South African manufacturing efficiently create employment? An analysis of the impact of trade and industrial policy. Informal Discussion Papers on the Economy of South Africa, Paper No. 1, Southern Africa Department, Washington DC: World Bank.

Levy, J.M. 1991. The US experience with local economic development. Mimeo.

Levy, J.M. 1990. What local economic developers actually do: Location quotients versus press releases. *Journal of the American Planning Association* Spring: 153-60.

Ligthelm, A.A. and L. Kritzinger-Van Niekerk. 1990. Unemployment: The role of the public sector in increasing the labour absorption capacity of the South African economy. *Development Southern Africa* 7, 4:629-41.

Lipton, M. 1988. *The Poor and the Poorest: Some Interim Findings*. Discussion Paper No. 25, Washington DC: World Bank.

Lovering, J. 1990. Fordism's unknown successor: A comment on Scott's theory of flexible accumulation and the reemergence of regional economies. *International Journal for Urban and Regional Research* 14, 1:159-74.

Luke, J.S., C. Ventriss, B.J. Reed and C.M. Reed. 1988. *Managing Economic Development: A Guide to State and Local Leadership Strategies*, San Francisco: Jossey Bass.

Lukhele, A.K. 1990. *Stokvels in South Africa*, Johannesburg: Amagi Books.

Mabin, A. 1991. The dynamics of urbanization since 1960. In M. Swilling, R. Humphries and K. Shubane (eds), *Apartheid City in Transition*, Cape Town: Oxford University Press, pp. 33-47.

Machimura, T. 1992. The rise and fall of urban restructuring coalitions in Tokyo. Paper delivered at the International Sociological Association, Research Committee 21, University of California, Los Angeles, 23-25 April 1992.

MacManus, S.A. 1990. Minority business contracting with local government. *Urban Affairs Quarterly* 25, 3:455-73.

Markusen, A.R. 1989. Industrial restructuring and regional politics. In R.A. Beauregard (ed), *Economic Restructuring and Political Response.* Newbury Park: Sage Publications, pp. 115-48.

Markusen, A.R. and V. Carlson. 1989. Deindustrialization in the American Midwest: Causes and responses. In L. Rodwin and H. Sazanami (eds), *Deindustrialization and Regional Economic Transformation: The Experience of the United States.* Boston: Unwin Hyman, pp. 25-59.

Maughan-Brown, M. 1992. Interview with J. Robinson and C. Boldogh, 16 November 1992.

Mazumdar, D. 1988. *Microeconomic Issues of Labor Markets in Developing Countries: Analysis and Policy Implications.* EDI Seminar Paper No. 40, Washington DC: World Bank.

McCaul, C. 1987. *Satellite in Revolt. KwaNdebele: An Economic and Political Profile.* Johannesburg: South African Institute of Race Relations.

McGrath, M. and S. Van der Berg. 1991. Growth, poverty and redistribution. Input paper for the Internal Imperatives Workshop, Project Economic Debate, organised by the Consultative Business Movement, 23 February 1991.

McKnight, J. and J. Kretzman. 1989. Community organizing in the 80s: Towards a post-Alinsky agenda. *Social Policy* 14, 3:15-17.

Meyer, M. 1987. Restructuring and popular opposition in West German cities. In M.P. Smith and J.R. Feagin (eds). *The Capitalist City: Global Restructuring and Community Politics.* Oxford: Basil Blackwell, pp. 343-64.

Mier, R. and K.J. Moe. 1991. Decentralized development: From theory to practice. In P. Clavel and W. Wiewel (eds), *Harold Washington and the Neighborhoods: Progressive City Government in Chicago, 1983-1987.* New Brunswick, NJ: Rutgers University Press, pp. 64-99.

Mji, D. 1990. Letter to M. Cohen, 24 September 1990.

Mohan, R. 1985. Labor force participation in a developing metropolis: Does sex matter? World Bank Staff Working Paper No. 749, Washington DC.

Molle, W. 1988. Regional policy. In P. Coffey (ed), *Main Economic Policy Areas of the EEC – Towards 1992: The Challenges of the Community's Economic Policies when the 'Real' Common Market is Created by the End of 1992.* Dordrecht: Kluwer Academic Publishers, pp. 67-98.

Molotch, H. 1976. The city as a growth machine: Toward a political economy of place. *American Journal of Sociology* 82, 2:309-32.

Molotch, H. and S. Vicari. 1988. Three ways to build: The development process in the United States, Japan and Italy. *Urban Affairs Quarterly* 24, 2:188-214.

Murray, R. 1989. From Bologna to Basildon: Regional initiatives for the 1990s. Paper presented to the Annual General Meeting of the South East Economic Development Strategy, 27 November 1989.

National Congress for Community Economic Development. 1989 Against all odds: The achievements of community-based development organizations. A survey published by the NCCED, Washington DC.

National Council for Urban Economic Development. 1984. *Establishing and Operating Private Sector Development Organizations: A Technical Guide Based on Model Approaches.* Prepared for the US Department of Housing and Urban Development, Office of Community Planning and Development, Washington DC.

National Council for Urban Economic Development. 1991. *Trends in Economic Development Organizations: A Survey of Selected Metropolitan Areas.* Washington DC: National Council for Urban Economic Development.

Nzimande, B. and M. Sikhosana. 1991. Civics are part of the National democratic Revolution. *Mayibuye* 2, 5:37-39.

Page Jr, J.M. and W.F. Steel. 1984. Small enterprise development: Economic issues from African experience. World Bank Technical Paper No. 29, Washington DC.

Peirce, N.R. and C.F. Steinbach. 1990. *Corrective Capitalism: The Rise of America's Community Development Corporations.* New York: The Ford Foundation.

Peterson, P.E. 1991. The urban underclass and the poverty paradigm. In C. Jencks and P.E. Peterson (eds), *The Urban Underclass.* Washington DC: The Brookings Institution, pp. 3-27.

Peterson, P.E., G.T. Kingsley and J.P. Telgarsky. 1991. Urban *Economies and National Development*. Policy and Research Series, Office of Housing and Urban Programs, USAID, Washington DC.

Pezzini, M. 1990. Networks in Italy – conditions underlying network formation. In *Proceedings of a Dialogue on Flexible Manufacturing Networks*. Conference organised by the Consortium for Manufacturing Competitiveness, Ramada Beach Resort, Fort Walton Beach, Florida, 16 January 1990.

Pickvance, C. 1991. The difficulty of control and the ease of structural reform: British local government in the 1980s. In C. Pickvance and E. Preteceille (eds), *Strategic Restructuring and Local Power: A Comparative Perspective*. London and New York: Pinter Publishers, pp. 1-17.

Planact. 1992a. Transition and development. In G. Moss and I. Obery (eds), *South African Review 6: From 'Red Friday' to CODESA*. Johannesburg: Ravan Press, pp. 201-15.

Planact. 1992b. *Resource Document: The Reorganization of Local Government in South Africa*. Yeoville: Planact.

Planact. 1992c. The theory and practice of local economic development: A guide. Mimeo.

Planact. 1992d. Local government in transition and the options for interim administrative arrangements. Mimeo.

Planact. 1990/91. *Annual Report 1990/91*. Yeoville: Planact.

Planact. 1989/90. *Annual Report 1989/90*. Yeoville: Planact.

Planact. 1989. *The Soweto Rent Boycott*. Yeoville: Planact.

Procter, C. 1992. Interview with J. Robinson and C. Boldogh, 8 September 1992.

Reich, R.B. 1991. *The Work of Nations: Preparing Ourselves for 21st Century Capitalism*. New York: Alfred A. Knopf.

Robinson, J. 1991. Post-apartheid or post-modernism: Local economic development initiatives in South Africa. Mimeo.

Robinson, P. 1992. Interview with J. Robinson and C. Boldogh, 5 November 1992.

Rodgers, G. 1989. Introduction: Trends in urban poverty and labour market access. In G. Rodgers (ed), *Urban Poverty and the Labour Market: Access to Jobs and Incomes in Asian and Latin American Cities*. Geneva: International Labor Organization, pp. 1-33.

Rodwin, L. 1989. Deindustrialization and regional economic transformation. In L. Rodwin and H. Sazanami (eds), *Deindustrialization and Regional Economic Transformation: The Experience of the United States*. Boston: Unwin Hyman, pp. 3-28.

Rodwin, L. and B. Sanyal. 1987. Shelter, settlement and development. In L. Rodwin (ed), *Shelter, Settlement and Development*. Boston: Allen and Unwin, pp. 3-31.

Rondinelli, D.A. 1991. Asian urban development policies in the 1990s: From growth control to urban diffusion. *World Development* 19, 7:791-803.

Rosenberg, T. 1992. Interview with J. Robinson and C. Boldogh, 7 December 1992.

Ross, D. and R.E. Friedman. 1990. The emerging third wave: New economic development strategies in the '90s. *Entrepreneurial Economy Review* Autumn, 3-10.

Rubin, H. 1988. Shoot anything that flies; claim anything that falls: Conversations with economic development practitioners. *Economic Development Quarterly* 2:236-51.

Sabel, C.F. 1989. Flexible specialization and the re-emergence of regional economies. In P. Hirst and J. Zeitlin (eds), *Reversing Industrial Decline: Industrial Structure and Policy in Britain and her Competitors*. Oxford: BERG Publishers, pp. 17-70.

Sayer, A. 1989. Postfordism in question. *International Journal of Urban and Regional Research* 13, 4:666-93.

Sazanami, H. 1991. Structural Transformation in Japan: Issues and prospects for regional development in the coming years. In L. Rodwin and H. Sazanami (eds), *Industrial Change and Regional Economic Transformation: The Experience of Western Europe*. London: Harper Collins, pp. 319-46.

Sbragia, A.M. 1990. Pittsburgh's 'Third Way': The nonprofit sector as a key to urban regeneration. In D. Judd and M. Parkinson (eds), *Leadership and Urban Regeneration: Cities in North America and Europe*. Newbury Park: Sage Publications, pp. 51-68.

Sbragia, A.M. 1989. The Pittsburgh model of economic development: Partnership, responsiveness, and indifference. In G.D. Squires (ed), *Unequal Partnerships: The Political Economy of Urban Redevelopment in Postwar America*. New Brunswick, NJ: Rutgers University Press, pp. 103-20.

Schlemmer, L. and R. Humphries. 1989. Metropolitan Witwatersrand: Trends, pressures and alternative futures. University of the Witwatersrand, Centre for Policy Studies, Mimeo.

Scott, A.J. 1988. Flexible production systems and regional development: The rise of new industrial space in North America and western Europe. *International Journal for Urban and Regional Research* 12, 2:171-86.

Seekings, J. 1992. Civic organizations in South African Townships. In G. Moss and I. Obery (eds), *South African Review 6: From 'Red Friday' to CODESA*. Johannesburg: Ravan Press, pp. 216-38.

Sellgren, J.M.A. 1991. The changing nature of local economic development activities: A longitudinal analysis of local authorities in Great Britain, 1981 to 1987. *Environment and Planning C: Government and Policy* 9, 3:341-62.

Sharp, E.B. 1990. *Urban Politics and Administration: From Service Delivery to Economic Development*. New York: Longman.

Sharpe, L.J. 1988. The growth and decentralization of the modern democratic state. *European Journal of Political Research* 16, 3:365-80.

Shearer, D. 1989. In search of equal partnerships: Prospects for progressive urban policy in the 1990s. In G.D. Squires (ed), *Unequal Partnerships: The Political Economy of Urban Redevelopment in Postwar America*. New Brunswick, NJ: Rutgers University Press.

Shiffman, R. 1990. A community-based development strategy for South Africa. Consultant report prepared on behalf of USAID, South Africa, final draft, 24 January 1990.

Shubane, K. 1991. Civil society in apartheid and post-apartheid South Africa. Paper delivered at a workshop of the Centre for Policy Studies, University of the Witwatersrand, July 1991.

Silver, H. 1986-87. Is industrial policy possible in the United States? The defeat of Rhode Island's Greenhouse Compact. *Politics and Society* 15, 3:333-68.

Silver, H. and D. Burton. 1986. The politics of state-level industrial policy: Lessons from Rhode Island's Greenhouse Compact. *APA Journal* Summer: 277-89.

Silverman, J.M. 1990. Public sector decentralization. Economic policy reform and sector investment programs. Division Study Paper No. 1, Public Sector Management Division, Africa Technical Department, World Bank.

Slabbert, F. van Zyl. 1992. *The Quest for Democracy: South Africa in Transition*. London: Penguin (Forum Series).

South African Institute of Race Relations. 1992. *1991/92 Survey*. Johannesburg: SAIRR.

South Africa, Republic of. 1991. Statistically unrecorded economic activities of coloureds, Indians and blacks: October 1990. Central Statistical Service, Statistical News Release P0315, Pretoria.

Southall, R. 1980. African capitalism in contemporary South Africa. *Journal of Southern African Studies* 7:38-70.

Sower, J. and B.L. Milkman. 1991. The bank community development corporation: An economic development tool for the nineties. *Economic Development Quarterly* 5, 1:3-8.

Sperry, C.W. 1985. What makes Mondragon Work? *Review of Social Economy* 43, 3:345-56.

Squires, G.D. 1989. Public-private partnerships: Who gets what and why. In G.D. Squires (ed), *Unequal Partnerships: The Political Economy of Urban Redevelopment in Postwar America*. New Brunswick, NJ: Rutgers University Press.

Starkey, R. 1992. Interview with J. Robinson and C. Boldogh, 12 November 1992.

Steffens, R. 1992. What the incubators have hatched. *Planning* 58, 5:28-30.

Stohr, W. and F. Todtling. 1978. An evaluation of regional policies – experiences in market and mixed economies. In N.M. Hansen (ed), *Human Settlement Systems*. Cambridge, MA: Ballinger, pp. 85-119.

Storper, M. 1990. Industrialization and the regional question in the Third World: Lessons of post-imperialism; Prospects of post-Fordism. *International Journal of Urban and Regional Research* 14, 3:423-44.

Sundquist, J.L. 1975. *Dispersing Population: What America can Learn from Europe*, Washington DC: Brookings.

Sutcliffe, M. 1992. Interview with J. Robinson and C. Boldogh, 26 November 1992.

Swilling, M. 1991. Socialism, democracy and civil society: The case for associational socialism. Mimeo.

Swilling, M. and K. Shubane. 1991. Negotiating urban transition: The Soweto experience. In R. Lee and L. Schlemmer (eds), *Transition to Democracy: Policy Perspectives 1991*. Cape Town: Oxford University Press, pp. 223-258.

Swilling, M., W. Cobbett and R. Hunter. 1991. Finance, electricity costs and the rent boycott. In M. Swilling, R. Humphries and K. Shubane (eds), *Apartheid City in Transition*. Cape Town: Oxford University Press, pp. 174-96.

Thomas, J.M. 1989. Detroit: The centrifugal city. In G.D. Squires (ed), *Unequal Partnerships: The Political Economy of Urban Redevelopment in Postwar America*. New Brunswick, NJ: Rutgers University Press.

Thurow, L. 1989. Regional transformation and the service activities. In L. Rodwin and H. Sazanami (eds), *Deindustrialization and Regional Economic Transformation: The Experience of the United States*. Boston: Unwin Hyman, pp. 3-25.

Tomlinson, R. 1992. Competing urban agendas in South Africa. *Urban Forum* 3, 1:97-110.

Tomlinson, R. 1990. *Urbanisation in Post-Apartheid South Africa.* London: Unwin Hyman.

Tomlinson, R. and M. Addleson. 1987a. Is the state's regional policy in the interests of capital? In R. Tomlinson and M. Addleson (eds), *Regional Restructuring Under Apartheid: Contemporary Perspectives on Urban and Regional Policies in South Africa.* Johannesburg: Ravan Press, pp. 55-73.

Tomlinson, R. and M. Addleson. 1987b. Export processing and free enterprise zones: The Ciskei and regional economic policy in South Africa. In R. Tomlinson and M. Addleson (eds), *Regional Restructuring Under Apartheid: Contemporary Perspectives on Urban and Regional Policies in South Africa.* Johannesburg: Ravan Press, pp. 278-93.

Tomlinson, R. and M. Addleson. 1985. Ciskei as a free enterprise zone. *Development Southern Africa* 2, 2:174-86.

Tongaat-Hulett. 1989. *The DFR – Planning for the Future: The Current Situation, Report 1.* Durban: Tongaat-Hulett Properties Ltd.

Topham, S. 1992. Work for all? Strategies for local economic development in post-apartheid South Africa. East London: Corplan discussion document, October 1992.

Trachte, K. and R. Ross. 1985. The crisis of Detroit and the emergence of global capitalism. *International Journal of Urban and Regional Research* 9, 2:187-216.

United Nations Industrial Development Organization. 1980. Export processing zones in developing countries. Working Papers on Structural Change 19, International Center for Industrial Studies, Geneva.

Urban Foundation. 1991. Policies for a New Urban Future. Urban Debate 2010, Income distribution model. Johannesburg: Urban Foundation.

Urban Foundation. 1990a. Policies for a New Urban Future. Urban Debate 2010, Housing for All. Johannesburg: Urban Foundation.

Urban Foundation. 1990b. Policies for a New Urban Future. Urban Debate 2010, Managing the Cities. Johannesburg: Urban Foundation.

Urban Foundation. n.d. Policies for a New Urban Future. Urban Debate 2010. Johannesburg: Urban Foundation.

Van der Berg, S. and J.C. Lotter. 1990. Metropolitan dominance, export promotion and the coastal metropolitan areas. *South African Journal of Economics* 58, 2:187-99.

Van Kralingen, M. 1990a. Letter to M. Cohen, 16 August 1990.

Van Kralingen, M. 1990b. Letter to S. Ndebele, 28 September 1990.

Walker, J.C. 1990. Revolving funds for economic development. In R.D. Bingham, E.W. Hill and S.B. White (eds), *Financing Economic Development: An Institutional Response*. Newbury Park: Sage Publications, pp. 177-90.

Wells Jr, L.T. and A.G. Wint. 1990. *Marketing a Country: Promotion as a Tool for Attracting Foreign Investment*. Washington DC: International Finance Corporation.

Western, J. 1987. *Outcast Cape Town*. Cape Town: Human and Rousseau.

Whyte, W.F. 1988. *Making Mondragon: The Growth and Dynamics of the Worker Cooperative Complex*. Ithaca, NY: ILR Press.

Wiewel, W. and J. Weintraub. 1990. Community development corporations as a tool for economic development finance. In R.D. Bingham, E.W. Hill and S.B. White (eds), *Financing Economic Development: An Institutional Response*. Newbury Park: Sage Publications, pp. 160-76.

Williams, K., T. Cutler, J. Williams and C. Haslam. 1987. The end of mass production? *Economy and Society* 16, 3:405-39.

Wilson, F. and M. Ramphele. 1989. *Uprooting Poverty: The South African Challenge*. Cape Town: David Philip.

Winter, M. 1992. Interview with J. Robinson and C. Boldogh, 25 November 1992.

Wolman, H. 1988. Understanding recent trends in central-local relations: Centralization in Great Britain and decentralization in the United States. *European Journal of Political Economy* 16, 3:425-35.

World Bank. 1991a. *Urban Policy and Economic Development: An Agenda for the 1990s*. World Bank Policy Paper, Washington DC.

World Bank. 1991b. South Africa: Urban Sector Reconnaissance Mission. Aide Mémoire, 10 May, Washington DC.

World Bank. 1991c. South Africa: Urban Sector Reconnaissance Mission. Aide Mémoire, 6 December, Washington DC.

Wyley, C. and C. Talbot. 1993. Durban's metropolitan development process. *Urban Forum*, 4, 1:107-15.

Yoder, R.A., P.L. Borkholder and B.D. Friesen. 1991. Privatization and Development. *Journal of Developing Areas* 25, 3:425-34.

Index